Reviews of Dr. James Ma̧

Positioning Africa for the 21st Century

"Dr. Magara has touched two critical ingredients that must underlay Africa's turnaround namely, transformational leadership and critical thinking backed by research. Development is intentional and knowledge intensive. Quality leadership and input from think tanks are indispensable for the process."

Stephen Adei, Ph.D., *Professor of Economics and Leadership, First Rector of Ghana Institute of Management and Public Administration (GIMPA), Accra, Ghana.*

"This book brings to the fore one of the fundamental issues that has restricted African development in the last six decades. Namely, the limited capacity of indigenous state and non-state think tanks in providing the planning framework that translates developmental aspirations and priorities into concrete results in terms of national policies and programs. As is stated in the book, 'A national think tank is to the nation what the brain is to the human body.' Has Africa for the most part been like a body without a brain? This book is a must-read for every leader, young and old - especially those from the continent of Africa.

Professor Vincent C. Anigbogu, Ph.D., *Director General, Institute for National Transformation International, Lagos, Nigeria.*

"Dr. Magara's well-researched global comparative analysis of Botswana, Malaysia, South Korea and Singapore present a compelling case for the value of think tanks. It leaves the reader absolutely convinced that creating and funding think tanks is worthy and necessary not only for Africa, but for the global economy as well."

Diane M. Wiater, Ph.D., *Regent University, Virginia Beach, Virginia, USA*

"It is high time African countries started thinking their development challenges through and making contexually relevant prescriptions and strategies. This book is a description of how think tanks can be a game-changer."

David Sseppuuya
Author, *Africa's Industrialisation & Prosperity*, (2017)
Consultant, World Bank Tanzania and Uganda country offices
Former Editor-in-Chief, 'The New Vision', and former Executive Editor, 'The Daily Monitor'
Kampala, Uganda

"This book guides the reader through important insights on how think tanks can be used to create effective teams, strategies and plans to achieve monumental goals. While the content can be applied to many nations, it serves as an important intervention tool for African leaders to unlock greater potential through think tanks and thereby help to accelerate the overall pace of development."

Dr. Virginia Richardson, BCC
Foresight Center, Inc. Founder & CEO, and
Doctoral Professor of Strategic Leadership & Foresight

POSITIONING AFRICA FOR THE 21ST CENTURY

The Pivotal Role of Leadership and Think Tanks

POSITIONING AFRICA FOR THE 21ST CENTURY

The Pivotal Role of Leadership and Think Tanks

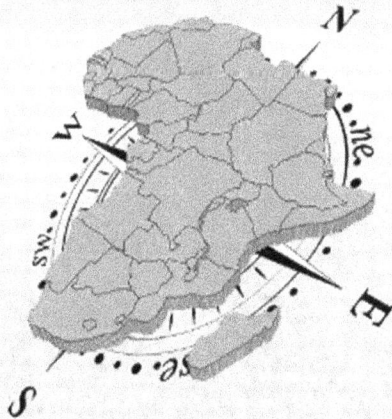

Dr. James Magara

Positioning Africa for the 21ˢᵗ Century
The Pivotal Role of Leadership and Think Tanks

by Dr. James Magara

Rights and Permissions
Text © James Magara, 2017

ISBN 978-9970-556-04-5

Produced and published by:
Beeranga Mwesigwa Foundation,
Suite B1, Adam House,
Portal Avenue, Kampala, Uganda

Dedication

To Barrister Emeka Nwankpa:

*Thank you for starting me off
on this leadership odyssey.*

Acknowledgements

This work was a result of my doctoral studies at the School of Business and Leadership, Regent University, Virginia Beach, USA. I would like to thank Dr. Virginia Richardson for her unwavering support and guidance throughout this work. Thank you for the excellent example you set in servant leadership even in times of personal difficulty. It has been an honor to be under your tutelage. I am very grateful to my study buddies Sam Odeke, Felistus Mbole, and in the earlier years, Robby Muhumuza, and Edward Mubiru for being my cheerleaders and companions in times of discouragement. Thanks too to the Resident Outcasts. Thank you, Kelly Whelan for putting that group of distance learners together.

Barrister Emeka Nwankpa ignited in me a passion for studying leadership. Professor Vincent Anigbogu urged me deeper into the leadership world. Professor Stephen Adei first opened my eyes to the existence of a "marketplace of ideas." Thank you all.

Deep appreciation goes to Emma Senginyunva, Eseza Mulyagonja and friends from the Institute for National Transformation (Uganda) for your contributions towards the design and production. Thank you Laban Jjumba and David Sseppuuya for your input at the final stages of the project.

I would like to specially appreciate my loving and supportive wife Lorna, who has been my greatest cheerleader. She patiently bore my absence as I worked on this book and helped in proofreading the text. Thank you, darling.

The views expressed in this treatise are mine, and should not be attributed to Regent University.

Dr. James Magara
Kampala, Uganda, October 2017

Contents

Foreword

The future is not a gift: it is an achievement. Every generation helps make its own future. This is the essential challenge of the present."
Robert Kennedy.

We Choose Our Future

Just four months after his inauguration, on May 25, 1961, President John F. Kennedy announced to his nation and the world his intention for the United States to put a man safely on the moon before the decade was out. This was a defining moment in history. The Soviet Union was already far ahead in the space race and many experts feared that whichever nation took a stronghold in space would likely dominate the world.

The pressure for the U.S. to take this seemingly impossible, far-reaching action was significant. President Kennedy felt he must act quickly and decisively without compromise to commit his nation to a free and peaceful future.

> Now it is time to take longer strides—time for this nation to take a clearly leading role in space achievement, which in many ways may hold the key to our future on Earth . . . Space is open to us now; and our eagerness to share its meaning is not governed by the efforts of others. We go into space because whatever mankind must undertake, free men must fully share (Kennedy, 1961). [1]

While the U.S. was rich with talent and resources, it faced a colossal challenge. On that Spring day in 1961 when President Kennedy cast his vision to win the "space race", no one had a plan or strategy on how to accomplish the monumental feat of putting a man safely on the moon.

Yet, in the following years, men and women from the U.S. and around the world worked together to accomplish something that had been only a dream in 1961. Even after the assassination

13

of President Kennedy in 1963, the mission to fulfill the vision continued. Finally, only months before the end of decade, on July 20, 1969 astronaut Neil Armstrong walked on the moon. He famously declared, "that's one small step for man, one giant leap for mankind".[2] The impossible dream framed in 1961 became a reality of the future by 1969.

A Vision Is Not Enough

President Kennedy created a vision for future space exploration. Yet his vision alone did not accomplish the objective. Many leaders cast visions full of great optimism for their organizations that all too often go unfulfilled. Their good intentions simply do not contain the substance for success. Indeed, it has been shown that less than forty percent (37%) of all project initiatives result in success.[3] That means sixty percent of all the visions with great intentions result in significant challenges causing them to fall considerably short of the objectives (42%), or the efforts fail all together (21%). If vision is not enough, what do we need to accomplish our goals? Even more importantly for leaders involved in efforts such as nation building, what must we do to accomplish our monumental goals requiring far-reaching efforts like putting a man on the moon?

Foresight Helps Us Anticipate the Future

Strategic Foresight played a key role in helping President Kennedy to anticipate what might happen if an adversarial nation took control of outer space and the skies surrounding our precious planet. For centuries, great battles have taken place across the globe as nations fought for control of land and waterways. While the casualties of war on land and water have been significant, by 1961, a growing number of experts feared the war of the skies had the highest potential to end the world for mankind.

President Kennedy came to realize that even without a war in the skies, a dominance of the airways could have far-reaching consequences if adversarial leaders were in control. Using the skills of strategic foresight, he could anticipate a future more fearful than the massive efforts necessary to put a man on the moon. For him, the direction became clear because he could anticipate two alternative futures: one he wanted to avoid, and one he could create.

Just as in the example with the space race, strategic foresight provides tools to help us explore what is on the horizon for the future. When we use foresight tools, we can keep a pulse on trends and current events to help us anticipate the potential alternative futures that might occur. Nearly all trends have the potential to go in many different directions, and foresight tools track the factors driving the trends forward and the things that might intervene to shift the trend in a new direction or even hold it back.

Think Tanks Help Nations Create A Brighter Future

Understanding the potential alternative futures provided many advantages for President Kennedy including the insight he needed to enter the space race. Yet, the efforts to put a man safely on the moon required three more elements: 1) a team that maximizes the use of the nation's intellectual resources through the collaborative expertise of a diverse group of exceptionally talented individuals, 2) a strategy on the tactical approach, and 3) a roadmap and plan to execute the strategy. Certainly, other elements played contributing roles, but the prospect of putting a man on the moon would have dwindled significantly without an effective team, strategy, and plan.

This book guides the reader through important insights on how think tanks can be used to create effective teams, strategies and plans to achieve monumental goals. While the content can be applied to many nations, it serves as an important intervention tool for African leaders to unlock greater potential through think tanks and thereby help to accelerate the overall pace of development.

Drawing from research on how think tanks are effectively used in other countries, it provides a global comparative analysis of Malaysia, South Korea and Malaysia. The many intervention tools offered throughout the book present a compelling case for the value of Think Tanks and can be used to create a solid foundation for Africa to strategically position for the complex, challenging road ahead.

In the book, Dr. James Magara provides a systematic and concise survey of African history and economics that helps to make the case for developing think tanks on the continent of

Africa. He explains why think tanks will be pivotal to help Africa achieve its monumental goals and paints insightful pictures of alternative futures describing an African future with think tanks and an African future without them. Magara's analysis provides a compelling argument for the creation and funding of think tanks.

Leaders With Monumental Dreams

This book is written for leaders who seek insight and direction on the most effective ways to achieve their monumental dreams. While we have the benefit of hindsight to learn from the ways in which President Kennedy's monumental dream was realized, we must not forget that in 1961 they were forced to figure out the team, strategy and plan as they went. Many mistakes were made and mishaps took place including great national tragedies and the loss of life due to working in unchartered territory.

The goal of this book is to learn from the successes and failures of others in Africa and other countries. African leaders have a genuine opportunity to incorporate strategic foresight to explore alternative futures on the horizon, cast visions based on their preferred future, and create think tanks to achieve far-reaching goals. In doing so, we can dream the impossible and bring those dreams into our future reality.

I am certain that you will find this book to be a genuine "game changer" and you will understand leading change from a refreshing new perspective. It was a sincere privilege for me to be a part of Dr. Magara's journey as he wrote it. He is a man of great substance and someone I am certain will help lead Africa into its preferred future. From this work, I learned much about human potential by incorporating think tanks, and the unwavering tenacity of the African people to make their way onto the global stage. The future is bright for Africa, especially for those leaders willing to take strategic steps using think tanks to go after their monumental dreams!

With Boundless Joy and Hope for Africa's Future,

Dr. Virginia Richardson, BCC
Foresight Center, Inc. Founder & CEO, and
Doctoral Professor of Strategic Leadership & Foresight

References

Kennedy, J. F. (1961). Special Message to the Congress on Urgent National Needs. [Delivered in person before a joint session of Congress May 25, 1961], *NASA*, Retrieved from https://www.nasa.gov/vision/space/features/jfk_speech_text.html.

NASA (2017). July 20, 1969: One Giant Leap For Mankind. Retrieved from https://www.nasa.gov/mission_pages/apollo/apollo11.html

Shore, D. (2014). *Launching and Leading Change Initiatives in Health Care Organizations.* San Francisco, CA: Jossey-Bass.

Endnotes

1   Kennedy, J. F. (1961). Special Message to the Congress on Urgent National Needs. [Delivered in person before a joint session of Congress May 25, 1961], *NASA*, Retrieved from https://www.nasa.gov/vision/space/features/jfk_speech_text.html.

2   NASA (2017). July 20, 1969: One Giant Leap For Mankind. Retrieved from https://www.nasa.gov/mission_pages/apollo/apollo11.html

3   Shore, D. (2014). *Launching and Leading Change Initiatives in Health Care Organizations.* San Francisco, CA: Jossey-Bass.

Preface

"Neither a wise man nor a brave man lies down on the tracks of history to wait for the train of the future to run over him."
Dwight D. Eisenhower

Is it not the ultimate irony that a thoughtful and philosophical leader like Kwame Nkrumah should turn around and persecute the intelligentsia, a short time after becoming Africa's first Independence leader? Was such an act of self-harm that was committed by this, the most famous of early post-Independence African leaders, who had started off promisingly by championing the development of intellectual capacity, not actually responsible for laying the spiritual foundations for the dearth of homemade solutions for Africa's interminable challenges?

Among his early accomplishments, the Ghanaian leader had formed the powerful state-supported think tank, the National Development Planning Commission, but this kind of vision was to disappear down a dark tunnel not only in Nkrumah's Ghana, but across the entire continent, as Dr. Magara so insightfully illustrates.

The absence of African thought, analysis and prescription to national development goes back in time. Africans were not invited to attend, nor were they consulted, when imperial powers met in Berlin, 1884-85, to carve up the continent into the political and economic entities that still exist today. That was in the 19th Century. A little over one hundred years later, Africans were present, though hardly influential, when the various rounds of the Paris Club of international creditors convened to dole out solutions to the continent's economic plight in the form of one-size-fits-all prescriptions made by the World Bank and the IMF in Washington, DC. That was in the 1980s and 1990s, as the 20th Century was drawing to a close.

In between, Africa had been at the recipient end of standard prescriptions made in Paris (Paris again!), London, Lisbon, Brussels and other colonial capitals, and imposed on hapless African nations. The countries and their people have since struggled to make economic and social headway, let alone become prosperous, two decades into the 21st Century.

Magara analyses and illustrates that the reason Africans have so little influence in the direction their countries and societies take, and continue to struggle in just about every area of public endeavor, is the absence of think tanks and local input. Himself a thinker and leadership trainer and mentor, who also happens to be a dental surgeon in Kampala, Magara argues that planning from without – that is, outsourcing our planning – is largely to blame for Africa's floundering fortunes. Countries that have made real headway have almost all invariably leaned on think tanks to weigh up local challenges and evolve homegrown solutions. He uses the study cases of Botswana, a rare African success story, and the East Asian upstarts of Malaysia, South Korea and Singapore, peers with Africa a mere sixty years ago but now world powers in their own right on account of garnering homemade solutions.

Revelations abound in this comprehensively researched thesis: for instance, in 1989 there were 100,000 donor-funded expatriate advisers working in the public sectors of 40 African countries, costing more than $4billion, or 35% of development assistance. And yet Africa has a lot of intellectual power that would inform think tank outlook, institutions whose viewpoints are either developed at home or honed overseas in world-class establishments. One standout, Ngonzi Okonjo-Iweala, is a Nigerian woman of great intellectual stature who has served as Managing Director of the World Bank. How much would she bring to a Nigerian or continental think tank? A lot of Africa's intellectual capacity, Magara observes, is lost either to country or to continent (former South African President, Thabo Mbeki, has noted elsewhere that Africa has lost 20,000 academics and 10% of highly skilled information technology and finance professionals).

A study of the intellectual history of Africa, right from the indirect rule of British colonialism, from which local chiefs did the master's bidding after all the thought and policy-formulation had been done in London, through the assimilation and association policy of the French that left Africans to thoughtlessly, so to speak, implement policies fashioned in Europe, shows the foundational challenge Africa finds itself in. There has been little or no independence of thought in the years after Independence. Policy-making in post-Independence Africa was initially dominated by ruling parties, which soon became single parties, further blunting thought and process. In such an environment, independent thought was often slapped down, even today when the scrambled thinking of governments sees leaders confuse alternative or dissenting views for dissidence, and even insurgency.

Yet independence of thought is critical for think tanks to play their vital role in national development. This book outlines the why and the how, and will be a valuable reference point as African leaders and policy makers put on their thinking caps for the continent to plot a way forward to what is a promising, if fraught, century ahead.

David Sseppuuya
Author, *Africa's Industrialisation & Prosperity,* (2017)
Consultant, World Bank Tanzania and Uganda country offices
Former Editor-in-Chief, 'The New Vision', and former Executive Editor, 'The Daily Monitor'
KAMPALA, UGANDA, October 2017

Preface

Introduction

In the early 1960s, one would not have been faulted to predict a better future for many sub-Saharan African countries compared with their East Asian peers. Endowed with abundant natural resources, vast amounts of arable land, and for some countries, a modest number of intellectuals and professionals, the newly independent African countries looked set for prosperous futures. Over the last sixty years, these sub-Saharan countries and their East Asian peers have charted different paths to where they are today. The latter have largely prospered while the former are still floundering. It is evident that the East Asian countries did some things that present and emerging African leaders would do well to learn. So what did they do differently? Some of the answers are traceable to the type of leadership they had, how those leaders exercised the practice of management, and how they approached the thinking about the future of their countries. This treatise submits that if African countries address the question of the quality of leadership and maximize the prudent use of their intellectual resources through fostering the use of think tanks in policymaking and planning for the future, Africa's pace of development would accelerate exponentially.

The failure of leadership and dearth of adequate development think tank capacity has been a major constraint on Africa's development. The deficiency of think tanks on the continent has resulted in African countries mortgaging their long range planning function to outsiders, and in some cases to a few indigenes, thus denying themselves the benefit of the participation and input from some of the best minds within the countries. As the continent journeys with the rest of the world deeper into the 21st century, this constraint must be removed to unfetter African countries into accelerated development, as happened in East Asia during the last sixty years of Africa's stagnation. This treatise is an effort to contribute towards unlocking Africa's leadership and thinking potential. It elucidates the genesis and development of think tanks in the last century and shows how countries have made use of them to accelerate their development.

Contrary to what some have alluded, Africa does not lack the minds to think critically. Most African countries today have citizens who have trained to the highest levels in some of the best institutions in the world. While at it, some of them have qualified at the top end of their classes. However, often at home, space has not been provided for them to exercise their mental capabilities. The sad tale is that other countries that do not need them as desperately as Africa does, have continued to reap the benefit. Furthermore, even the cream of professionals raised and trained in Africa with the scant resources available on the continent, continue to leave Africa's shores for work abroad in the developed world, leaving the continent further impoverished in intellectual capital. A 2013 United Nations report showed that 2.9 million Africans, that is, one in nine Africans with a tertiary education were living in developed countries - in Europe, North America and elsewhere. This indicated a 50 percent growth in the years leading up to 2013, more than any other region in the world.

Chapter 1 covers a discussion of definitions, concept, types and genesis of think tanks. Chapter 2 gives a brief overview of leadership and policymaking on the African continent from the pre-colonial era to the present time. It covers the impact of the failure of leadership and planning on Africa's development.

Chapter 3 is a short case study of the country of Botswana, which has stood out as an increasingly prospering country in the last five decades of African Independence, registering remarkable economic growth throughout this time. What are the lessons in leadership and policymaking?

Chapter 4 case studies Malaysia, South Korea, and Singapore to illustrate the role leadership and think tanks played in the development of the three East Asian countries in the last sixty years and to draw lessons.

The twentieth century witnessed the most rapid changes the world has ever experienced. The African continent felt the impact more profoundly than any another continent. Chapter 5 examines the impact of the shock wave of globalization on African and East Asian countries. It delves into the rapid social change the continent is experiencing, and how African countries can reposition themselves to ride the wave.

Chapter 6 discusses the importance of leadership, and advocates for a different leadership paradigm from the one that characterized Africa in the last sixty years. It emphasizes the fact that in all situations, quality leadership is what makes the difference. Chapter 7 presents roles that think tanks can play in the development of African countries.

Chapter 8 touches the thorny issue of financing African think tanks. Various avenues for funding are explored bearing in mind the peculiarities of working on the African continent. The argument is that no country should be too poor to fund its brain center, a national think tank. Every state must invest in a national policy think tank to support political leaders to elaborate a national vision, an agenda for development, and growth strategies to deliver it.

Finally, Chapter 9 crystallizes the main points raised in the book and makes actionable recommendations to carry them further. Every country faces unique challenges, so the transferability of development approaches and the drawing of lessons will always be questioned. Political, economic and social factors will have to be taken into account when attempting to apply lessons from one country to another. However while it is true that many experiences may not have cross-country application, there is still much to learn for those that are open to learning. The countries highlighted are not perfect and some still have serious challenges however, they have experienced success where many others have failed. Wisdom requires one to take note and learn from those who have been more successful.

This book introduces the concept of think tanks to leaders who are not versed in it. It emphasizes ways that African countries can benefit from the growing phenomenon of think tanks. It is a call for current and emerging African leaders to avoid mirroring the leadership mistakes of the past five decades. It is a call for clear-sightedness and decisiveness so that the growing opportunities for the continent do not slip through its fingers. It is my hope that this brief discourse will play a role in elevating the level of thinking on the continent particularly regarding decision and policy making as Africa journeys further into the twenty-first century. May those who read the future accounts of the present times resound with gratitude for the positions taken at this time. I pray this book gets into the hands, eyes, and minds of every policy maker and executor on the African continent. If the ideas herein translate to action, a new day awaits the African homeland.

1

Think Tanks 101

"The existence of think tanks is of great consequence to any society."
James G. McGann

The term "think tank" is relatively modern, however the concept has existed in various parts of the world for a long time. The African continent has long been a center of knowledge for generations. Many of the famed Greek philosophers like Socrates, Thales, Aristotle, and Pythagoras spent many years studying in North Africa, which at that time was the educational center of the ancient world.[1,2] Also, North Africa hosted the ancient library of Alexandria, one of the largest and most significant of the ancient world.[3] The African continent is home to a rich history of higher education and knowledge creation including the University of Al Karaoulne at Fez in Morocco, founded in CE 859 as a madrasa and identified by many as the oldest degree awarding institution in the world.[4] The Egyptian Al-Azhar University was established in 970.[5] Centuries before Europe colonized the continent and questioned the primitive character of African mentality, local African scholars in places like Timbuktu discussed Aristotelian logic.[6]

In Europe, arguments between rulers and the Catholic Church about taxes in the 800s resulted in the hiring of teams of independent lawyers to advise about financial and political prerogatives against the clergy.[7] Both popes and monarchs turned to lawyers, who were often independent nobles or clerics in their own right, to get advice; these consultants retained a degree of intellectual independence.[8]

Academic societies in Peru, South America, in the 1790s, and liberal and conservative newspapers in Colombia in the second half of the nineteenth century functioned in ways that would fall under the definition of modern day think tanks.[9] Independent research teams became common in the late 16th and early 17th centuries when states often depended on independent scholars and their expertise.[10]

Chinese rulers and aristocracy had a tradition of valuing counsel from scholars and people with diverse backgrounds. Lord Mengchang who ruled more than 2,000 years ago is known to have supported up to 3,000 people as retainers in his home.[11] He was known to take copious notes during many discussions while wining and dining his entourage and his family almost every night.[12]

Modern Day Think Tanks

The modern-day term, "think tank" has its origins in the military. It was the name given to the secure places that American military and civilian experts met to strategize during World War II.[13] In the post-war period, the term was applied to contract researchers that did work for the military. Later on in the 1960s, the term was expanded to describe experts who formulated policy recommendations. By the 1970s, the application of the term had expanded to include those engaged in political, economic and social issues. In the wake of the end of the cold war, hundreds of think tanks were established in former communist nations.[14]

In the past five decades, public policy research organizations, or think tanks, have emerged as forefront leaders for policy formulation. More than 90 percent of all think tanks were created since 1951 and 58 percent in the last twenty years of the last century.[15] Globally, think tanks present a broad spectrum of sizes and activities. As of 2015, 6,486 think tanks were working to help bridge the gap between knowledge (academia) and policy (politicians and policymakers).[16] This great surge has transformed local, national, and international politics and created a demand for public policy analysis and research.[17]

What Exactly are Think Tanks?

There is no single accepted definition of a think tank. Stone defines them as organizations, "that collect, synthesize and create a range of information products, often directed towards a political or bureaucratic audience, but sometimes for the benefit of the media, interest groups, business, international civil society and the general public of a nation".[18] Dr. James G. McGann of the Lauder Institute defines them as, "Public policy research analysis and engagement organizations that generate policy-oriented research, analysis, and advice on domestic and international issues, thereby enabling policymakers and the public to make informed decisions about public policy".[19] Think tanks produce research products with the aim of informing policy debates. And while providing policy advice is perhaps their underlying purpose, think tanks have had and can have other uses too – for instance, legitimizing government or party policies or existing as a space for debate.

They are usually not-for-profit in their legal statute, though some operate on a for-profit basis. The extent to which think tanks are either more rooted in the private sector or the realm of government varies across countries and within a given institutional, legal and cultural context. Think tanks become political actors as an integral part of the civil society and serve as an important catalyst for ideas and action in emerging and advanced democracies around the world. Increasingly, think tanks are seeking unique niches to attract funding, media attention, and the attention of policymakers.[20, 21]

The roles of think tanks differ from country to country. Ideally, think tanks are considered policy-idea advocates, and their targeted consumers are government branches - such as the executive and the legislative, and social groups influencing the policymaking processes. It helps when policymakers are teachable and willing to listen because unless policymakers hear their voice, think tanks are of little use [22].

Think Tanks and Universities

Universities are repositories of some of the best and most well developed minds that a country has. While both universities and think tanks deal with the merchandise of knowledge, there are differences between the two. Universities seek to produce new knowledge for the sake of expanding the horizons of a field, while policy research actively aims to put practical information in the hands of opinion leaders who shape policy debates and decision makers who make the final choices.[23] A challenge that academics face is that they know their subjects so well that often they tend to share too much detail of what they know, or fail to present it in a way that their intended audiences can easily understand. Think tanks are not content with just producing good research; they want the research used in shaping policy thinking. They improve the understanding of issues and influence thinking in a particular direction. Think tanks thus bridge the academic and policymaking communities, and the state and civil society. They serve the public interest by being independent voices that translate applied and basic research into a language that is understandable, reliable, and accessible for policymakers and the public.[24] They create accessible and relevant materials for specific audiences. They understand that good research is useless if not delivered to those who will use it. They also know that decision makers require actionable information; experts require depth; and the general public and the media require engaging analysis that is relevant to them.[25] Effective think tanks ensure that they have efficient and appropriate communication strategies.

Types Of Think Tanks

Though there is no single prototype of what a think tank should be, most share a common goal of producing high-quality research and analysis combined with engaging the public in some way.[26] There is a wide variation in what think tanks do and the extent to which they do it depending on their host societies. Think tank expert, Dr. James G. McGann offers a typology that takes into consideration the relative differences in political systems and civil societies. In the global context, most think tanks tend to fall into the broad categories outlined in Table 1.1

Table 1.1: Categories of Think Tank Affiliations

CATEGORY	DEFINITION
AUTONOMOUS AND INDEPENDENT	Significant independence from any one interest group or donor and autonomous in its operation and funding from government
QUASI INDEPENDENT	Autonomous from government but controlled by an interest group, donor, or contracting agency that provides a majority of the funding and has significant influence over operations of the think tank.
GOVERNMENT AFFILIATED	A part of the formal structure of government
QUASI GOVERNMENTAL	Funded exclusively by government grants and contracts but not a part of the formal structure of government
UNIVERSITY AFFILIATED	A policy research center at a university
POLITICAL PARTY AFFILIATED	Formally affiliated with a political party
CORPORATE (FOR PROFIT)	A for-profit public policy research organization, affiliated with a corporation or merely operating on a for-profit basis

Source: McGann, J. G. (2016). *2016 Global Go To Think Tank Index Report.* Philadelphia, PA USA: Think Tanks and Civil Societies Program, International Relations Program, University of Pennsylvania. Retrieved from http://repository.upenn. edu/cgi/viewcontent.cgi?article=1011&context=think_tanks

Government Affiliated (or State) Think Tanks

Government affiliated state think tanks can play a pivotal role in the economic development of countries as has been shown in some East Asian nations. They have a role in working out a national vision and can also serve in elaborating and guiding the implementation, monitoring, and evaluation of the same.[27] When they are absent or not consulted, national policies are determined by the influence of lobby and special interest groups, political advantage, or on the impulses and whims of a leader only "playing politics." These factors rarely reflect the totality of the dimensions that have to be considered in national policy, program formulation and implementation.[28] Depending on the leadership styles of both government and think tank leaders, government-funded think tanks may face the challenge of intellectual independence. Prudent governments ensure that government think tanks retain intellectual independence and provide unbiased information for good decision-making.

Professor Steve Adei of Accra, Ghana advances five characteristics that are mandatory if state think tanks are to be effective.[29] First, qualified and competent researchers must administer them. Second, they must have autonomy of voice and not be just a reflector of "the master's voice." Third, they must be patriotic and nationalistic but not political so as to be able to generate scenarios without bias. Fourth, they must be sufficiently funded. Fifth they must be committed to the common and long-term good of the country. Examples of think tanks affiliated with governments are the Economic Development Board of Singapore (EDB) and the Korea Development Institute of South Korea.

Non-Government (Non-State) Think Tanks

Non-government think tanks are also sometimes referred to as independent think tanks. Four main models have emerged:[30]

i. Academic think tanks are either affiliated with universities or are independent. These typically are nonpartisan and focus on public policy research.

ii. Contract research think tanks are professional specialists paid by government contracts.

iii. Advocacy think tanks are distinguishable by their goal-oriented work, which is to effect change rather than merely inform a client or decision maker.

iv. Political party think tanks serve the interests of the political parties that they represent.

The first two are very similar, and so are the last two. Academic and contract types of think tanks try to portray a middle-of-the-road, centrist image, maintaining a balance in a political sense and presenting a broad middle ground of policy. They have a standard feature: sound research based on high academic standards.[31] On the other hand, advocacy and party think tanks champion specific ideas and want to be known for a set of political values they espouse. They nurture a more particular, easily identifiable, coherent and persistent political image. Usually, their specific names, mission statements, and funding mechanisms leave no doubt about their closeness with the ideas and political principles of their parties.[32]

Non-state think tanks serve an important role in the development of ideas for nations and the progress of the world. They bring on board independence of thought and are useful in articulating positions and causing paradigm shifts in political positioning.[33] Independent think tanks provide an alternative source of policy information to that of the government. Alternative ideas and analysis are indispensable in functional democracies. Non-state think tanks play vital roles in providing these. They provide governments with a necessary check on policies that might otherwise pass without adequate scrutiny. In advanced and emerging economies, there are more non-state think tanks than state or government ones. In these countries, it is common for the government to contract independent think tanks to provide specific inputs to policy formulation. However, their role is not to replace state think tanks but rather to complement them, and more so in the developmental state.

Credible and accessible information can shape public policy debates and decision making. Think tanks constitute a marketplace of ideas where politicians, bureaucrats, and the public shop for research and analysis.[34] In western democracies, they serve as alternative expertise repositories for new governments trying to fill policymaking positions from outside the government ranks.[35] They also help in training future policymakers through their intern and fellows programs.[36] In fulfilling their roles, think tanks bring new issues to public attention and provide alternatives for decision makers to consider. They thus have the potential to change the way both policymakers and the public think about, and ultimately act on issues.

The Global Scene

For most of the twentieth century, think tanks were an organizational phenomenon found only in the advanced industrial democracies of the West, primarily in the United States, Canada, Western Europe, and Japan. They have now become a global phenomenon providing information and advice for policymakers and civil society representatives in countries as diverse as India, Lebanon, Chile, Bulgaria, Senegal, and Thailand.[37] Asia that had lagged behind with Africa now has a growing research footprint. China recently pledged support for 100 new think tanks to expand ministerial analytical capacity.[38]

James McGann reports that as of 2015, close to 55 percent of all think tanks were in North America and Europe; there are 1931 think tanks in North America (Mexico, Canada, and the US) and 1770 think tanks in Europe.[39] The United States has the largest number of think tanks in any single nation totaling 1835.[40] American think tanks also dominate the top echelons of global think tanks in rankings, which is not too surprising considering that they are extremely well resourced.[41]

The U.S. think tanks benefit from the style of government where officials are appointed, serve a relatively short period in government, make contacts and then return to the research sector in the so-called revolving-door practice. In the staff line-up of any of the U.S. think tanks is a host of former senior government officials making up the ranks. Further, there is a long-established culture of ideas generation boosted by the ease with which former politicians and government officials move in and out of the think tanks.[42] Conversely, in parliamentary systems such as the UK, where members of parliament typically fill cabinet positions, when a British minister's term in government ends, he or she returns to the backbenches, rather than becoming a fellow at a think tank like Chatham House.[43]

Table 1.2: Number of Think Tanks in the World (2015)

Number of Think Tanks in the World in 2015					
2015 Global Think Tank Total = 6,846					
Asia		Europe		North America	
1262	774	1770	398	1931	615
	Central and South America		Middle East & North Africa	Oceania (96) →	Sub-Saharan Africa

Source: McGann, J. G. (2016). *2016 Global Go To Think Tank Index Report.* Philadelphia, PA USA: Think Tanks and Civil Societies Program, International Relations Program, University of Pennsylvania. Retrieved from http://repository.upenn.edu/cgi/viewcontent.cgi?article=1011&context=think_tanks

As think tanks expanded geographically to Asia, Africa, Latin America, Central Europe, and the former Soviet Union, they faced different challenges that forced them to develop innovative ways to maintain their operations. The problems included securing stable funding, hostile tax environments, maintaining their independence, and authoritarian governments intolerant to independent voices.[44, 45] Also, there were mounting institutional challenges, such as the competition for top analysts that is threatening the viability of some think tanks. Nevertheless, many think tanks in these regions have attained a highly visible presence and participate actively in their countries' policy debates.

Bringing expert knowledge to bear in government decision-making is a challenge faced by governments and private policymakers throughout the developed and the developing world.[46] There is still much room for growth for think tanks globally as the need increases for understandable, reliable, accessible, and useful information about societies, possible alternatives plus their implications, and for information on the progress of current policies.[47]

Table 1.3: Countries with the Largest Number of Think Tanks (2015)

Rank	Country	Number of Think Tanks
1	United States	1835
2	China	435
3	United Kingdom	288
4	India	280
5	Germany	195
6	France	180
7	Argentina	138
8	Russia	122
9	Japan	109
10	Canada	99
11	Italy	97
12	Brazil	89
13	South Africa	86
14	Sweden	77
15	Switzerland	73
16	Australia	63
17	Mexico	61
18	Iran	59
19	Bolivia	59
20	Israel	58
21	Netherlands	58
22	Spain	55
23	Romania	54
24	Kenya	53
25	Belgium	53

Source: McGann, J. G. (2016). *2016 Global Go To Think Tank Index Report.* Philadelphia, PA USA: Think Tanks and Civil Societies Program, International Relations Program, University of Pennsylvania. Retrieved from http://repository.upenn. edu/cgi/viewcontent.cgi?article=1011&context=think_tanks

The African Scene

Modern think tanks in sub-Saharan Africa began in the 1920s. The South African Institute of Race Relations (SAIRR), established in 1929 during the challenging times of great depression, is the oldest known think tank in SSA in modern times.[48] The South African Institute of International Affairs (SAIIA) followed in 1934. However, these institutes remained uncommon in Sub-Saharan Africa until the 1960s when many African countries became independent. The Institute of Statistical, Social and Economic Research (ISSER) and Centre for Development Studies in Ghana were established in 1962 and 1969 respectively.[49] CODESERIA in Senegal, Freedom Market Foundation in South Africa and the Nigerian Institute of International Affairs were all founded in the early 1970s.[50]

James McGann outlines some trends that favored the growth of think tanks on the continent, and they include:[51]

a) The fall of the Berlin Wall and the third wave of democratization

b) Information revolution

c) End of government monopoly on information

d) Complexity and technical nature of policy problems

e) Size of government and crisis in confidence in government officials

f) Globalization and the growth of state and non-state actors

g) Need for timely and concise information and analysis "in the right form at the right time."

These trends transformed the economic, social and political debates in most countries of the world, which in turn, created a greater demand for policy research and advice.[52] In 2008-2009, of the 53 states in Africa, only 42 states had think-tank representation.[53] Of these 42 only 14 African countries had 10 or more think tanks, namely, Burkina Faso (16), Cameroon (20), Cote d'Ivoire (12), Ethiopia (20), Ghana (36), Kenya (56), Malawi

(13), Namibia (11), Nigeria (45), Senegal (16), South Africa (84), Tanzania (11), Uganda (23), and Zimbabwe (21).[54] It is important to note that the number of think tanks in a country does not necessarily indicate their impact. The influence of think tanks is more a function of the quality of their research products, the access they have with policymakers and decision makers, and whether their voice is heard.

As Figure 1.1 indicates, of the 2015 global total of 6846 think tanks, 9 percent (only 615) are in sub-Saharan Africa whereas 18 percent (1262) are in Asia. Sub-Saharan Africa is clearly underrepresented in this industry. Table 1.3 shows the number of think tanks in Africa per country as of 2015. Unlike ancient times, the Africa continent is currently a significant net consumer of knowledge and not a net producer.

Think tanks are ideas factories and as the common saying goes, "ideas are the most powerful force in the world." There is no question that ideas generated out of think tanks have had a profound influence on the world. On the social front, it was the work of the Thomas Clarkson's Society for the Abolition of the Slave Trade in the eighteenth century that led to the abolition of slave trade in Britain, changing the destiny of the black race. In more recent times, on the economic front, the spread of liberal economic ideology especially during the Reagan-Thatcher era was a result of the work of think tanks like the Adam Smith Institute in the UK and the Reason Foundation in the USA. On the political front, African intellectuals who gathered, mainly in Europe, in the 1940s and 1950s conceived and later led the movements that resulted in independence for the modern African states.

Table 1.3: Number of Think Tanks by African Country (2015)

Algeria	9	Libya	2
Angola	4	Madagascar	5
Benin	15	Malawi	15
Botswana	13	Mali	12
Burkina Faso	16	Mauritania	2
Burundi	5	Mauritius	8
Cape Verde	2	Morocco	15
Cameroon	21	Mozambique	4
Central African Republic (CAR)	2	Namibia	15
Chad	3	Niger	4
Comoros		Nigeria	48
Dem. Rep. of the Congo (DRC)	7	Rwanda	7
Republic of the Congo	3	Sao Tome/Principe	
Cote d'Ivoire	12	Senegal	16
Djibouti		Seychelles	3
Egypt	35	Sierra Leone	1
Equatorial Guinea		Somalia	6
Eritrea	5	South Africa	86
Ethiopia	25	South Sudan	5
Gabon	2	Sudan	5
Gambia	6	Swaziland	4
Ghana	6	Tanzania	15
Guinea	2	Togo	4
Guinea-Bissau	1	Tunisia	18
Kenya	53	Uganda	28
Lesotho	4	Zambia	13
Liberia	3	Zimbabwe	26

Source: McGann, J. G. (2016). *2016 Global Go To Think Tank Index Report.* Philadelphia, PA USA: Think Tanks and Civil Societies Program, International Relations Program, University of Pennsylvania. Retrieved from http:// repository.upenn.edu/cgi/viewcontent.cgi?article=1011&context=think_ tanks

Notes & References

1   Onyewuenyi, I. C. (2010). *The African origin of Greek philosophy: An exercise in Afrocentrism.* Nsukka Nigeria: University of Nigeria Press.

2   Asante, M. K. (2004). *An African Origin of Philosophy: Myth or Reality?* Retrieved from http://www.asante.net/articles/26/afrocentricity/

3   MacLeod, R. M. (2014). *The library of Alexandria: Centre of learning in the ancient world.* New York, NY: Palgrave Macmillan.

4   Adams J. King C., & Hook D. (2010). *Global research report Africa. (2010).* Leeds, UK: Evidence. Retrieved from http://researchanalytics.thomsonreuters.com/m/pdfs/globalresearchreport-africa.pdf

5   ibid.

6   Diagne, S. B. (2008). *Toward an intellectual history of West Africa: the meaning of Timbuktu.* In Shamil J. & Diagne S. B. (Eds), *The Meanings of Timbuktu* (pp.19-28). Pretoria, South Africa: The Human Sciences Research Council Press.

7   Soll J. (2017). How think tanks became engines of royal propaganda. *Tablet Magazine.* Retrieved from http://www.tabletmag.com/jewish-news-and-politics/222421/think-tanks-jacob-soll-propaganda.

8   ibid.

9   Kimenyi, M. S. & Datta, A. (2011). *Think tanks in sub-Saharan Africa: How the political landscape has influenced their origins.* Overseas Development Institute. Retrieved from https://www.odi.org/sites/odi.org.uk/files/odi-assets/publications-opinion-files/7527.pdf

10 Soll J. (2017). How think tanks became engines of royal propaganda. *Tablet Magazine.* Retrieved from http://www.tabletmag.com/jewish-news-and-politics/222421/think-tanks-jacob-soll-propaganda.

11 Xiangwei, W. (2017, February). China's think tanks overflow, but most still think what they're told to think. *South China Morning Post.* Retrieved from http://www.scmp.com/week-asia/opinion/article/2069944/chinas-think-tanks-overflow-most-still-think-what-theyre-told

12 ibid.

13 McGann J. G. & Sabatini, R. (2011). *Global think tanks: Policy networks and governance.* New York: NY: Routledge

14 ibid.

15 McGann, J. G. (2000). How think tanks are coping with the future. *The Futurist,* 34(6), 16-23.

16 McGann, J. G. (2016). *2016 Global Go To Think Tank Index Report.* Philadelphia, PA USA: Think Tanks and Civil Societies Program, International Relations Program, University of Pennsylvania. Retrieved from http://repository.upenn.edu/cgi/viewcontent.cgi?article=1011&context=think_tanks

17 McGann, J. G. (2000). How think tanks are coping with the future. *The Futurist,* 34(6), 16-23.

18 Stone, D. (2004). *Introduction: think tanks, policy advice and governance.* In Stone, D., & Denham, A, (Eds), *Think Tank Traditions.* Manchester, UK: Manchester University Press. p.3

19 McGann, J. G. (2016). *2016 Global Go To Think Tank Index Report.*

20 McGann, J. G. (2000). How think tanks are coping with the future. *The Futurist, 34*(6), 16-23.

21 McGann, J. G., & Weaver, R. K. (2009). *Think tanks & civil societies: Catalysts for ideas and action.* New Brunswick, N.J: Transaction Publishers.

22 Stone, D. (2010). Think tank transnationalisation and non-profit analysis, advice and advocacy, *Global Society 14* (2), 154-55.

23 Selee, A. D. (2013). What should think tanks do? A strategic guide to policy impact. Stanford, CA: Stanford Briefs.

24 McGann J. G. (2007). *Think Tanks and Policy Advice in the US.* New York: NY: Routledge

25 Selee, A. D. (2013). What should think tanks do? A strategic guide to policy impact. Stanford, CA: Stanford Briefs.

26 McGann J. G. & Sabatini, R. (2011). *Global think tanks: Policy networks and governance.*

27 Adei, S. (2009, July). *The critical role of the development of think tanks for Africa's development.* Paper presented at the meeting of SALT Institute, Kampala, Uganda.

28 ibid.

29 ibid.

30 McGann, J. G., & Weaver, R. K. (2009). *Think tanks & civil societies: Catalysts for ideas and action.* New Brunswick, N.J: Transaction Publishers.

31 Braml, J. (2006). U.S. and German Think Tanks in Comparative Perspective. *German Policy Studies, 3*(222-267).

32 ibid.

33 Adei, S. (2009, July). *The critical role of the development of think tanks for Africa's development.*

34 McGann, J. G. (2000). How think tanks are coping with the future. *The Futurist, 34*(6), 16-23.

35 ibid.

36 ibid.

37 ibid.

38 Biswas, A. K. & Hartley, K. (2015). The Rise of Asia's Think Tanks: Regional think tanks are proliferating. Is the quality keeping pace? *The Diplomat.* Retrieved from http://thediplomat.com/2015/09/the-rise-of-asias-think-tanks/

39 McGann, J. G. (2016). *2016 Global Go To Think Tank Index Report.*

40 ibid.

41 Miks, J. (2012). India's Think Tank Failure. *The Diplomat.* Retrieved from http://thediplomat.com/2012/01/indias-think-tank-failure/

42 ibid.

43 ibid.

44 Mbadlanyana, T., Cilliers, J., & Sibalukhulu, N. (2011). Shaping African futures: Think tanks and the need for endogenous knowledge production in sub-Saharan Africa. *The Journal of Futures Studies, Strategic Thinking and Policy, 13*(3), 64-84.

45 McGann, J. G. (2000). How think tanks are coping with the future. *The Futurist, 34*(6), 16-23.

46 McGann, J. G. (2016). *2016 Global Go To Think Tank Index Report.*

47 ibid.

48 Mbadlanyana, T., Cilliers, J., & Sibalukhulu, N. (2011). Shaping African futures: Think tanks and the need for endogenous knowledge production in sub-Saharan Africa.

49 ibid.

50 ibid.

51 McGann, J. G. (2016). *2016 Global Go To Think Tank Index Report.*

52 McGann, J. G., & Weaver, R. K. (2009). *Think tanks & civil societies: Catalysts for ideas and action.*

53 Mbadlanyana, T., Cilliers, J., & Sibalukhulu, N. (2011). Shaping African futures: Think tanks and the need for endogenous knowledge production in sub-Saharan Africa.

54 ibid.

2

An African Odyssey
In Policymaking

*"Thinking is the hardest work there is, which is probably
the reason why so few engage in it."*
Henry Ford

In 2014 the former Vice President of USA Joe Biden speaking
in the United States - Africa summit, referred to the continent of
Africa as the "nation of Africa".[1] This view of the continent as a
singular unit by commentators from other parts of the world is
not uncommon. It is however very erroneous because present
day Africa consists of 54 sovereign states (Figure 2.1).

Another common misconception about Africa is its size.
Africa is the second largest of the earth's seven continents. With
its adjacent islands, it covers a land area of about 30 million square
kilometers or about 22 percent of the world's total land area.[2] It
has a land area that can contain USA, Europe, India, Argentina,
China and New Zealand put together.[3] All these countries have a
total land area of 11,668,035 square miles compared with Africa's
11,706,166 square miles (Figure 2.2). Africa stretches 8,050 km
from its northernmost point of Cape Blanc in Tunisia to its
southernmost tip of Cape Agulhas in South Africa. The equator
cuts the continent almost into two halves.

Figure 2.1: A Political Map of Africa

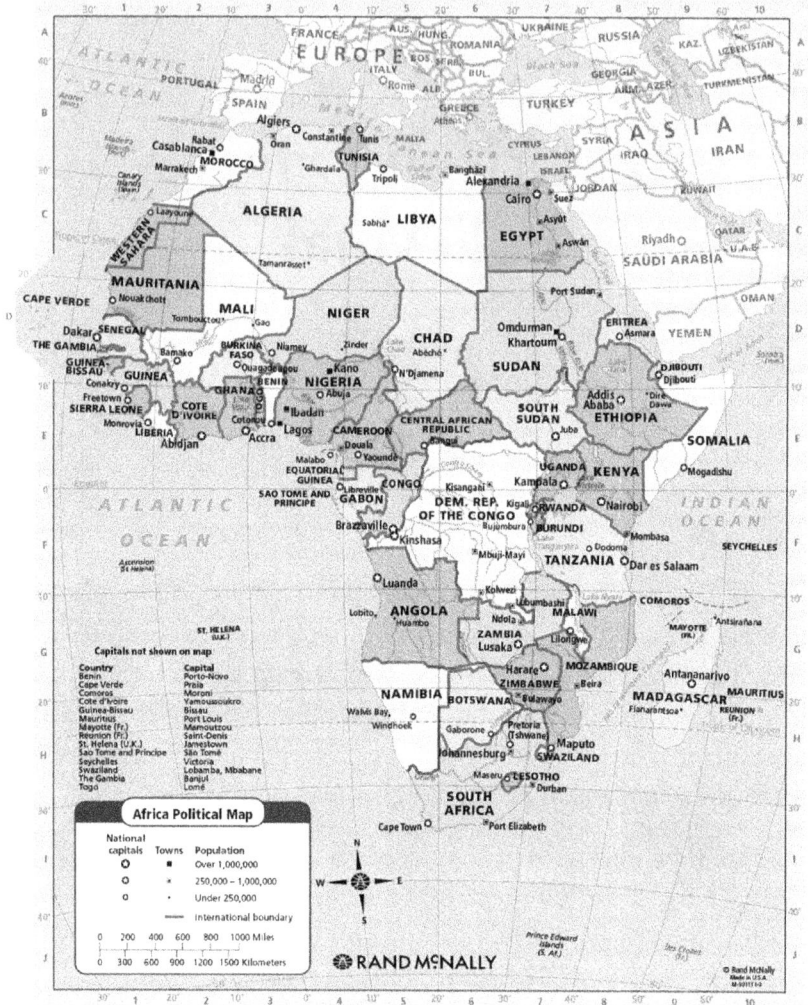

Source: Rand McNally. Retrieved from http://seccionzobel.blogspot.ug/2014/11/
political-africa.html

By the time the scramble for Africa by the Europeans was over in the late nineteenth century many diverse and independent people groups with differing history, culture, languages, and religion, were amalgamated and enclosed as part of new territories.[4] In all some 10,000 African polities had been amalgamated into 40 European colonies and protectorates.[5] Changes to this initial land grab occurred as a result of the First and Second World Wars. Africa is currently home to 1.2 billion people.[6]

Figure 2.2: The True Size of Africa

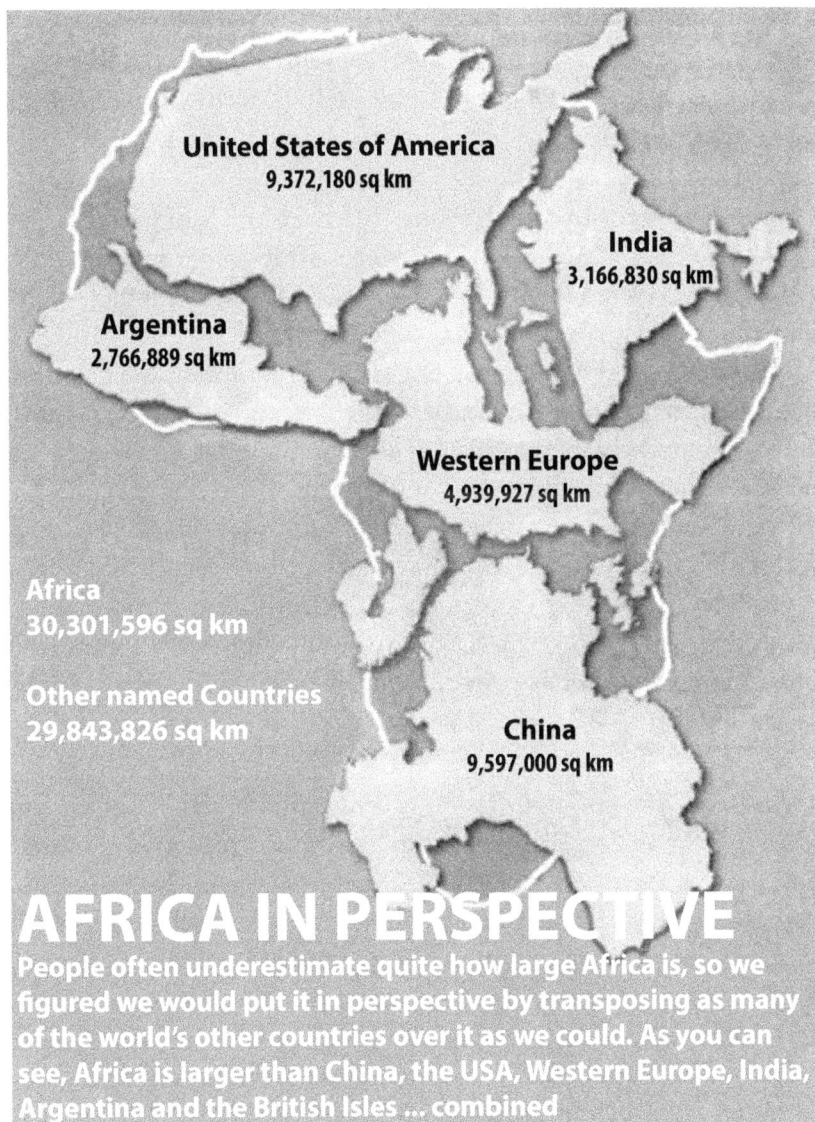

United States of America
9,372,180 sq km

India
3,166,830 sq km

Argentina
2,766,889 sq km

Western Europe
4,939,927 sq km

Africa
30,301,596 sq km

Other named Countries
29,843,826 sq km

China
9,597,000 sq km

AFRICA IN PERSPECTIVE
People often underestimate quite how large Africa is, so we figured we would put it in perspective by transposing as many of the world's other countries over it as we could. As you can see, Africa is larger than China, the USA, Western Europe, India, Argentina and the British Isles ... combined

Source: White African. Retrieved from http://whiteafrican.com/2006/04/19/africa-in-perspective/

The range of political development on the continent has been diverse. Most African countries obtained political independence in the 1960s however some did so as early as 1847 (Liberia) and others as late as in 1990 (Namibia), and 2011 (Southern Sudan). There has also been a range of experiences regarding democracy, autocratic civilian, and military rule. While there have been regional and country variations, there have also been general trends. Therefore, the brief treatise that follows is a generalization of events that portray a broad trend on the continent.

Pre-colonial Africa

Pre-colonial Africa had many different forms of governance closely related to the level of economic organization and production. While some pre-colonial African societies were hunting-gathering economies, other societies had agriculture-based economies.[7] African societies were predominantly agrarian with their foundations in land and its uses.[8] In both hunting and gathering, and small agricultural societies, a village government with a council of elders and village chiefs predominated.[9] In intensive-agricultural societies with a crafts-manufacturing sector like Buganda, Ethiopia, Ghana, Mali, and Songhay, centralized governments capable of collecting taxes, regulating commerce, and mobilizing armies were common.[10, 11] Political power in most societies rested in family or kinship groups.

Policy and Decision Making in Pre-colonial Africa

In the pre-colonial era, absolute monarchs ruled most societies. Practices differed from polity to polity. A modern day African relic of this system of governance is the Kingdom of Swaziland, which remains an absolute monarchy. Most pre-colonial African societies had a council of elders with the responsibility of resolving conflicts, maintaining societal order, and advising the rulers.[12] For example, even in present times, traditionally the council of elders in the Karamojong and Teso communities in Uganda resolves disputes. That council among the Karamojong is called the *Akiriket* while among the Teso it is called *Arriget*.[13]

Another example of a polity where rulers interacted and conferred with their followers was among the Batswana of Southern Africa. Through the custom of tribal gatherings called the *kgotla,* Batswana chiefs consulted and interacted with their subjects.[14] These fora were akin to modern-day town hall meetings. *Kgotlas* helped the Chiefs stay closely connected to men in their societies; they were the main fora for political discussion. A *kgotla* gave adult males the opportunity to criticize and advise the chief. In comparison with other African tribes, Botswana's pre-colonial leadership set-up was quite tolerant of dissent.[15]

Broadly speaking though, across most of pre-colonial Africa, decision making for the polity was reserved for an individual, or at best, a few people at the top. At the start of the colonial period, most African societies, unlike the Asian ones, had not acquired much experience in the management of people and space, nor were they accustomed to thinking in terms of multi-ethnic communities. The colonial period disrupted the governance modes that existed on the continent before its advent. It brought about an important change that resulted in the formation of new countries and a new approach to governance that included aspects of focused management.

Colonial Africa
(Late 19th Century to 1950s)

The driving force behind the colonization of Africa was not altruistic as is often portrayed; it was economic. The fact that the first Europeans to stake a claim on the continent were not politicians but businessmen like Lord Lugard attests this. He was not initially employed by the British Government, but rather by companies. He was first an employee of the East Indian Company, the Royal East African Company, and then the Royal Niger Company. It was from there that he transferred to the British government.[16]

The Industrial Revolution in Europe created a need for both raw materials and foreign markets. Africa, having the largest deposit of almost every mineral on the planet and 30,330,000 square kilometers of mainly un-colonized land provided a perfect solution for Europe's need. These facts led European countries to compete vigorously for Africa. At the end of the 19th Century, after meetings in Berlin, Paris, London, and other capitals by European statesmen and diplomats in the scramble for Africa, European powers finally staked claims to virtually the entire continent. The most significant of these meetings was the Berlin Conference (1884-1885), where fourteen European nations met to decide how to divide up Africa. There wasn't a single African representative at the conference. The carving up of the colonial territories was not consistent with ethnic considerations but rather with the defense of the strategic and commercial interests of the colonial rulers. The biggest winners at the conference, Britain and France (Figure 2.3), became the two dominant colonial masters in Africa. Each approached the governance of their colonies differently.

Figure 2.3: Colonies & Protectorates in Africa around 1914

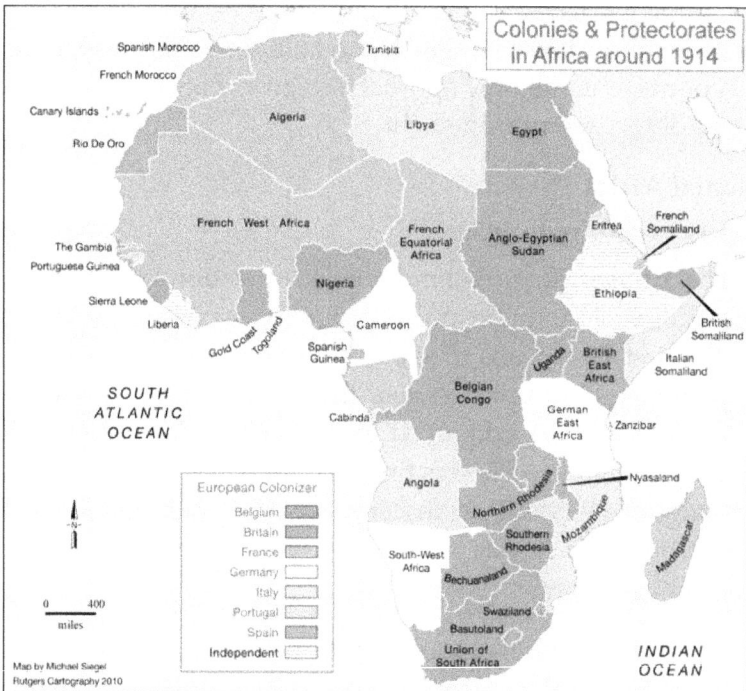

Source: Siegel M. (2010). *Colonies and protectorates in Africa around 1914.* Retrieved from http://exhibitions.nypl.org/africanaage/maps.html

Policy and Decision Making in Colonial Africa

The British used indirect rule. They delegated power to local chiefs and others with pre-existing claims to power.[17] These local leaders had to be sympathetic to British interests. They were given authority for limited decision-making and put in charge of tax collection, local conflict resolution and most importantly, quelling anti-British feeling among the people. They reported to British colonial officers, who in turn reported to, and received orders from the government in London. Critical policy decisions were made in London without local input.[18]

The policies of assimilation or association characterized the French style of direct rule.[19] The policy of assimilation employed in some colonies like Senegal in West Africa, gave the right to freedom, equality, and fraternity to anyone who was offered French citizenship, regardless of race or color. A very small number of the African elite in each colony benefited from this arrangement. This privileged group was then used to ensure that the status quo functioned with minimal resistance to French colonial policies. Though each colony had an African Council-General to represent them in France on various issues, these representatives had little input into policy decisions. Association, employed in the majority of French colonies, was a system where the Minister of Colonies and the government in Paris directed policies. Colonial policies were uniformly formulated in Paris. French governors based in the colonies implemented them and reported back to Paris.[20]

Gradually even the traditional leaders were left out of the management of the new countries. They became increasingly marginalized as the colonial powers produced the multi-ethnic territories that would become Nation-States. These new areas were difficult for the traditional authorities to rule because of their ethnic and cultural diversity. In many territories, the colonial powers neglected training alternative national elite.[21]

These approaches to governance to a large extent truncated the development of original thinking on the continent, as there was little or no consultation with the African elite. Broadly speaking, it was not in the interest of the colonialists to give Africans a say in colonial policy.[22] Policies were designed in Europe with little if any African input. In some cases, colonial administrations set up research institutions such as the West African Institute for Social and Economic Research, established in 1950 in Nigeria.[23] These institutes helped them govern, improve the lives of settler populations and expand the growth of export-oriented cash crops.[24] In East Africa, to cater for farming interests, the British set up research institutions that focused on agriculture and livestock.[25]

The Early Post Independence Period (Single Party Rule) (The 1960s)

The front-runners for African independence were Ghana (from Britain in 1957) followed by Guinea (from France in 1958). Within a decade the majority of African countries were independent of colonial rule. Agitation for independence mainly came from the African elite and not from the traditional chiefs. Even if the African elite were opposed to colonial power and did not have any significant influence on colonial policy, they were, in fact, closer to the colonial mentality as reflected in the states they created. From 1960 to 1970 the elite who managed political power were mainly teachers and a handful of doctors and African Union leaders.[26] Nationalism, considered to be indispensable for freedom from the colonial yoke and for laying the foundations of viable states, guided their actions.[27]

The early years of independence gave the illusion of bringing about radical change. There was a great optimism for the future. Income levels were higher than in many Asian regions and on a par with Latin America, the continent held great riches in natural resources and Africans were finally free to form their own destiny. The State was perceived as the ideal entrepreneur, bringing overall progress and social justice.[28] African nationalist politicians started out proclaiming nationalistic objectives, and selecting party candidates regardless of ethnic origin. As the stakes grew higher with the approach of independence, ambitious politicians changed the basis for campaigning - they found they could win votes by appealing for ethnic support and, in return, promise improved government services and new development projects in their ethnic regions.[29] Soon the personalization of power was affirmed in virtually every country by *coups d'état,* the introduction of one-party rule, or simply the monopoly of power by autocrats.[30]

In justifying the establishment of a one-party state, the common reason given by African leaders was that unlike Western societies that were divided along class lines, African societies were classless and homogeneous and did not warrant a pluralistic political system based on social classes.[31] The political arena became a platform upon which different ethnic groups contested for scarce resources.[32] The continent soon became troubled by ethnic and racial conflict, political unrest, violent crime, ravaging poverty, economic failure and resignation, predatory leaders and rampant corruption.

Atrocious post-colonial African leadership bears a large part of the responsibility for the African tragedy.[33] Most political parties that led Africa to independence adopted Marxist platforms. Examples are the African Independence Party in Senegal, the African Democratic Rally, founded in Bamako in 1946, with notable members: Félix Houphouët-Boigny (Côte d'Ivoire), Ahmed Sékou Touré (Guinea), and Modibo Keita (Mali). Others were the Action Group of Chief Obafemi Awolowo in Nigeria, the Convention People's Party of Kwame Nkrumah in Ghana, and the Mau Mau of Jomo Kenyatta in Kenya.[34] The rejection of colonialism and Western institutions was understandable. But there was an overreaction in attempting to eradicate all the vestiges of Western colonialism. Ghanaian economist George Ayittey notes that after independence, many African leaders, proclaiming themselves "free and independent under black rule," hauled down the statues of European monarchs and erected, not those of African heroes, but of another set of aliens - Marx and Lenin.[35]

The new leaders, with a desire to consolidate power, barred political competition. Many countries on the continent slid into single-party rule even where the law permitted multi-party politics. As post-independence African countries moved toward single-party rule, 'big man' politics increasingly dominated. Any attempts to introduce party competition met repression. Regimes become increasingly predatory as those in power tended to favor members of their own ethnic and religious group. The policies that emerged from the process were more about concentrating benefits on some groups and individuals and less about promoting economic development.[36]

Policy and Decision Making During Single Party Rule

For a brief period after independence, African politicians hobnobbed with academics, often seeking their mainly socialist ideas for policymaking.[37] [38] Former colonial research institutions were reconfigured to promote growth and development, while new governments invested considerable sums of money in expanding state infrastructure, including research and development. Examples of research units included the Planning Statistics and Research Unit of Botswana's Ministry of Education, the Research Unit of the Zambian Ministry of Finance and Planning, and the Research Unit of the Ministry of Finance and Economic Planning in Ghana.[39]

Governments also still relied heavily on foreign experts and intellectuals for inspiration.[40] For instance, Ghana's Kwame Nkrumah drew inspiration from pan-Africanists, such as George Padmore and W.E.B. Dubois. Similarly, Tanzania's Julius Nyerere had a band of foreign 'Fabian socialists'; and Zambia's Kenneth Kaunda invited John Hatch, a close intellectual associate, to be the first director of the Institute for Humanism.[41] Later, European and American 'radicals' were to appear as itinerant advisors to some regimes in Africa.[42]

As governments moved towards monocratic rule, a rift emerged in this erstwhile positive relationship resulting in suspicion, mistrust, antagonism and lack of cooperation.[43]

Academics faced a dilemma as the resulting acrimony forced them to consider exile, persecution, or maintenance of a low profile. Some politicians like Kwame Nkrumah assumed the role of philosopher king (he took on the title of "Osagyefo" meaning "Redeemer" in the Akan language). As contrary views were increasingly not tolerated, academic work was reduced from intellectual work to the incantation of the thought of the leader.

Political space for academics vanished as they were treated with suspicion and mistrust. Outsiders funded the few spaces in which academics could exercise their autonomy and placed limits on their intellectual independence. At the peak of Ghana's drive for economic emancipation its first President, Kwame Nkrumah put emphasis on building intellectual capacity in the country. He created various state-supported think tanks and a powerful National Development Planning Commission. Scientific think tanks like the Cocoa Research Institute and the umbrella Council of Scientific and Industrial Research (CSIR) were also established.[44] Ironically when Nkrumah became dysfunctional in his latter days, the intellectuals and independent thinkers became part of the group he persecuted.[45]

Many leaders at this time deemed the development of an intellectual class as a threat to their rule. In some countries, the freedom fighters that became government leaders in post-independence Africa were not highly educated and consequently became insecure with any criticism of policy. Finding little or no room to exercise their abilities, African intellectuals resorted to civil society, providing mostly foreign-funded research institutes with research, though even these did not offer full intellectual independence. Ironically, often the very governments that had shunned African intellectuals became consumers of their research only now dressed as donor-contracted reports - a practice common even today.[46]

Much like during the rule of absolute monarchies, by and large, policymaking in the post-independence period, from the late 1950s to the 1970s, was particularly dominated by ruling parties, particularly presidents or the 'big man,' with little input from other groups in society.[47] In that period just a few individuals held decision-making powers. The personalization of power had the effect of centralizing authority in the presidency and the executive at the expense of other institutions.[48]

After political independence, a number of these new countries initiated some forms of development planning and achieved some levels of success.[49] The first phase of development planning in Africa was during the 1960s and was characterized by centralized planning with fixed-term development planning phases. Countries like Uganda, Botswana, and Nigeria had plans promoting state-engineered economies. It was notably the time of state-owned enterprises operating in most of the productive sectors. In this phase, at least 32 African countries had a National Development Plan.[50] However, due to a variety of reasons mainly stemming from failures in governance and lack of think tank capacity to analyze and vet these plans, Africa's development plans of the 1960s had limited success. Some of the reasons for failure were: deficiencies in the plan documents; failure in implementation; ambitious formulation of targets; institutional and bureaucratic weaknesses; exogenous shocks; and political factors.[51] Another major reason was the absence of analytical think tank capacity.[52]

Military Rule
(The 1970s)

The single-party rule period was marked by a variety of failures including poor economic performance, political repression, denial of civil freedoms, widespread corruption and inability to provide essential services such as education and health to the majority of the population, and sectarianism.[53] The resulting widespread discontent provided militaries with the justification to overthrow civilian governments so much so that in most cases, the populace enthusiastically welcomed military coups. From 1970 to 1990 almost all African States, with a few exceptions were ruled by the military and autocratic rule was prevalent even in those rare countries whose leaders were not from the military.[54] By the year 2000, of the 53 independent African states, approximately 40 had been affected by the 'coup d'état epidemic'.[55] In 2004 the Chairman of the African Union Commission, Alpha Oumar Konare, reminded an African Union summit that the continent had suffered from 186 "coup d'etats".[56]

Policy and Decision During Military Rule

Unfortunately for the African people, the transition to military rule in many cases was like the proverbial jumping from the frying pan into the fire. The ensuing military governments mostly ruled by decree and in many cases were very cruel. Political parties were disbanded, constitutions suspended and legislative assemblies dissolved. In many countries, the new military leaders, like Uganda's Idi Amin, became absolute dictators, declared themselves life Presidents, and eliminated anyone deemed a political threat. As a result, there were no political, institutional avenues for public input into policymaking.[57] It was also the height of the Cold War, during which African countries became pawns for the super powers. So long as the African dictators pledged allegiance, powerful nations chose to look the other way even as the population was butchered.

At the time, state-sponsored research institutes in most cases only performed legitimizing roles; otherwise, they risked harsh consequences from ruling regimes.[58] The periodic planning that had been initiated in the 1960s was largely discontinued. Much like the decade of the 1960s, decision-making was the preserve of just a few individuals. The production of research and policy ideas got little or no priority. Funding for tertiary education and state and university-affiliated research institutes was massively cut. Those who stood up to military regimes were persecuted. Africa lost its best minds as academics went into exile, made themselves inconspicuous, or 'toed the line'.[59] The cost to the continent as a result of the loss of intellectual capital is hard to quantify, but is probably one of the biggest losses Africa has experienced second only to the slave trade. The value of the intellectual loss from slave trade and the brain drain certainly surpasses the centuries-old loss Africa has experienced from the exploitation of her natural resources by foreigners. One only has to see the role intellectuals and professionals played in the rise of the Asian Tigers to get an idea how different African countries could have been today, if the intellectual capital had been retained and utilized. Predictably, the era of military rule resulted in the continental economic recession seen in the 1970s and 1980s together with the effects that are still evident today. Failure of leadership on the African continent had resulted in the tragedy of the slave trade followed on its heels by colonization. Once again, the failure of leadership on the continent made African countries vulnerable to outside actors, this time leading to economic enslavement.

Economic Liberalization Era
The Structural Adjustment Period (1980s and 1990s)

The period from 1980 to 1990 was attendant with difficulties for African countries due to the widespread economic recession and high debt levels resulting from the leadership failures. Donor agencies began to play an increasing role in sub-Saharan Africa's economic policies. In the early 1980s the World Bank and the International Monetary Fund (IMF) (known collectively as the Bretton Woods Institutions) [60] prescribed and imposed economic policies for developing countries referred to as the Structural Adjustment Programs (SAPs). SAPs were designed to reduce the role of the State in production and service delivery, and placed emphasis on macroeconomic stability, downsizing of public sector institutions, privatization and cutting government spending and budget deficits.[61]

SAPs were meant to provide temporary financing to borrowing countries so that they could stabilize their economies. It was expected that governments would be enabled to repay their debts, reduce deficits in spending, and close the gap between imports and exports.[62] Gradually, these loans evolved into a core set of economic policy changes required by the World

Bank and IMF.[63] According to the dictum, African countries would further integrate into the global economy, the role of the international private sector would strengthen, and African countries would grow through trade. However debt repayment among other economic polices were made the priority as poor countries were forced to reduce spending on health, education, and development.

The Poverty Reduction Strategy Papers Period (2000s)

The late 1980s saw the fall of the Soviet Union and the demise of socialist systems of governance. With SAPs deemed a failure in the early 1990s, and changes in the global environment, donor policy demands now focused on political reforms, including the establishment of democratic institutions, and improving 'efficiency', transparency and accountability of bureaucracies - the latter more commonly known as the good governance agenda.[64] In the early 2000s, Poverty Reduction Strategy Papers (PRSPs) replaced SAPs, with the intention of reversing the adverse effects on welfare and social conditions resulting from a decade of Structural Adjustment. Many African countries embarked on at least two generations of PRSPs with a strong emphasis on poverty reduction as a condition for debt relief.[65]

While PRSPs introduced the principle of ownership and consultations, which were lacking in SAPs, they were still externally driven and therefore lacked credibility. There were serious questions about their sustainability because they tended to place disproportionate emphasis on the social sector at the expense of the productive sector.[66] PRSPs were short sighted in not holding a long-term view for the countries involved.

In many ways, the PRSPs were a repackaging of the SAPs. According to a statement issued in Kampala, Uganda in 2001, rather than enabling local people to decide their content, PRSPs meant more IMF and World Bank control not only over financial and economic policies, but also over every aspect and detail of national policies and programs.[67] One of the enduring criticisms of the Bretton Woods recipes for the continent has been the "one-size fits all" approach.[68]

Consequences of SAPs and PRSPs

The results of SAPs especially in the social sector were disastrous. Budget restrictions compromised social service delivery and human capital development. There were net job losses due to the downsizing of the public sector institutions and massive privatizations. Most importantly SAPs did not result in the envisaged growth outcomes as the annual economic growth for Africa over the 1990s averaged only 2.1 per cent.[69]

African countries were forced into the global marketplace before they were economically and socially stable and ready. They were told to concentrate on similar cash crops and commodities resulting in the semblance of a large-scale price war.[70] Most African countries signed up to the General Agreement on Tariffs and Trade (GATT), which in 1995 became the World Trade Organization (WTO). This rules-based system, whereby member states adhere to over 60 agreements covering goods, services and intellectual property, committed them to altering their national laws, regulations and administrative procedures.[71] Commodity prices dropped favoring consumers in the West. Governments then needed to increase exports just to keep their currencies stable and earn foreign exchange with which to help pay off debts. Gradually the value of labor decreased and social unrest resulted.[72] As donors, like the IMF kept the exchange rates in their favor, African countries found it increasingly difficult to escape the poverty trap.[73]

The public sector job losses and wage cuts associated with the Bretton Woods programs increased hardship in many African countries. During the 1980s, when most African countries came under World Bank and IMF tutelage, per capita income declined by 25 percent in most of sub-Saharan Africa.[74] Reduced access to health care services increased the spread of diseases and the vulnerability to HIV infection.[75] The resultant economic insecurity reinforced migrant labor patterns, which in turn increased the risk of infection. The spread of HIV / AIDS in Africa was facilitated by worsening poverty and by the conditions of inequality intensified by World Bank and IMF policies.[76]

Food security was compromised, for example the Malawian government was humiliated in 2002 when it was forced by the IMF to sell its surplus grain in favor of foreign exchange just before famine struck.[77] This was akin to forcing the head of a household to sell food reserved for his family and then watch the children starve to death. Malawi was forced to remove any subsidies towards agriculture to allow the forces of "demand and supply" to operate. The rich countries preach but do not practice this. For example The U.S. government has been subsidizing farmers against unpredictable hardships such as severe weather since the 1930s, when drought and the Great Depression devastated the nation's agriculture industry. Today, the U.S. government pays farmers about $20 billion annually in agricultural subsidies and insurance.[78] The laws of "demand and supply" are obviously not allowed to operate and yet the Bretton Woods organizations did not hesitate to impose such polices on hapless African countries.

Further, aid was often used inappropriately. For example, it was reported that about twenty-five per cent of an aid package sent to Malawi in 2005 (£700,000 of £3 million) was misspent on U.S. firms' hotel and meal bills.[79] Even notebooks and pens were flown in from Washington rather than purchased locally. In her New York Times bestseller, *Dead Aid,* Zambian born international economist, Dambisa Moyo convincingly argues that aid is fueling corruption on the continent. She contends that it is precisely because of aid that the majority of sub-Saharan countries flounder in a seemingly never-ending cycle of corruption, disease, poverty and aid-dependency despite having received more than US$300 billion in development assistance since 1970.[80] She further contends that if the aid taps are turned off, within a few years, African countries will be able to fend for themselves. Similarly, historian, journalist, and biographer, Martin Meredith noted that since independence, Africa had received more Western aid than any other region but with no discernible results.[81]

Policy and Decision Making During the SAPs and PRSPs Period

During the SAP and PRSP periods, there was a wholesale abandonment of indigenous planning as African countries essentially mortgaged their planning responsibility to the Bretton Woods Institutions. American economist and recipient of the 2001 Nobel Memorial Prize in Economic Sciences, Joseph Eugene Stiglitz, states that the IMF was not particularly interested in hearing the thoughts of its "client countries" on such topics as development strategy or financial austerity and so all too often, the Fund's approach to the developing countries has had the feel of a colonial ruler.[82] As large-scale structural adjustment took hold across sub-Saharan Africa, state financial support to research was rolled back resulting in government research institutes being scaled or shut down.[83] Foreign-funded U.S.-style non-state think tanks begun to proliferate. Not surprisingly, these legitimized the mainstream policy agenda at the time.[84] Institutional donors and foundations increasingly became the source of funds to bridge the resource gaps in university research centers. This inevitably influenced the research agenda at these institutions. The age-old adage, 'He who pays the piper calls the tunes,' became evident.

The dependence of poor and highly indebted African countries on World Bank and IMF loans gave these institutions leverage to control economic policymaking. Financial control effectively led to political control. The policies mandated by the World Bank and IMF forced African governments to orient their economies towards greater integration in international markets at the expense of social services and long-term development priorities. Poverty reduction strategy papers (PRSPs), initially seen as a requirement for receiving debt relief (through the Heavily Indebted Poor Countries – HIPC - initiative) from the IMF and World Bank came to dominate African economic and social policies in the 1990s.[85] The Millennium Development Goals (MDGs) became a key framework through which donor aid was disbursed and linked to the New Partnership for Africa's Development (NEPAD).

Even universities, the traditional bastion of research and independent thinking became increasingly reliant on external support from (often U.S.) foundations such as Ford and Rockefeller, and agencies such as Canada's International Development Research Centre (IDRC), the Swedish Agency for International Development Cooperation (SIDA) and the World Bank.[86] During economic and political liberalization in the 1980s and 1990s, university professors who had been hibernating in the one-party and military rule eras often returned to the policy fold by setting up their own (donor-funded) research centers. Examples include the Development Policy Centre in Nigeria, the Economic and Social Research Foundation in Tanzania and the Centre for Policy Studies in South Africa.[87]

During the liberalization period new non-government think tanks proliferated in response to increased donor funding.[88] This funding often came from the same donors that were lending to African governments with neoliberal conditionalities. Not surprisingly such think tanks legitimized donor positions and provided a mechanism for donors to hold recipient governments accountable. These institutions prioritized policy issues related to political and economic liberalization, such as trade liberalization, regional integration, the 'good governance' agenda, poverty reduction, and achievement of the MDGs.[89] The World Bank's African Capacity Building Foundation played a key role in establishing think tanks in Botswana, Ghana, Kenya, Nigeria, Tanzania and Uganda.[90] Indigenous think tanks often found themselves competing for government influence with international institutions such as the World Bank and their research units.

Role Of Foreign Experts

To further compound the situation, donors often conditioned the provision of aid to employment of their own experts, resulting in a huge number of foreign advisors and consultants working in African policymaking institutions.[91] In 1989 it was reported that there were over 100,000 donor-funded expatriate advisors working in the public sectors of 40 sub-Saharan African countries, at a cost of more than $4 billion, nearly 35 percent of official development assistance to the region.[92] The salaries of these experts which were part of the loans, were determined by the donors, including perks like furnished family accommodation, free transportation, business-class fares to home base (plus spouse), medical cover and evacuation in event of illness or injury. Africa thus contributed at an inordinate cost, to solving unemployment challenges in the developed world.

The employment of experts at exorbitant costs further marginalized local specialists and academics who in some cases, were more qualified than the foreign experts and had a better understanding of the local situation. In many countries in sub-Saharan Africa, policymaking and policy analysis were increasingly undertaken by a small number of technocrats, typically based on the presidency and Central Bank, in collaboration with officials from international financial institutions.[93] Reform programs designed in Washington passed through a few local staff members who often did not even read them before they were signed off by governments.[94] Further, in some cases national debate on economic policy issues was actively discouraged.[95]

Perhaps a silver lining in this dark phase was the fact that donor inspired, political liberalization saw competitive politics replace single-party rule and autocratic military dictatorships in virtually all African countries. This opened up some space for civil society input in development planning. Policymakers and decision-makers were by now alerted to the need to broaden the agenda of public sector reforms and of the importance of good institutions in the development process.

In Summary

This overview reveals the extent to which external actors have had a strong influence on domestic policy processes in Africa. In the pre-colonial era, decision making varied from polity to polity. While absolute monarchs ruled most polities, there was often a council of elders available for consultation. In the colonial times decision and policymaking was almost exclusively external. After independence, though African countries had the opportunity to design their own policies, they did not become independent in their thinking. Rather they remained dependent on mainly European experts, for support and policy advice. Gradually African countries became increasingly dependent on foreign aid and loans. This is still the case in a large part of Africa today.

Donor dependence has provided development partners with significant policy leverage, and raises questions as to the extent to which African countries can claim 'ownership' over their economic policy choices. On the global scene, international treaties and development paradigms were accepted and agreed on by members of the UN and the WTO. This among other things influenced the development of domestic policy across sub-Saharan Africa.[96]

It is noteworthy, as will be elucidated in chapter 4, that in the same time period the East Asian countries that took a different approach to leadership were able to escape the poverty trap and prosper in unprecedented ways. Unlike the East Asian examples African countries mostly mortgaged their thinking and planning to the Bretton Woods organizations. The respective outcomes sixty years down the road are a lesson in contrasts. African countries are still dependent on the rest of the world despite possessing abundant natural resources, while their East Asian peers that did not have the same resources are prospering. African countries populate the lists of the poorest countries on earth while East Asian countries have largely escaped the poverty trap. There were some exceptions though in this dark tale. One notable African country that took a different approach to leadership, thinking, and the management of resources escaped from economic enslavement: the country of Botswana.

Notes & References

1   Lawyer, K. (2014, August 6). Biden Calls Continent of Africa a 'Nation'. *CNS News.* Retrieved from http://www.cnsnews.com/mrctv-blog/kelly-lawyer/biden-calls-continent-africa-nation August 6, 2014 | 10:38 AM EDT

2   Sayre, A. P. (1999). *Africa.* Twenty-First Century Books.

3   Krause, K. (n.d.). The true size of Africa. Retrieved from http://kai.sub.blue/en/africa.html

4   Meredith, M. (2006). *The state of Africa: A history of sixty years of independence.* London, UK: Simon & Schuster, Inc.

5   ibid.

6   World Population Review. (2017). *Africa Population 2016.* Retrieved from http://worldpopulationreview.com/continents/africa-population/

7   Lumpkins, C. (2016). *Precolonial African economies.* The College of the Liberal Arts., Penn State University. Retrieved from http://elearning.la.psu.edu/afam/100/lesson-2-part1/african-roots-of-african-american-life-under-slavery/pre-colonial-african-economies.

8   Mafeje, A. (1998). *Kingdoms of the Great Lakes Region.* Kampala, Uganda: CODESRIA.

9   Lumpkins, C. (2016). Precolonial African economies.

10 ibid.

11 Mafeje, A. (1998). *Kingdoms of the Great Lakes Region.* Kampala, Uganda: CODESRIA.

12 Kariuki, F. (n.d). *Conflict resolution by elders in Africa: Successes, challenges and opportunities.* Retrieved from https://www.ciarb.org/docs/default-source/centenarydocs/speaker-assets/francis-kariuki.pdf?sfvrsn=0

13 Chapman C., & Kagaha, A. (2009). Resolving Disputes using Traditional mechanisms in the Karamoja and Teso Regions of Uganda. *Minority Rights Groups International.* Retrieved from http://www.refworld.org/pdfid/4a97dc232.pdf

14 Ayittey, G. B. N. (1992). *Africa betrayed.* New York: St. Martin's Press.

15 ibid.

16 Perham, M. F. (1960). *Lugard: The years of adventure 1858-1898.* London: Collins.

17 Tarikh 11. (1970). *Indirect rule in British Africa.* Longman for the Historical Society of Nigeria.

18 ibid.

19 Gardinier, D. E. (1971). *French colonial rule in Africa: A bibliographical essay.* New Haven: Yale University Press.

20 ibid.

21 Cour, J.-M., Snrech, S., Sahel Club., African Development Bank., & Permanent Inter-State Committee for Drought Control in the Sahel. (1998). *West Africa Long Term Perspective Study.* Paris: OECD. Retrieved from https://www.oecd.org/swac/publications/38512525.pdf

22 Kimenyi, M. S. & Datta, A. (2011). *Think tanks in sub-Saharan Africa: How the political landscape has influenced their origins.* Overseas Development Institute. Retrieved from https://www.odi.org/sites/odi.org.uk/files/odi-assets/publications-opinion-files/7527.pdf

23 ibid.

24 ibid.

25 ibid.

26 Igue, J. O. (2010). A new generation of leaders in Africa: what issues do they face? *International Development Policy.* The Graduate Institute Geneva. Retrieved from https://poldev.revues.org/139

27 ibid.

28 Cour, J.-M., Snrech, S., Sahel Club., African Development Bank., & Permanent Inter-State Committee for Drought Control in the Sahel. (1998). West Africa Long Term Perspective Study.

29 Meredith, M. (2006). *The state of Africa: A history of sixty years of independence.*

30 Cour, J.-M., Snrech, S., Sahel Club., African Development Bank., & Permanent Inter-State Committee for Drought Control in the Sahel. (1998). West Africa Long Term Perspective Study.

31 Mboya, T. (1986). *Freedom and after.* Nairobi: Kenya. Heinmann Kenya Ltd.

32 Meredith, M. (2006). *The state of Africa: A history of sixty years of independence.*

33 Ayittey, G. B. N. (1992). *Africa betrayed.*

34 Igue, J. O. (2010). A new generation of leaders in Africa: what issues do they face?

35 Ayittey, G. B. N. (1992). *Africa betrayed.*

36 Brough, W. T. & Kimenyi, M. S. (1985). On the Inefficient extraction of rents by dictators. *Public Choice 48*(1) 37-48.

37 Kimenyi, M. S. & Datta, A. (2011). *Think tanks in sub-Saharan Africa: How the political landscape has influenced their origins.*

38 Rashid, S. (1994). Social sciences and policy-making in Africa: A critical review. *Africa Development, 19*(1), 91-118.

39 Kimenyi, M. S. & Datta, A. (2011). *Think tanks in sub-Saharan Africa: How the political landscape has influenced their origins.*

40 ibid.

41 Mkandawire, T. (2000). *Non-organic Intellectuals and 'Learning' in Policy-making Africa.* Stockholm: Learning in Development Co-operation EGDI Publication.

42 ibid.

43 ibid.

44 CSIR (2017). Council for Scientific and Industrial Research. Available at http://www.csir-iir.org/about.html

45 Meredith, M. (2006). *The state of Africa: A history of sixty years of independence.*

46 Kimenyi, M. S. & Datta, A. (2011). *Think tanks in sub-Saharan Africa: How the political landscape has influenced their origins.*

47 ibid.

48 Chazan, N., Lewis, P., Mortimer, R. A., Rothchild, D. S., & Stedman, S. J. (1999). *Politics and society in contemporary Africa.* Boulder, CO: Lynne Rienner Publishers.

49 Obadan, M. (2011, September). *Past development plans in Nigeria: Performance, problems and prospects.* Paper presented at the 52nd Annual Conference of the Nigerian Economic Society, Covenant University, Ota.

50 Lopes, C. (2013). 50 years of Development Planning in Africa – lessons and challenges. *United Nations Economic Commission for Africa*. Retrieved from: http://www.uneca.org/es-blog/50-years-development-planning-africa---lessons-and-challenges.

51 ibid.

52 Adei, S. (2009, July). *The critical role of the development of think tanks for Africa's development*. Paper presented at the meeting of SALT Institute, Kampala, Uganda.

53 Kposowa, A. J. & Jenkins, J. C. (1993). The structural sources of military coups in postcolonial Africa, 1957-1984. *The American Journal of Sociology 99*(1), 126-163.

54 Igue, J. O. (2010). A new generation of leaders in Africa: what issues do they face?

55 Kieh, G.K (2000). Military Rule in Liberia. *Journal of Political and Military Sociology, 28*(2), 327-342.

56 Plaut, M. (2006, January). Africa's hunger: A systemic crisis. *BBC News*. Retrieved from: http://newsvote.bbc.co.uk/mpapps/pagetools/print/news.bbc.co.uk/2/hi/africa/4662232.stm

57 Anene, J. (1997). Military administrative behavior and democratization: Civilian cabinet appointments in military regimes in sub-Saharan Africa. *Journal of Public Policy, 7*(1), 63-80.

58 Kimenyi, M. S. & Datta, A. (2011). *Think tanks in sub-Saharan Africa: How the political landscape has influenced their origins*.

59 ibid.

60 In 1944, 730 delegates from 44 countries met at the United Nations Monetary and Financial Conference held at the Mount Washington Hotel in Bretton Woods, New Hampshire, USA form July 1 to July 22 to create a new international monetary system. The main goals of the meeting were to ensure a foreign exchange rate system, prevent competitive devaluations and promote economic growth. One of the major results of the conference was the creation of the International Monetary Fund to monitor reserve rates and lend reserve currencies to nations. The IMF was formally introduced in 1945 when 29 members signed the Articles of Agreement. The other was the creation of the World Bank Group to provide assistance to countries during the reconstruction post World War phase. Being in the colonial era, Africa was only represented by Egypt, Ethiopia, Liberia and the Union of South Africa. The agreement collapsed in the early 1970s during the Nixon Presidency.

61 World Bank. (1994). *Adjustment in Africa: Reforms, results, and the road ahead*. New York, N.Y: Oxford University Press.

62 ibid.

63 Colgan, A. L. (2002). Hazards to health: The World Bank and IMF in Africa. *Africa Action*. Retrieved from https://www.africa.upenn.edu/Urgent_Action/apic041802.html

64 Kimenyi, M. S. & Datta, A. (2011). *Think tanks in sub-Saharan Africa: How the political landscape has influenced their origins*.

65 Lopes, C. (2013). 50 years of Development Planning in Africa – lessons and challenges.

66 ibid.

67 The Bretton Wood Project, (2001, June). *PRSPs just PR say civil society groups.* Bretton Woods Project. Retrieved from http://www.brettonwoodsproject.org/2001/06/art-15999/

68 Stiglitz, J. (2002), *Globalization and its Discontents.* New York: W. W. Norton Press.

69 Shah, (2013) Structural Adjustment a Major Cause of Poverty. *Global Issues.* Retrieved from: http://www.globalissues.org/article/3/structural-adjustment-a-major-cause-of-poverty

70 ibid.

71 Kimenyi, M. S. & Datta, A. (2011). *Think tanks in sub-Saharan Africa: How the political landscape has influenced their origins.*

72 Shah, (2013) Structural Adjustment a Major Cause of Poverty.

73 ibid.

74 UNICEF. (2000, September). Balance sheet of human progress in Africa. Retrieved from http://www.unicef.org/miscellaneous/balance.htm

75 Colgan, A. L. (2002). Hazards to health: The World Bank and IMF in Africa.

76 ibid.

77 Pettifor A. (2002). World Bank IMF forces famine on Malawi. *GMWatch.* Retrieved from http://www.gmwatch.org/news/archive/2002/2876-world-bankimf-forces-famine-on-malawi

78 The Economist. (2017). *Farm subsidies milking tax payers.* The Economist. Retrieved from http://www.economist.com/news/united-states/21643191-crop-prices-fall-farmers-grow-subsidies-instead-milking-taxpayers

79 Hencke, D. (2005, August). Anger as £700,000 of £3m British aid to Malawi spent on US firms. *The Guardian.* Retrieved from https://www.theguardian.com/politics/2005/aug/29/uk.internationalaidanddevelopment

80 Moyo, D. (2010). Dead aid: *Why aid is not working and how there is a better way for Africa.* New York: Farrar, Straus and Giroux.

81 Meredith, M. (2006). *The state of Africa: A history of sixty years of independence.*

82 Stiglitz, J. (2002), *Globalization and its Discontents.*

83 Kimenyi, M. S. & Datta, A. (2011). *Think tanks in sub-Saharan Africa: How the political landscape has influenced their origins.*

84 ibid.

85 ibid.

86 ibid.

87 ibid.

88 ibid.

89 ibid.

90 ibid.

91 ibid.

92 World Bank (1989) *Sub-Saharan Africa: From crisis to sustainable growth.* Washington, DC: IBRD.

93 Van de Walle, N. (1999). Economic Reform in a Democratizing Africa. *Comparative Politics 32*(1), 21-41.

94 ibid.

95 ibid.

96 Kimenyi, M. S. & Datta, A. (2011). *Think tanks in sub-Saharan Africa: How the political landscape has influenced their origins.*

3

Botswana The Outlier

"When a king has good counselors, his reign is peaceful."
Ashanti Proverb

At independence in 1966, few would have believed that within sixty years Botswana would become the most successful state on the African continent, and a beacon of hope for sub-Saharan Africa, even dubbed the African miracle by Western countries and donor agencies. How did Botswana succeed where most of her sub-Saharan peers failed? Several authors have attributed this outlier success to the limited colonial influence, good political institutions, wise leaders, and prudent economic policy.[1, 2, 3, 4, 5, 6, 7]

Geography

Botswana is a landlocked country in southern Africa with neighbors: Zimbabwe to the northeast, Namibia to the north and west, South Africa to the east and south, and Zambia at one spot on the Zambezi River in the north (Figure 2.1). Most of Botswana is uninhabitable and unfriendly to agriculture with the Kalahari Desert accounting for 84 percent of the 581,730 square kilometers land mass. Only 0.6 percent of the country's area is suitable for agriculture.[8] Its current population is 2,209,208 million people (July 2016 estimate).[9]

Historical Background

Pre-colonial Botswana

Indigenous conditions in Bechuanaland, as it was called at the time exhibited a fair amount of cultural and ethnic homogeneity.[10] Tribal chiefs were revered. They determined the allocation of land for hunting, farming, or residences, and presided over conflict resolution within the tribe and with other tribes.[11] Despite their immense political power, they were readily accessible by their subjects, since they were treated as their equal as evidenced in the traditional tribal gatherings called *kgotlas* explained in Chapter 2.

From 1818 through the early 1830s, Bechuanaland suffered repeated, albeit unsuccessful attacks by the Zulus from the South. Later the Boers did the same until the Tswana tribe mounted a successful defense at the Battle of Dimawe in 1852.[12] Chief Sechele, the ruler at the time, reached out to the British for protection but was promptly spurned. British interest at the time, beside appeasement of the Boers through peaceful diplomacy, was an all out colonization of Bechuanaland rather than granting it protectorate status.

Colonial Rule

When Germany presented a threat to British colonialism in South Africa by annexing South West Africa (present-day Namibia) in 1884, British policy changed drastically.[13] Britain now offered Bechuanaland protection against the Boers and Germans. In 1885, Sechele accepted Britain's offer, and Bechuanaland, which covered most of present-day Botswana became a protectorate. Under the agreement, the British prohibited any invasions into Bechuanaland.[14]

Besides promising protection to Bechuanaland (for the selfish interest of keeping land access open to further north of Africa), the British had no real interest in actively managing Bechuanaland.[15]

So they armed the Batswana to protect themselves against the Germans to the west and the Boers to the south.[16] They however did not engage in any nation-building project in Bechuanaland. There were hardly any social and physical infrastructure projects during the colonial era. Colonial excesses in India, South Africa, and Rhodesia had stretched the British Empire's budget, and no promising returns on investment were envisioned in Bechuanaland since it was not known to possess any valuable natural resources. Bechuanaland was left alone with the hope that there would be no military conflicts.[17] British expenditure on the protectorate at the time exposes the colonial priorities: seventy-five percent was on administration, and another significant portion went to upgrading tribal militants.[18] Another sign of lack of British interest and commitment to the territory was that they administered it from Mafikeng in South Africa, and not from within the territory itself.[19]

One thing the British did at this time is worthy of note. A harsh British policy practiced in its African colonies was the levying of a "hut tax" on a per hut or household basis. The tax was payable in money, labor, grain, or stock. It enabled the colonialists to raise funds, broaden the cash economy, and was also used to force Africans to work in the colonial economy (like working in the mines).[20] When it was introduced in Botswana in 1899, all Batswana families in possession of a hut were required to pay a one-pound tax.[21] The policy remained in place throughout most of Botswana's colonial history. The effect of the tax was severe. Since a large part of the population lived on subsistence budgets, they were unable to pay the tax. Many chose not to comply; others responded by entering the formal labor market.

The British guaranteed employment in their colonial mining operations. There was a resultant massive emigration of Batswana men into South Africa in search for jobs. At its peak in 1943, nearly 50 percent of the adult male population had immigrated to South Africa.[22, 23] The impact on the physical, economic, and social infrastructure of up to half of the adult male population abroad most of each year was devastating.[24] On the family scene, generations of children were raised without male influence at home as women stepped up to take on a larger role in the household, thus straining the very fabric of civil society.[25] Economically, skilled artisans and entrepreneurs were no longer able to service the missing male population, and the political institutions were crippled.[26]

After World War II, Bechuanaland successfully thwarted British attempts to combine the Protectorate with their South African colony. The 1948 election of the National Party government, which instituted apartheid in South Africa, and the 1961 withdrawal of South Africa from the Commonwealth ended any prospect of the incorporation of Bechuanaland into South Africa.[27] Chief Seretse Khama of Bechuanaland was banned from the protectorate in 1948. While a student in England he married a white Englishwoman. The interracial marriage was a breach of tribal custom and an anathema for the white South African leaders who had just instituted apartheid, and they insisted that the British prohibit Khama from ruling Bechuanaland.[28] They pressured the British not to allow him to return to Bechuanaland. The British complied hoping the ban would ease tensions in South Africa. However, because Khama enjoyed widespread support in Bechuanaland, this political issue divided South Africa and Bechuanaland. In 1956, Khama rescinded his claim to chieftainship and returned to Bechuanaland.[29] By 1960, an anti-apartheid, anti-colonial party, the Botswana People's Party (BPP) had been formed. In response, Khama helped to form the Botswana Democratic Party (BDP), which unlike the urban-based BPP, appealed to the rural commoners and tribal chiefs alike.[30] The story of Sir Seretse Khama and his wife Ruth has now been dramatized in the 2016 biographical romantic drama film, *"A United Kingdom"*.

Status at Independence

In the late 1950s and early 1960s, Britain was losing control of the protectorate as political parties and nationalism were on the rise. In the spring of 1965, Britain officially recognized Botswana's national independence and, in the fall of 1965, elections were held. The BDP, led by Khama, enjoyed a landslide victory, and he became Botswana's first president in a Westminster parliamentary system.[31] The government had a single chamber, 31-member Assembly responsible for legislation. The Parliament also had a House of Chiefs separate from the Assembly that served as an advisory body.[32]

The state in Botswana was in a disadvantaged position in many ways. At that time, it was undeveloped and seldom heard of - one of the poorest countries in the World. The country had no army, a fragile bureaucracy and a weak middle class.[33] There was no basic infrastructure. Only 22 km of paved road linked the capital, Gaborone with the South African border. It also lacked a skilled workforce with 22 university graduates and a mere 100 graduates from secondary school.[34] The population at independence was about 612,950.[35]

The post-independence government had limited ability to govern. As with other parts of Africa, the colonialists had designed the bureaucracy for supporting the administration and not for the promotion of economic development. Two years before independence the entire civil service consisted of 607 officers of whom 502 were expatriates.[36] Though there was no armed conflict at the time, powerful chiefs, who managed the country's eight tribal reserves, dominated the domestic political structure the new government inherited.[37] In 1968 agriculture dominated the economy, representing over 40 percent of GDP.[38] Financially, Botswana depended on Britain for 50 percent of its national budget.[39]

Fortunately for the country, diamonds were only discovered in the year after the end of colonial rule. If the discovery had happened in the era of colonialism, Botswana's story would certainly have been very different. Most importantly, the country got wise and selfless post-independence leaders. These leaders prudently utilized the diamond wealth (without any other comparatively valuable natural resources), to uplift the country to the level of an upper middle-income country with a 2015 per capita GDPPP of $17,700.[40] They used the discovery of diamonds in the year after independence for the rapid post-colonial growth that helped Botswana break financial ties with the British Exchequer by 1972/73.[41] Unlike many developing countries with abundant mineral resources that were characterized by mismanagement and corruption, the Botswana government utilized diamond revenues for the development of human capital, infrastructure, and mining technology.[42]

The Role of Leadership and Institutions

In hindsight, it is clear that the future of the post-independence countries rested on the decisions made by the first generation of leaders. Botswana's crucial moment came in 1965 when the BDP and Seretse Khama won the elections. Unlike other African leaders who chose reform paths that were not conducive to long-term economic growth, Khama and his administration were determined to pursue a policy aimed at economic growth; they adopted pro-market policies.[43] Right from independence, Khama set out to establish Botswana's government as a "financially viable entity".[44] The strategy deployed to achieve this was to pursue market-based development, with the state having a vital role.[45] In 1966, government policy established that the role of the state would be one of providing infrastructure and education, while it was up to the private sector to develop manufacturing.[46] Foreign investment came into diamond mining.[47]

President Khama successfully persuaded his Bangwato tribe to relinquish their collective mineral rights over the newly discovered diamond reserves.[48] Once the Bangwato agreed, all other tribes followed suit - thus the state secured mineral rights for the national treasury, rather than being captured by local ethnic interests.[49] Then in 1975 the state successfully negotiated with De Beers Diamond Company for a 50/50-share ownership in all of the country's diamond mines (compared to the previous 85/15 percent share for De Beers).[50]

The Government then wisely invested the revenue in a wide variety of development schemes building roads, dams, clinics, schools, and water reticulation projects.[51] Botswana ended its dependence on British grants in aid as early as 1972/73, now referred to as the "Year of Our Second Independence".[52] By the beginning of the 1980s, diamonds had replaced beef as Botswana's leading foreign exchange earner; in 1981, diamond exports accounted for 40 percent of total exports - in the first quarter of 2001 it was 87 percent.[53]

The government provided 'cheap' capital through loans directed to state-owned enterprises and indirectly to the public through the state development banks. This encouraged domestic investment, supported by the government's investment in social and infrastructural development such as educational facilities, energy, and transportation, which became the foundation for success.[54, 55]

Khama's exposure to Western education and British common law may have played a part in making him sympathetic to markets. The government promised low and stable taxes to mining companies, liberalized trade, increased personal freedoms, and kept marginal income tax rates low to deter tax evasion and corruption. Also, Khama preserved the *kgotlas* and many elements of customary law.[56] It is evident that the strong leadership and foresight of Khama and Masire was critical in Botswana's success.

Despite the wounds inflicted by colonialism, Khama's government never got hang up on the past as attested by his interracial marriage to a Briton, Ruth Wilson. The national leadership's prudent policy choices at the time of independence signaled a genuine commitment to long-term development. They resisted the pressure for rapid Africanization (or 'localization,' as it was called in Botswana) - of the civil service. President Khama made it clear in his first presidential speech in 1966 that he would 'never sacrifice efficiency on the altar of localization'.[57] They wisely recognized that proceeding too quickly on this matter would undermine administrative efficiency and professionalism as long as there was a shortage of qualified African officers.

The leaders also prioritized the strengthening of the state's institutional capacity to enable it to coordinate and manage economic development. The creation of an efficient state administration became a top priority. They set out to strengthen the Economic Planning Unit set up shortly before independence within the Ministry of Finance and set up a Central Statistics Office.[58] Vice-President Masire, the main driving force for ongoing development planning in the government, was put in charge of these units, and expatriates or former colonial administrators who had served in Bechuanaland or elsewhere in Africa manned key posts.[59] To ensure bureaucratic efficiency, the politicians gave the administration a high degree of independence and refrained from intervening in bureaucratic decision-making.[60, 61] Politicians however defined the policy framework within which the administration worked. They also sketched the broader outlines of development plans and left the skilled technocrats to craft the details and then implement the programs.[62] Though there was resistance to this approach by some of the remnants of the colonial administration, the new leadership prevailed.

Two other government institutions were especially important. First, was the Botswana Meat Commission (BMC) - the sole agency responsible for the slaughter and marketing of beef, as well as the only exporter of meat and meat products from the country.[63] It ensured high standards of production through monitoring by state veterinary services. As a monopolist, the BMC determined the prices that cattle producers got for their cattle. Prices were set at relatively high levels. Thus, producers were assured of a safe and reliable market. In sharp contrast to parastatals in other African countries, the BMC recorded a surplus almost every year from its inauguration. The surpluses returned to the suppliers and not to the government.[64] The state substantially expanded the country's capacity in the cattle industry, by building abattoirs and providing veterinary services and vaccines and by funding the erection of fences.

The second was the fully state-owned Botswana Development Corporation (BDC) established in 1970. It served as the country's main promoting and financing agency for commercial and industrial development.[65] It was clarified from the beginning that the BDC was to be profitable or it would be shut down.[66, 67] Although many of its investments in industry and agriculture were unprofitable, its success in other areas, especially finance and real estate development, more than made up for these losses.[68] The state significantly expanded the provision of services in areas such as health and water supply. Thus, by 1998, 88 per cent of the population lived within 8 km of a government health facility, and 97 per cent had access to safe drinking water.[69]

Botswana has a powerful presidency however, the position of the Ministry of Finance and Development Planning is also robust and autonomous. This has meant that the country has two power centers rather than one.[70] Unlike many African countries where there is a high degree of patrimonialism (a form of governance in which all power flows directly from the leader), in Botswana appointment to high-level positions has not been used to buy support or to co-opt potential opponents. The number of ministries has been limited, and there has been a relatively low turnover of ministers and senior administrative staff.[71] Using Bratton and van de Walle's three empirical indicators of patrimonialism - concentration of power with the leader, provision of personal favors and misuse of state resources - it has been showed that although elements of patrimonialism can be found in Botswana, it has been relatively restricted and significantly less widespread than in other African countries.[72, 73] Also, the government has established one of the longest running multiparty democracies on the continent. The Botswana government machinery over the years has had its hallmark as being non-corrupt and free of patronage. Rankings like those provided by the World Bank, UNDP and Transparency International, have consistently ranked Botswana as the least corrupt country in Africa. Botswana is a leading country in Africa on good governance, which is a reflection of the high quality of its institutions, its independent legal system and the relatively low level of corruption.

Role of the Bretton Woods Organizations

Traditionally, embracing the IMF and World Bank has proven the kiss of death for developing countries however Botswana's leadership seemed to recognize the danger involved in depending on the IMF and World Bank.[74] Though the IMF and World Bank aided Botswana throughout the 1980s, they played more of an advisory role.[75] Botswana's leaders embarked on a massive program in search of more private capital investment and indeed, since gaining its independence significant amounts of foreign direct investment have flowed into Botswana.[76] As Botswana improved its credibility and lowered mining taxes to 10 percent, significant amounts of foreign direct investment poured in. The leaders kept marginal income taxes low to deter tax evasion and corruption. Investors gained confidence from the fact that the tax structure of the mining industry was seldom adjusted.[77]

Fiscal Discipline

Among the strategies used by the government was the accumulation of significant reserve with the Bank of Botswana.[78] Due to fiscal discipline, an increase in government revenue did not mean increased government spending. For instance, whenever booms in the commodity prices resulted in increased government revenue, the government of Botswana would not alter its expenditure pattern but rather dedicated such 'windfalls' gains to future development.[79] So the government expenditure remained reasonably close to a long-run growth pattern. Accountability and consultation were adequately emphasized as the institutional framework was put in place to protect the public interest during the planning process.

On the contrary in Nigeria, the excess crude oil account was "shared" between the three tiers of government - Federal, State and Local government.[80] Following the dramatic rise of the Organization of Petroleum Exporting Countries, Nigeria became the fifth largest producer of petroleum in the world and should have joined the more prosperous forces of globalization. The habit of consumption and the shortage of relevant skills plunged the Nigerian economy into mismanagement, corruption, and debt.[81] Long lines at petrol stations and chronic shortages of fuel were the order of the day. Ironically, despite being a petroleum producer, shortages of petroleum products - diesel, kerosene, cooking gas, and other commodities often disrupted commercial activity.

Comparing the economic outcomes of dependence on natural resource between Botswana and Nigeria, the resource curse is more prevalent in Nigeria compared to Botswana because of the different qualities of their institutions.[82] The quality of institutions in a country is the predominant factor that transcends resource abundance towards economic growth.[83] Among these institutions are functional national think tanks.

The Role of Planning

Since independence in 1966, Botswana's development process has been guided by successive National Development Plans (NDPs). These have provided a medium-term planning and budgeting framework (typically 5-6 years) for capital and recurrent expenditure, and have been a key feature of Botswana's system of development management.[84] The plans outline the government's development priorities for the project period as well as the policies, program, and projects required to achieve those priorities.

The NDPs and accompanying process have retained the importance and respect they have enjoyed since independence.[85] In many ways, the key features and characteristics remain unchanged. That said, significant innovations have occurred over time to improve the relevance and effectiveness of the planning and budgeting process in response to a changing domestic and international social and economic climate.[86]

Development Pathway and Achievements

Botswana has experienced remarkable economic growth since independence. The exploitation of deposits of diamonds and minerals, a beef export industry that has preferred status with Europe, and a tourism policy that has courted the top-end of the market, have driven the growth.[87] The domestic cost of production of diamonds is little compared to their overseas sales value resulting in a hugely profitable venture for the country.[88] So the economic history of Botswana is to a large extent the story of natural resource management. It is most unlikely that the Botswana growth miracle would have occurred if diamonds had not been found soon after independence, and the government had not nationalized all subsoil mineral resources in 1967, thereby gaining control over future revenues.[89] Diamonds have been the engine of economic growth.

From 1965 to 1995, Botswana had the fastest growing economy in the world.[90] During that 30-year stretch, Botswana's average annual rate of growth was 7.7 percent, hitting a staggering GDP per capita increase of 13 percent per annum in the years 1980-89.[91] In 2001, Botswana's real per capita income was $7,820, nearly twice as high as the average East Asian Tiger's per capita income of $3,854, and more than four times the $1,826 average per capita income of an individual living in sub-Saharan Africa.[92, 93] Botswana has moved from being the third poorest country in the world to being an upper middle income nation.[94] Through fiscal discipline and sound management, Botswana has managed to transform itself from one of the poorest countries in the world with a per capita GDP of US$70 to an upper-middle income country with a 2015 per capita GDP of US$17,700 PPP (current International $).[95] Education expenditure is among the highest in the world, at around 9 percent of GDP, and includes the provision of nearly universal and free primary education although the sector has not created the skilled workforce.[96] Adult literacy was 88.2 percent as of 2015.[97]

At independence, Botswana had approximately 22 km of paved road, which linked the capital of Gaborone with the South African border. As of 2011, there was a total of 17,916 km of roads including 8,916 km of Public Highway Network roads (6,116 km paved and 2,800 km unpaved) and 9,000 km of District Council roads linking all the key towns and district capitals.[98] An infrastructure of roads, rail lines, and ports closely link Botswana to the South Africa. The Trans-Kalahari Highway connects Botswana to the Namibian port of Walvis Bay.

Challenges Botswana faces

Much of Botswana's economic growth can be attributed to its very low starting point. Despite impressive growth, political stability, improved infrastructure, prudent financial management, material modernization and investments in human capital, the country faces many challenges. Botswana has been unable to emulate the developmental states in Asia such as South Korea or Taiwan in building up a large-scale competitive manufacturing base.[99] The country's contemporary economy is not substantially diversified from what it was at Independence.[100, 101] The government did appreciate the need to expand beyond mining and agriculture into high productivity industry, and some assistance schemes have been launched over the years, unfortunately, these became subject to increasing abuse and subsequently failed.[102] When it came to expanding beyond the traditional and well-established sectors, Botswana exposed itself as resembling other corrupt African countries from which it is generally set apart.[103] Starting from the mid-1970s, there was an intra-sectoral diversification, and significant overall growth in value added, but not in relative terms in the percentage of GDP.[104, 105]

Unfortunately, low levels of technology and productivity are also characteristic of the agricultural sector, which is further restrained by a hostile environment. Absolute agricultural production could never be expected to become high in a country that is as climatically challenged as Botswana, with roughly two-thirds of the country comprising the Kalahari Desert and only four percent of the country suitable for agriculture.[106] In the 1930s, Batswana farmers grew 90 percent of the country's cereals consumption, but production decreased in the 1980s to about 50 percent. Consequently, in 1991 the Botswana government abandoned its previous goal of self-sufficiency in food production, and instead adopted a policy of food security.[107]

Despite the strong growth record of Botswana, the country suffers from persistent and increasing unemployment and under-employment.[108] Unemployment has remained persistent at nearly 17.8 percent due to not only the poor state of the agricultural sector but also to the insufficient employment provided by non-agricultural sectors. [109] A notable part of the country's inhabitants are engaged, if at all, in low-productivity activities either in the informal sector such as hawking or in the traditional agricultural sector and as a consequence, the country faces high levels of poverty and inequality, as well as low human development indicators.[110] Poverty rates declined from 50 percent at independence to just over 19 percent in 2016.[111] Significant pockets of poverty remain, especially in rural areas. Not everyone has benefited meaningfully from raised incomes or higher standards of living - although the extensive provision of health and education facilities, as well as access to water and a decent transport infrastructure, tends to muddles this.[112]

The HIV/AIDS adult prevalence rate remains one of the highest in the world at 22 percent, contributing to education and health outcomes that are below those of countries in the same income group. [113] Lack of water security presents a significant challenge to sustaining economic growth. Acute shortages of energy threaten agricultural, industrial, and tourism sectors.[114]

Botswana's growth opportunities and poverty reduction will only be achievable over the long term if sustainable sources of energy are made available.

Further Botswana faces a key policy dilemma of how to grapple with the predicted decline in previously buoyant diamond revenues. Natural resources are characteristically uncertain. Without diversification, only modest real growth in the largest component of government's current revenue sources can be expected. While diamonds may not be entirely exhausted for another generation, the output is already well past its peak.[115] Botswana has made some progress in reducing its dependence on diamonds in the past 20 years, nonetheless, the level of economic diversification needed to offset diminishing mineral revenues remains a challenge.

The advances that have occurred are indeed very promising, but they are only pre-conditions for turning growth into development. Botswana could use the foundation it has created through its diamond wealth to diversify industry, transform agriculture, and become a modern society. Diversification is necessary for long-run economic sustainability because it is development and not diamonds that lasts forever.[116]

Lessons from Botswana for African Countries

Until the 1970s, economists, in general had a favorable view of abundant natural resources. After World War II, the post-independence developing countries that were rich in natural resources were considered guaranteed to prosper. The following decades however unexpectedly saw the economic growth and development of the newly industrializing economies in East Asia that did not have natural resources, stagnation in Latin America, and economic and political failure in sub-Saharan Africa.[117] The most resource-abundant countries on the continent in the last sixty years have been characterized by corrupt leaders selling off natural assets and pocketing the profits, individuals and international companies becoming wealthy while governments stayed poor.[118]   This apparent paradox where countries and regions with an abundance of natural resources like minerals and fuels tend to have less economic growth and worse development outcomes than countries with fewer natural resources is referred to as the "resource curse".[119]

These countries have also been characterized by a decline in other sectors as one sector prospered (the so-called "Dutch disease" – the term was coined to describe the decrease in the manufacturing sector in the Netherlands after the discovery of large deposits of natural gas). A general negative correlation between natural resource endowments and economic growth has been demonstrated.[120] This is paradoxical because incomes from natural resources should raise wealth and increase purchasing power thereby also increasing investment levels and growth rates. Explanations given for the failure of many resource-abundant countries vary including the higher prevalence of laziness, rent seeking, the conflict between stakeholders, corruption, and predation, compared with economies relying on other comparative advantages.

Though one of the largest resource exporters in the world,[121] Botswana has managed to avoid both the resource curse and Dutch disease, by creating a long-term plan for the extraction of natural resources and good policy for continued growth.[122, 123] This achievement makes it a member of a very exclusive group of developing countries, including only a few others such as Mauritius and Malaysia.[124] Botswana stands out a class apart and is a testament to what could have happened to most of Africa in the last sixty years if there had been prudent self-sacrificing leadership, and thinking applied to economic planning.

Botswana has demonstrated that even one natural resource can promote growth if there is leadership to prudently manage and leverage for investments in infrastructure and human capital. Other resource-rich countries in Africa have much to learn from Botswana's example about the importance of prudent leadership, original thinking, and careful management to avoid the natural resource curse and Dutch disease. It can thereby be a model on how to achieve necessary pre-conditions for development, but it cannot be a model for actual development since there has been no transformation into modernization.[125] For lessons on this, African countries have to look further afield to East Asian countries that gained independence at about the same time as African countries but traveled a different road to where they are today.

Notes & References

1   Acemoglu, D., Johnson, S. & Robinson, J. (2003). *Botswana: An African success story*. In Rodrik, D. (Ed.), *In search of prosperity: Analytical narrative on economic growth*. Princeton, NJ: Princeton University Press (pp. 80-122).

2   Beaulier, S. A., & Subrick, J. R. (2006). The political foundations of development: The case of Botswana. *Constitutional Political Economy, 17, 2,* 103-115.

3   Harvey, C. & Lewis Jr. S. R. (1990). *Policy Choice and Development Performance in Botswana*. London: Macmillan in association with the OECD Development Centre.

4   Iimi, A., & IMF. (2006). *Did Botswana escape from the resource curse?* Washington, DC: International Monetary Fund, African Dept.

5   Leith, C. (2005). *Why Botswana prospered*. Montreal, Canada: McGill-Queen's University Press.

6   Mpabanga, D. (1998). *Constraints to industrial development*. In Salkin, J. S. (Ed.), *Aspects of Botswana economy: Selected papers*. Gaborone: Lentswe la Iesedi.

7   Samatar, A.I. (1999). *An African miracle: State and class leadership and colonial legacy in Botswana*. Portsmouth, UK: Heinemann.

8   CIA World Factbook. (2016b). Country profile Botswana. Retrieved from https://www.cia.gov/library/Publications/the-world-factbook/geos/bc.html

9   ibid.

10   Acemoglu, D., Johnson, S. & Robinson, J. (2003). *Botswana: An African success story.*

11   ibid.

12   ibid.

13   ibid.

14   Beaulier, S. A., & Subrick, J. R. (2006). The political foundations of development: The case of Botswana.

15   Acemoglu, D., Johnson, S. & Robinson, J. (2003). *Botswana: An African success story.*

16   Parson, J. (1984) *Botswana: Liberal Democracy and the Labor Reserve in Southern Africa*. Boulder, Co: Westview Press.

17   Acemoglu, D., Johnson, S. & Robinson, J. (2003). *Botswana: An African success story.*

18   Parson, J. (1984). *Botswana: Liberal Democracy and the Labor Reserve in Southern Africa.*

19   Hope, K. R., & Somolekae, G. (1998). *Public administration and policy in Botswana.* Kenwyn: Juta

20   Pakenham, T., & Abacus. (1994). *The scramble for Africa 1876-1912.* London: Abacus.

21   Massey, D. (1978). A Case of Colonial Collaboration: The Hut Tax and Migrant Labour. *Botswana Notes and Records, 10,* 95-98. Retrieved from http://www.jstor.org/stable/40979541

22   Parson, J. (1984). *Botswana: Liberal Democracy and the Labor Reserve in Southern Africa.*

23   Schapera, I. (1947). *Migrant labour and tribal life: A study of conditions in the Bechuanaland protectorate.* London: Oxford University Press.

24   Beaulier, S. A., & Subrick, J. R. (2006). The political foundations of development: The case of Botswana.

25   ibid.

26   ibid.

27   ibid.

28   ibid.

29   ibid.

30   ibid.

31   ibid.

32   Botswana. (1966). *Transitional plan for social and economic development.* Gaborone: Department of Government Printing.

33   Molutsi, P. (1989). *Whose interests do Botswana's politicians represent?* In Holm, J. & Molutsi, P. (Eds.), *Democracy in Botswana* (pp. 120-131). Athens: Ohio University Press.

34   Acemoglu, D., Johnson, S. & Robinson, J. (2003). *Botswana: An African success story.*

35   Botswana Population. (2015). Increases in Botswana's population. *Expansion.* Retrieved from http://countryeconomy.com/demography/population/botswana

36   Picard, L. (1987). *The politics of development in Botswana: A model of success?* Boulder, CO: Lynne Rienner.

37   Samatar, A.I. (1999). *An African miracle: State and class leadership and colonial legacy in Botswana.*

38   Hillbom, E. (2008). Diamonds or development? A structural assessment of Botswana's forty years of success. *The Journal of Modern African Studies, 46*(2), 191-214.

39   Samatar, A.I. (1999). *An African miracle: State and class leadership and colonial legacy in Botswana.*

40   CIA World Factbook. (2016b). Country profile Botswana.

41   Beaulier, S. A., & Subrick, J. R. (2006). The political foundations of development: The case of Botswana.

42   Van Wyk, J. (2010). Double diamonds, real diamonds: Botswana's national competitiveness. *Academy of Marketing Studies Journal, 14*(2), 55-76.

43   Beaulier, S. A., & Subrick, J. R. (2006). The political foundations of development: The case of Botswana.

44   Botswana. (1966). *Transitional plan for social and economic development.* Gaborone: Department of Government Printing.

45   Samatar, A.I. (1999). *An African miracle: State and class leadership and colonial legacy in Botswana.*

46   Hillbom, E. (2008). Diamonds or development? A structural assessment of Botswana's forty years of success.

47   Hartland-Thunberg, P. (1978). *Botswana: An African Growth Economy.* Boulder, CO: Westview Press.

48   Taylor, I. (2005). Botswana's Developmental State and the Politics of Legitimacy. Retrieved from http://www.rrojasdatabank.info/devstate/Botswana.pdf

49   ibid.

50   ibid.

51   ibid.

52   Tsie, B. (1998). *The state and development policy in Botswana.* In Hope, K.R. & Somolekae, G. (Ed.), *Public Administration and Policy in Botswana.* Johannesburg: Juta Press.

53   Gaolathe, B. (2002). *Budget Speech 2002.* Gaborone: Department of Government Printing. Retrieved from http://www.bankofbotswana.bw/assets/uploaded/ Budget percent20Speech percent202002.pdf

54   Acemoglu, D., Johnson, S. & Robinson, J. (2003). *Botswana: An African success story.*

55   Leith, C. (2005). *Why Botswana prospered.*

56   Beaulier, S. A., & Subrick, J. R. (2006). The political foundations of development: The case of Botswana.

57   Picard, L. (1987). *The politics of development in Botswana: A model of success?*

58   ibid.

59   ibid.

60   Samatar, A.I. (1999). *An African miracle: State and class leadership and colonial legacy in Botswana.*

61   Leith, C. (2005). *Why Botswana prospered.*

62   Samatar, A.I. (1999). *An African miracle: State and class leadership and colonial legacy in Botswana.*

63   ibid.

64   ibid.

65   Sebudubudu, D. (2005). *The institutional framework of the developmental state in Botswana.* In Mbabazi, P. & Taylor, I. (Eds.), *The potentiality of developmental states in Africa: Botswana and Uganda compared* (pp. 79-89). Dakar, Senegal: Codesria.

66   Samatar, A.I. (1999). *An African miracle: State and class leadership and colonial legacy in Botswana.*

67 Leith, C. (2005). *Why Botswana prospered.*

68 Eriksen, S. S. (2011). The possibility of state formation: The experience of Botswana in a theoretical perspective. *The European Journal of Development Research, 23*(3), 444-458.

69 UNDP. (2005). Botswana Human Development Report 2005. Retrieved from http://hdr.undp.org/sites/default/files/botswana_2005_en.pdf

70 Eriksen, S. S. (2011). The possibility of state formation: The experience of Botswana in a theoretical perspective.

71 ibid.

72 Soest, C. (2009). *Stagnation of a "miracle": Botswana's governance record revisited.* Hamburg: German Institute of Global and Area Studies.

73 Van de Walle, N. (1999). Economic Reform in a Democratizing Africa. *Comparative Politics 32*(1), 21-41.

74 Easterly, W. (2002). *The Elusive quest for growth: Economists' adventures and misadventures in the tropics.* Cambridge MA: MIT Press

75 Beaulier, S. A., & Subrick, J. R. (2006). The political foundations of development: The case of Botswana.

76 Van Wyk, J. (2010). Double diamonds, real diamonds: Botswana's national competitiveness.

77 Beaulier, S. A., & Subrick, J. R. (2006). The political foundations of development: The case of Botswana.

78 Leith, C. (2005). *Why Botswana prospered.*

79 Osabuohien, E. & Salami A. (2012). *Planning to fail or failing to plan: Institutional response to Nigeria's development question.* Abidjan: African Development Bank.

80 ibid.

81 Kefela, G. T. (2011). Driving forces of globalization in emerging market economies developing countries. *Asian Economic and Financial Review, 1*(2), 83.

82 Fosu, A. K. (2011). *Terms of trade and growth of resource economies: A tale of two countries.* Oxford: Centre for the Study of African Economies.

83 Mehlum, H., Moene, K. & Torvik, R. (2006). Institutions and the resource curse. *Economic Journal, 116,* 1-20.

84 Land, M. A. (2010). *Strengthening of national capacities for national development strategies and their management: An evaluation of UNDP's contribution, Country Study – Botswana.* UNDP. Retrieved from http://web.undp.org/evaluation/documents/thematic/cd/btoswana.pdf

85 ibid.

86 ibid.

87 Taylor, I. (2005). Botswana's Developmental State and the Politics of Legitimacy.

88 Jefferis, K. (1998). Botswana and diamond-dependent development. In Edge, W., & Lekorwe, M. H. (Eds), *Botswana, politics and society.* Pretoria: J.L. van Schaik.

89 Hillbom, E. (2008). Diamonds or development? A structural assessment of Botswana's forty years of success.

90 Beaulier, S. A., & Subrick, J. R. (2006). The political foundations of development: The case of Botswana.

91 Mpabanga, D. (1998). *Constraints to industrial development.*

92   Beaulier, S. A. (2004). *Explaining Botswana's success: The critical role of post-colonial policy.* Retrieved from http://object.cato.org/sites/cato.org/files/serials/files/cato-journal/2003/11/cj23n2-6.pdf

93   World Bank (2002). *World Development Indicators Online Database.* Washington: World Bank.

94   Beaulier, S. A., & Subrick, J. R. (2006). The political foundations of development: The case of Botswana.

95   CIA World Factbook. (2016b). Country profile Botswana.

96   World Bank (2016a). Literacy Rate, Adult Total for Botswana [SEADTLITRZSBWA]. Retrieved from https://fred.stlouisfed.org/series/SEADTLITRZSBWA

97   ibid.

98   CIA World Factbook. (2016b). Country profile Botswana.

99   Taylor, I. (2005). Botswana's Developmental State and the Politics of Legitimacy

100 Leith, C. (2005). *Why Botswana prospered.*

101 Siwawa-Ndai, P. (1998). *Industrialisation in Botswana: evolution, performance and prospects.* In Salkin, J. S. (Ed.), *Aspects of Botswana economy: Selected papers.* Gaborone: Lentswe la lesedi.

102 Leith, C. (2005). *Why Botswana prospered.*

103 Beaulier, S. A. (2004). *Explaining Botswana's success: The critical role of post-colonial policy.*

104 Harvey, C. & Lewis Jr. S. R. (1990). *Policy Choice and Development Performance in Botswana.*

105 Owusu, F. & Samatar, A. I. (1997). Diamonds or development? A structural assessment of Botswana's forty years of success. *Canadian Journal of African Studies 31*(2), 268-99.

106 Parson, J. (1984). *Botswana: Liberal Democracy and the Labor Reserve in Southern Africa.*

107 Silitshena, R. M. K. & McLeod, G. (1998). *Botswana: a physical, social and economic geography.* Gaborone: Longman Botswana, 2nd edition.

108 Taylor, I. (2005). Botswana's Developmental State and the Politics of Legitimacy.

109 CIA World Factbook. (2016b). Country profile Botswana.

110 Taylor, I. (2005). Botswana's Developmental State and the Politics of Legitimacy.

111 CIA World Factbook. (2016b). Country profile Botswana.

112 Taylor, I. (2005). Botswana's Developmental State and the Politics of Legitimacy.

113 CIA World Factbook. (2016b). Country profile Botswana.

114 ibid.

115 ibid.

116 Hillbom, E. (2008). Diamonds or development? A structural assessment of Botswana's forty years of success.

117 Beaulier, S. A., & Subrick, J. R. (2006). The political foundations of development: The case of Botswana.

118 ibid.

119 Warner, A. M., Sachs, J. D., & National Bureau of Economic Research. (1995). *Natural Resource Abundance and Economic Growth.* Cambridge, Mass: National Bureau of Economic Research.

120 ibid.

121 Iimi, A., & IMF. (2006). *Did Botswana escape from the resource curse?*

122 ibid.

123 Hill, C. (1991). Diamonds or development? A structural assessment of Botswana's forty years of success, *World Development 19*(9), 1185-96.

124 Warner, A. M., Sachs, J. D., & National Bureau of Economic Research. (1995). *Natural Resource Abundance and Economic Growth.* Cambridge, Mass: National Bureau of Economic Research.

125 Hillbom, E. (2008). Diamonds or development? A structural assessment of Botswana's forty years of success.

4

Wisdom From The East

The ideal country in a flat world is one with no natural resources
because countries with no natural resources tend to dig inside themselves.
They try to tap the energy, entrepreneurship, creativity, and intelligence of
their own people – men and women – rather than drill an oil well.

Thomas Friedman

While African countries were grappling with the challenges
addressed in Chapter 2, some East Asian countries were facing
similar problems albeit with a different approach to finding
solutions. African countries like Nigeria in West Africa, Botswana
in South Africa, Uganda in East Africa, and East Asian countries
like South Korea, Singapore and Malaysia are similar in that they
were all colonized. Countries in both regions shook off the specter
of colonialism at about the same time - soon after the Second
World War. South Korea gained independence from Japan in 1945
in the aftermath of the devastating Second World War. Malaysia
got independence from Britain in 1957, Nigeria from Britain in
1960, Uganda from Britain in 1962, Singapore from Britain in
1963 (then from the Malaysia Federation in 1965), and Botswana
from Britain was in 1966. After their independence, all these
countries faced post-independence development challenges, but
with varying approaches and different results.

In the early 1960s, one would not have been faulted to predict a better future for the African countries compared with their East Asian peers. With abundant natural resources, vast amounts of arable land, and for some countries, a modest number of intellectuals and professionals, the newly independent African countries looked set for prosperous futures. At the time, Ghana had an income per capita higher than that of the Republic of Korea (Table 4.1). By 2013, Korea's income per capital was fourteen times greater than Ghana's (Table 4.1). Even as late as the 1970s, Malawi, Burundi and Burkina Faso were economically ahead of China on a per capita basis.[1] In 1960, the average continental GDP per capita in Africa was roughly three times the East Asian average ($425 versus $135 in constant 2000 US dollars) while in 2004, Asia's per capita income was twice as high as the African average ($536 versus $1,140 using the same measure).[2]

Over the last sixty years, these East Asian countries and sub-Saharan countries have charted their different paths to the different destinations they are in today. Table 4.1 compares the GDP per capita of selected African and Asian countries over a sixty-year period. The difference could not be starker. It is evident that the East Asian countries did some things that present and emerging African leaders would do well to learn. So how did they approach their challenges? Some of the answers are traceable to the type of leadership they had and how leaders approached the thinking about the future of their countries. For example, the gains Korea made compared to Ghana have been attributed not only to the former's increased political stability but also to its greater success in acquiring and using knowledge.[3]

Figure 4.1 A Map of East Asia

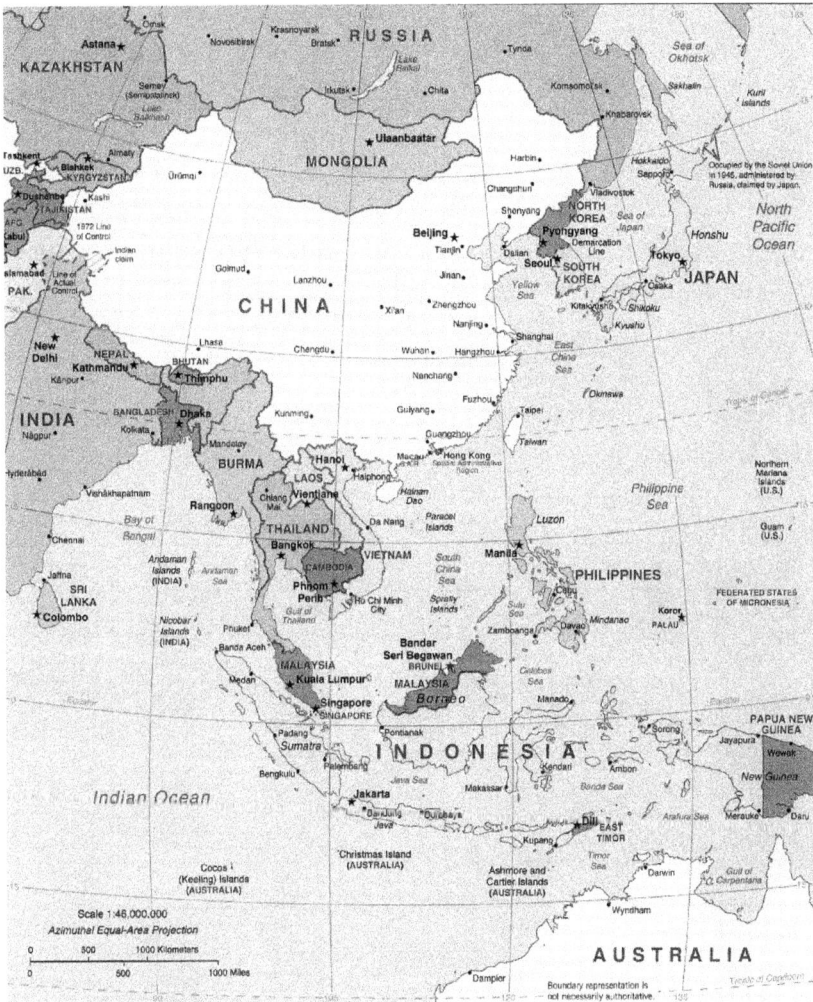

As seen in Chapter 2, the post-independence years of many African countries were characterized by dictatorships and the specter of neoliberal economics pushed by the Bretton Woods organizations. "Benevolent dictators" ruled some of the East Asian countries reviewed in this chapter. The major difference was that these leaders were thinkers, very open and even desirous of an evidence-based approach to leadership. They correctly discerned that a neo-liberal approach to the economy was not suitable as a state policy aimed at accelerating socio-economic development long before this ideology became the world dominating doctrine. They chose a different path: the developmental state. In his book, *The Development State,* Woo-Cumings describes the theory of the developmental state as the explanation for the East Asian industrialization.[4] It is often conceptually positioned between a free market capitalist economic system and centrally planned economic system, and called a plan-rational capitalist system, 'conjoining private ownership with state guidance'.[5]

Table: 4.1 Comparison of GDP per capita - selected countries (US Dollars)

Country	GDP PPP 1964 (US$)	GDP PPP 2013 (US$)
African Countries		
Botswana	71.8	7,315
Kenya	108.5	1,245.51
Uganda	76.1	571.96
Rwanda	41.1	638.67
Ghana	230.4	1858.24
Nigeria	112.9	3,005.51
Zambia	236.9	1844.80
Burundi	86.6	267.11
Malawi	50.2	226.46
Burkina Faso	80.5	683.97
Asian countries		
China	84.6	6807.43
South Korea	120	25,976.95
Singapore	485.3	55,182.48
Malaysia	312.2	10,583.06

Adapted from information from the World Bank

THE MALAYSIAN EXPERIENCE

Malaysia is more naturally endowed than Botswana. It has a wealth of minerals and natural resources that include tin, petroleum, timber, copper, iron ore, natural gas, bauxite, palm trees, and rubber. It is multicultural, and unlike Botswana, but like many African countries, it experienced racial tension in its nascent years of independence leading to countrywide riots in 1969. Malaysia is perhaps the best example of a country in which the leadership has pragmatically managed the economic roles and interests of various racial groups in the long-term without significant loss of growth momentum.[6] The Malaysian experience provides an example of leaders working out an approach to building consensus in a fractious society divided by race, religion, and culture.[7] Faced with unique local race situations, the leaders contemplated the challenges confronting the country and came out with indigenous tailor made solutions that lifted the country and its peoples out of poverty into middle-income status.

Geography

Malaysia is a peninsula located in southeastern Asia, bordering Thailand in the north and also occupying the northern one third of the island of Borneo. Other neighbors are Indonesia, Brunei, and the South China Sea, south of Vietnam (Figure 4.1). It has a total land area of 329,847 square kilometers of which 328,657 square kilometers is land area while water covers 1,190 square kilometers; sixty-two percent of the land is forest covered.[8] The July 2016 estimate of the population was 30,949,962.[9]

Historical Background

Malaysia was known from the early centuries A.D. for internationally valued exports like gold, tin, and exotics such as birds' feathers, edible birds' nests, aromatic woods, and tree resins.[10] Due to an ideal positioning on the sea trade routes from the Indian Ocean to East Asia, Arab, Indian, and Chinese merchants regularly visited it.[11] From the early sixteenth century, the Portuguese, the Dutch, and the English followed suit. By the late eighteenth century, the Dutch East India Company (VOC) was dominant in the Indonesian region while the English East India Company (EIC) acquired bases, beginning with Penang (1786), Singapore (1819) and Melaka (1824).[12] Opportunities for trade attracted Chinese migrants over the centuries.[13]

Britain used its colonies as suppliers of raw materials for its industries and as an outlet for manufactured goods, so British interest in the Malay Peninsula was more about the economics of the commodities trade rather than politics. Unlike Botswana, Malaysia was therefore of interest to the British due to its relative abundance of raw materials.

The Japanese occupied the colony during the Second World War from 1942 to 1945. In 1948, the British-ruled territories on the Malay Peninsula apart from Singapore formed the Federation of Malaya, which became independent in 1957. Malaysia was formed in 1963 when the former British colonies of Singapore, as well as Sabah and Sarawak on the northern coast of Borneo, joined the Federation.[14] A Communist insurgency, confrontation with Indonesia, Philippine claims to Sabah, and Singapore's expulsion in 1965 marred the first several years of the country's independence.[15]

Status at Independence

At independence from the United Kingdom in 1957, Malaysia's founders inherited a low-income agrarian economy, whose backbone was rubber and tin production, and entrepôt trade. Business enterprises were small-scale, mostly localized, and predominantly family-based.[16] The country had a population of 7.4 million with the majority residing in rural areas where the incidence of poverty was the greatest.[17] In 1947, agriculture employed more than two-thirds of the labor force, 22.5 percent were in the tertiary sector, 2.5 percent in mining, and 6.7 percent in manufacturing;[18] these proportions remained virtually unchanged until independence.

Industrialization was very low consisting of the processing of the primary exports, rubber, and tin, together with the limited production of manufactured goods for the domestic market.[19]

Role of Leadership, Think Tanks and Planning

The post-independence leaders and policymakers in Malaysia inherited institutions that were the legacy of more than 100 years of British colonial rule and appeared to be stronger and functioning better than those in other developing countries.[20] In 1969 Malaysia experienced racial riots between the Chinese (who were more wealthy) and Malays across the country. Equitable distribution of wealth became a pressing issue that had to be addressed. In the post-1970 period, the leaders discussed the challenge of distributive demands, the massive ethnic economic imbalances arising from the racial riots at the end of the 1960s, and the need to raise the pace and intensity of industrialization.[21] The post-independence leadership subsequently based the economic development strategy on three long-term policies: the New Economic Policy (NEP), 1970–90, the National Development Policy (NDP), 1990–2000, and the National Vision Policy (NVP), 2001-10.[22] The leaders wisely placed policy emphasis on economic growth with an equal benefit for all groups and communities in society.[23] The overriding objective of the NEP maintained in the NDP, and the NVP was to preserve national unity by eradicating poverty irrespective of race, and by restructuring Malaysian society to reduce the identification of race with economic function and geographical location.[24] At the heart of the distributive strategy were policies to assist the *Bumiputera* (a Malaysian term to describe the Malay race and other indigenous peoples of Southeast Asia) obtain parity with the non-*Bumiputera* in income and wealth.[25]

The post-independence leadership incorporated the Malaysia Industrial Development Authority (MIDA) in 1967 as the principal government agency promoting and coordinating industrial development and investment in Malaysia.[26] It had the responsibility of researching and recommending trade policies and strategies relevant to the promotion of industries. Later with the passing of the Promotion of Investment Act in 1986, MIDA assumed a greater role in investment promotion. The leadership decision to establish MIDA in the mid-1960s was a landmark in the drive towards industrialization.

As of 2011, the three most prominent think tanks in Malaysia were the Institute of Strategic and International Studies (ISIS), the Malaysian Institute for Economic Research (MIER), and the Asian Strategic and Leadership Institute (ASLI). These often got engaged by the government to make policy recommendations on national and international economic issues, defense, security and foreign policy issues, strategies for nation building, and other matters such as the environment.[27] The government expects the think tanks to provide recommendations during the policy formulation stage. For instance, MIER participated in formulating the Third Industrial Master Plan (IMP) for the Ministry of International Trade and Industry (MITI).[28] ISIS formulated the "Vision 2020" strategy in 1993 that seeks to transform Malaysia into a developed nation with a united Malaysian race by the year 2020.[29] Malaysian think tanks give input in the formulation of Malaysia's Five-Year development plans.[30] They often play an active role in developing and advancing domestic policies and agendas, by providing valuable input into the annual government budget process. They focus on micro-issues such as employment, race relations, and education opportunities. They also highlight training and employment opportunities for both political party members and the public, both in the private and public sectors.[31]

Development Pathway

Economic diversification has been and continues to be a key theme of the long-term strategy in Malaysia. The leadership decided on two approaches: first was the diversification of agriculture from rubber into other crops like palm oil on a large scale; and second was the diversification away from primary into secondary industries, especially manufacturing.[32] In following these approaches, Malaysia went further than Botswana was able to.

The post-independence growth of the Malaysian economy falls into four broad phases detailed below.[33] The first phase (1957-1970) covered the years immediately after the country gained independence from British rule. At that time the post-independence leadership was uneasy with the fact that the economy mainly depended on natural rubber and tin mining. Forecasting information from a variety of sources indicated that rubber prices were on a downslide, partly due to the growing competition with synthetic rubber. This competition was worrisome for development planners and decision makers.[34] In light of this and the high volatility in the prices of these commodities, the leadership made diversifying production and income the major strategic policy thrust.[35]

A significant policy shift after analysis of the situation was the decision to increase the cultivation of oil palm in the 1960s as a key component of agricultural diversification and the overall industrialization strategy.[36] As a result of the policies enacted, from 1966-1970 covering the First Malaysia Plan period, the acreage shares of the two crops almost reversed; oil palm acreage increased from about 99,000 acres in 1960 to 335,000 acres in 1970, a more than three-fold increase. Palm oil production increased from about 90,000 tons in 1960 to 396,000 tons in 1970.[37] Malaysia attests the argument that a natural-resource-based industrialization strategy can bring benefits to economies that produce primary commodities.[38]

In the second phase of economic growth (1971-1990), after contemplating ways to increase foreign direct investment, the national leadership enacted new policies. They included the Investment Incentives Act of 1968, Free Trade Zone Act of 1971, and later the Promotion of Incentives Act of 1986.[39] Before this investment promotion drive, import substitution strategy drove industrial growth. FDI in export-oriented firms was actively promoted, and as a result, the 1970s ushered in a new phase of economic growth, marked by the rapid rise of construction and export-oriented manufacturing industries.[40] During the colonial period, agricultural processing had been the primary manufacturing activity. Now newer industries such as beverages, textiles, chemicals and chemical products, and transport equipment began to emerge, almost entirely in the private sector.[41] The leaders decided to keep external tariff rates modest mainly for revenue raising purposes, unlike other countries that were industrializing during that period.[42] In this period the Malaysian economy weathered shocks like oil crises of 1973-1974 and 1978-1979, and the global slowdown in demand for electronics and primary commodities in 1985-1986.

The third growth phase (1991-2000) traversed the difficult years of the Asian financial crisis and the period of exchange controls. The fourth phase (2001- 2007) was one of slow growth following the terrorist attacks in the United States on September 11, 2001, as well as more competitive external economic conditions that have heightened some of Malaysia's vulnerabilities.

Diversification beyond agriculture and primary commodities has been successful. Manufactured goods now account for a larger share of GDP and total exports. Malaysia is currently aiming at achieving high-income status by 2020 and moving up farther up the value-added production chain by attracting investments in finance, high technology industries, biotechnology, and services.[43]

Achievements

Once a producer of raw materials, Malaysia has transformed to an emerging multi-sector middle-income country.[44] GDP per capita was estimated at U.S. $27,200 in 2016.[45] In 2014 Malaysia was estimated to have an installed electricity generation capacity of 30 million kW.[46] Gross exports of goods and services constitute more than 80 percent of GDP. As an oil and gas exporter, Malaysia has previously profited from higher world energy prices, which supplied about 29 percent of government revenue in 2014. Agriculture still plays a part in the economy with 3800 square kilometers of arable land under irrigation.[47] Urbanization has been rapid: in 2005, 63 percent of Malaysia's population lived in urban areas, compared with 25 percent in 1957.[48]

Factors that have contributed to Malaysia's economic success like its early exposure to international commerce due to its strategic positioning along major trade routes, and the fact that its openness to globalization forces brought in foreign capital, which has been instrumental.[49] Social and political traps mired the movement of many developing countries towards industrialization based on the natural endowments. The pivotal role wise, discerning leadership had in navigating Malaysia past these snares is often overlooked. The Malaysian economic miracle can be attributed to a knowledge-based development policy trajectory.

Lessons from Malaysia for African countries

Malaysia, like Botswana, has demonstrated that the resource curse is avoidable. However the Malaysian experience goes further. It is an example of how an economy relatively rich in natural resources can transform itself into a more industrialized economy over a period of about 20 years. Malaysia demonstrates that diversification is essential for growth. It also shows that openness and international integration too are helpful for growth if managed carefully and thoughtfully. International trade and long-term capital flows made significant contributions to the growth of the Malaysian economy. The case study highlights the importance of export-led growth. The growth of labor-intensive manufacturing industries absorbed the surplus labor, especially from the rural areas, openning up employment opportunities and raising income levels.

Private investment, domestic as well as FDI, is vital for economic growth as reliance on substantial public investment is not sustainable. Competition for FDI has and will intensify, and policy reforms and strong institutions will be needed to attract and retain FDI. Industrial policies are critical for economic diversification and FDI. Fiscal incentives and infrastructure support, including industrial estates and free trade zones (FTZs), must undergird the export-led growth of manufactured products. FDI can make outstanding contributions to the growth of manufacturing industries and exports.

The key lessons of policymaking from Malaysia over the past 50 years are anchored in state-led attempts to diversify sources of income for the Malaysian economy, even as sociopolitical engineering was used to build the Malaysian nation.[50] An appropriate system of policymaking and implementation - aligned with developmental objectives, technical capacities, and political and social imperatives - needs to be in place to sustain economic growth.[51] To cultivate domestic enterprises, specifically to encourage the rise of large business groups the political leadership intervened actively in the economy to plan and structure industrial and corporate development. The Malaysian experience strongly underscores the importance of strong national leadership supported by strong institutions including think tanks to forecast, plan and anticipate issues looming on the horizon and make adjustments accordingly. The capacity to make prudent farsighted decisions played a crucial role in the growth and development of Malaysia. There was a deliberate and not a laissez-faire approach to development.

THE SOUTH KOREAN EXPERIENCE

Unlike Malaysia and most African countries, the only natural resources South Korea could boast of were coal, tungsten, graphite, molybdenum, lead, and hydropower potential. Rising out of the ashes of the Second World War and the Korean War that devastated the country, within one generation South Korea has emerged as one of the leading countries in the world. In the 1960s, South Korea's GDP per capita was comparable with levels in the poorer countries of Africa and Asia. In 2004, South Korea joined the trillion-dollar club of world economies. The South Korean experience offers many lessons for post-war African countries

Geography

South Korea, also known as the Republic of Korea, is located in Eastern Asia, in the southern half of the Korean Peninsula bordering the Sea of Japan and the Yellow Sea (Figure 4.1). It has a total area of 99,720 square kilometers; of which 96,920 square kilometers is land, while 2,800 square kilometers is water.[52] It has a 2,413 kilometer coastline and shares a 237 kilometer land border with North Korea. South Korea is made up of mostly hills and mountains.[53] Vast coastal plains in the west and south provide the only 18.1 percent agricultural land it has, of which 7,780 square kilometer is under irrigation. 63.9 percent of the land area is forest covered.[54]

Historical Background

Korea has an ancient history dating back to 2333BC.[55] Japanese imperialism led to the colonization of the Korean peninsular from 1910 to 1945. When the Japanese Empire unraveled at the end of World War II, Korea fell victim to the Cold War. It was divided into two spheres of influence along the 38th parallel line. The Americans controlled south of the line - the Russians installed a communist regime in the north, later ceding power to China. The Republic of Korea was formed three years later in 1948. Two years later the massively destructive Korean civil war (1950-53) followed leaving the country divided into two. Some estimates place the loss of life from the Korean conflict of 1950 to as high as 5 million. More than half of these - about 10 percent of Korea's prewar population of 20 million in 1950 - were civilians. Estimates put the loss of physical infrastructure as a result of physical damage at 25 per cent and the cost at $6.9 billion at the market rate (nearly five times the GDP in 1953).[56] The country's production in all sectors is estimated to have fallen by 48 percent from 1949 to 1951.[57] In the aftermath of the relatively short but exceptionally bloody Korean War, South Korea was one of the poorest countries in the world.

Status at Independence

Before 1964 there was pessimism about South Korea's future. Despite massive amounts of aid from the U.S., not many gave the country a chance of climbing out of economic stagnation in the decade after the Korean War. In 1963 the country was regarded as a "basket case," a "hopeless bottomless pit" and donors talked of pouring money into a "Korean rat hole".[58] The period 1962 - 1964 is viewed as the "turning point" or the "take off" in the remarkable economic achievements attained by South Korea. Like happened in later years in many African countries, the country experienced a military coup in 1961. However, unlike the era of military rule in Africa, the military governments in Korea concentrated on economic growth and initiated a series of ambitious five-year economic development plans aimed at transforming the overwhelmingly agricultural economy into an industrial one.[59]

The Role of Leadership, Think Tanks and Planning

At the beginning of his first term when a military coup brought General Park Chung-hee to power in 1961, much like happened in many African countries, the Korean people greeted him as a hero. In contrast however, in subsequent years he was seen as a benevolent dictator in recognition of how his authoritarian regime initiated a series of successful economic reforms. Unfortunately a declared intent to entrench himself in the presidency on a permanent basis eventually undermined his popularity. In the early 1960s, President Park laid the foundation for rapid economic growth, and successfully initiated long-term planning for the first time. His planning strategy worked quite well, and the economy grew rapidly. He launched a national campaign, the "New Village Movement" which emphasized the spirit of self-help and self-support, and provided rewards to competent and honest bureaucrats.[60]

Though often criticized for his personality and his style of government, President Park must be credited for encouraging education (that nurtured the Korean bureaucracy for two decades) and for his interest in learning and discussing economic issues with experts.[61] He was a visionary and had the capacity to understand the economic context and identify the stages of the modernization process that he was leading.[62] From the late sixties, he recognized the need to integrate information and knowledge to facilitate the formulation of comprehensive, coherent, and theoretically attainable five-year plans, in a politically consistent and economically viable way.[63] With the increasing complexity of the modernization process, the information generated by the bureaucracy became inadequate. In response to this, the president fostered the formation of government think tanks to systemize necessary knowledge. The cultural environment paid high respect to scholarly work as well as its practical needs for professional advice. Korea Development Institute (KDI) was founded in 1971 as an official government research institution, which provided a much more autonomous base for drafting economic plans as confidence in indigenous capabilities rose due to significant economic success during the 1960s.[64] Government resources and foreign aid mainly from the United States, initially financed the KDI. The U.S. Agency for International Development (USAID) allowed the Korean government to spend 1.3 billion won from the aid account for development and granted another 1.5 million dollars to finance several KDI programs. The government gave 500 million won directly. However, even though U.S. advisors recommended the creation of the KDI, the U.S. eventually kept its distance.[65]

In addition to creating national think tanks, the leadership employed the best-educated human resources, the "gray matter" of the country, into its bureaucratic machinery, and President

Park surrounded himself with competent and qualified academic technocrats and empowered them. An example is the role of "political professors" interested in modernization theories and development such as Nam Duck-woo, who became a high-ranking public officer as well as Kim Chung-yun, who previously was a central banker, Park's chief of staff and Minister of Finance and Minister of Commerce.[66]

Though initially the bureaucracy and scholars recruited as advisors provided policy ideas, a practice established early was to create discussion committees. In addition to these committees and minister's conferences, Korean intellectuals were organized in special advisory groups in framing and developing policy ideas for President Park.[67] These committees, formal and informal, were consulted as secondary sources of knowledge. For this reason, even if the political regime was vertical and authoritarian, the policies were not designed on the basis of false information or without a view of the involved actors.[68] When issues of great importance emerged, Park Chung-hee himself would assist and participate actively in the discussions made in the framework of the Economic Ministers' Conference and the State Council.[69]

The practice of consulting and discussing enabled government agencies to develop their capacity to get, generate, and analyze information. The Korean case shows that in addition to reliance on highly educated bureaucrats; there must also be a scheme of incentives to make the best use of them. Korea benefited from at least three key institutional factors: the tradition of the career civil service, the implementation of exams to recruit the most capable minds, and a merit-based system that permitted the promotion of personnel into each ministry's bureaucratic level.[70] These factors resulted in a bureaucracy that was considerably motivated and stable when it came to personnel mobility, which in turn translated into the possibility to accumulate knowledge and develop outstanding analytical abilities.[71] Though the national vision came from the highest levels of government, the intermediate-level bureaucracy, the holders of technical knowledge, had the responsibility of translating the ideas and knowledge into content for policies. It was also at this level that consultations and feedback with the economic actors were (and still are) made.[72]

In the earlier years, the emerging private sector lacked the intellectual resources to contribute significantly to the planning process, which required a high level of education that, at the time, was scarce and expensive.[73] The private sector was also reliant on the government's instructions and projects formulated within the five-year economic development plans; hence, to divert resources to support private research centers and independent analysis was probably considered unnecessary.[74] Furthermore, unlike in the United States or Europe, there was no philanthropic culture to fund these projects.

During the first decade of Park Chung-hee's military regime, the macroeconomic planning was entirely in the hands of the government. The existence of a professional bureaucracy reduced-not disregarded- the need for or dependency on external experts to rationalize ideas, formulate economic policies, and provide intelligence, analysis, and consultancy.[75] From the very beginning of his rule, Park created two "super" ministries mainly in charge of these tasks: the Ministry of Finance (MOF) and the Economic Planning Board (EPB).[76] While the MOF, was responsible for fiscal policy and could intervene actively in banking and foreign exchange, and even trade policies, the EPB was the center of talented Korean economists, many of whom studied in the United States. It centralized economic information, controlled the budget, the foreign aid, the loans, and also the management of national statistics.[77] The functions of the EPB represented Park's compromise to establish systematical and sustainable long-term growth and development plans with a civilian face.[78] The EPB served a pivotal role within the government's structure. Its director was also deputy prime minister. It controlled the other ministries' information and coordinated the policies regarding the purposes mentioned.[79] The EPB became the organizational pillar of the developmental project of President Park, and "was the brain of economic policy".[80] Both the EPB and President's office were manned by the most brilliant minds available in Korea at the time and become his most trusted sources of knowledge to define his preferences and make his choices.[81]

President Park was a listening and teachable leader. He was also skillful enough to bring about intellectual synergies between the EPB and the selected circle of economic secretaries within the President's Office (PO). Though he had the last word at the Economic Ministers' Conference, his ambition and personality drove him to understand the logic of economic-growth policies. He consequently sought advice, listened and received feedback from his advisors and secretaries, most of whom were high-ranking scholars, as well as from people in business.[82, 83] The macroeconomic ideas and policies during the 1960s came out of the EPB, the PO, and the MOF.[84]

Development Pathway

The South Korea planning model had short-term interconnected plans with specific objectives. Of the six economic development plans undertaken between 1962 and 1991, all but one exceeded expectations in growth rates.[85] The South Korean government aimed at becoming self-reliant through these plans. Each five-year phase had specific objectives, targeted specific industries in the economy and was designed to promote rapid industrialization and exports.

The first phase of the planning model (1962-1966) aimed at building a self-reliant industrial structure. The Government directly participated by heavily investing in the energy sector (Korea Electric Company). There was strong political will, and a high level of commitment to attaining these plans. The results were better than expected with annual growth under the first plan averaging 8.5 per cent against a target of 7.1 per cent.[86]

The second phase (1967-1971) aimed at modernizing the industrial sector to become internationally competitive, and enhancing import substitutive production capacity. Again government massively invested in the steel industry to enhance economic development.[87] The third phase (1972-1976) termed the 'Big Push' era, aimed at massive investment in chemical industrialization and export-oriented industrial development, resulting in the production of iron and steel, transport machinery, household electronics, and chemical productions.[88] Previous plans were assessed, and lessons learned incorporated in the next planning phase. In this phase, there was an effort in curbing some socioeconomic issues (e.g. rural unemployment, and inequality) by encouraging industrialization outside the major cities.

The fourth phase (1977-1981) targeted developing internationally competitive industries. The government emphasized manufacturing efficiency comprising of technology and skilled labor production processes, thus boosting export capacity.[89] Consequently, South Korea became competitive in the international market as high-quality production at low cost was emphasized. Industries involved in power generation, integrated machinery, diesel engines, and heavy construction equipment received financial assistance from the government.

The fifth phase (1982-1986) targeted technology-intensive industrialization. There was ongoing consultation and flexibility as think tanks followed trends in the international market to determine the objective of the industrialization plan. For example, when the global demand for technology-oriented products was foreseen, a decision was made to heavily invest in technology production such as manufacturing of electronic televisions, videos, semi-conductor related products, among others.

The goals of the sixth Five-Year Economic and Social Development Plan (1987-91) were based on the previous plan. In this phase, after establishing that the country was strong enough for competition, the government focused on less protective mechanisms by import liberalization, the removal of trade restrictions and non-tariff barriers on imports.[90] The government further expanded human resources training, research, and development for industrial utilization, especially for small and medium-sized firms.

The seventh phase (1992-1996) aimed at developing high-technology production including microelectronics, fine chemicals, bioengineering, optics, and aerospace. Public-private partnership was encouraged to enhance the even geographical spread of industrialization to provincial cities and other locations outside the major cities of South Korea.

Achievements

The economic policies that have underpinned South Korea's growth have emphasized the development of a dynamic, export-oriented manufacturing industry, with a gradual shift towards high technology. South Korea remains more dependent upon manufacturing than nearly all Organization for Economic Cooperation and Development (OECD) countries.[91] South Korea has experienced rapid and sustained economic growth since the 1960s when South Korea's gross domestic product (GDP) per capita was comparable to levels in the poorer countries of Africa.[92] Forty-five years after the full-scale, government-led industrialization drive that started in the early 1960s, South Korea's GDP per capita has increased from US$67 in 1953 to US$20,050 in 2007and currently stands at $37,900 – 2016 dollars - (2016 est.).[93, 94, 95] According to a 2016 estimate, services contribute 60.2 percent, industry 37.6 percent, and agriculture 2.3 per cent, to the economy. Electricity production in 2014 stood at 582.1 billion kWh, while consumption was 497 billion kWh.[96] Electricity access by the population is 100 per cent.

Financial constraints did not inhibit the achievement of the national plans. Resources were prudently used, for example, the country reduced government expenditure to widen the resource gap and enhance self-reliant economic progress in the first three phases of the planning.[97] The result has been that that South Korea has dramatically transformed from an under-developed economy to an industrial powerhouse. By 1986 the country had attained a more or less self-sufficient economy with a balance of trade (the ratio of export/GDP to import/GDP) at about 1.[98] By 2005, South Korea was the most wired country in the world with broadband Internet coverage in 72 percent of households.[99] Real GDP expanded about 14 times in the 50 years (1953 – 2003) from 15.1 billion in 1953 to 567.7 billion in 1996 and $680.1 in 2004, (all in 2000 U.S. prices).[100] During this period there was an average annual growth rate in real GDP of 8 per cent and GDP per capita growth of almost 5.9 per cent.[101]

Concurrently South Korea improved the quality of its labor force. In its global competitiveness report of 2001- 2002, the World Economic Forum ranked South Korea among the top ten in higher education, Internet use and school connections to the Internet.[102] By 1970, the literacy (defined as people over 15 years of age who can read and write) had gone up to 87.6 percent from 22 percent in 1945. This progress continued to a literacy rate of 97.9 by 2011. (99.2 percent of males and 96.6 percent of females).[103] The students enrolled in secondary school as a percentage of their age group increased from 25 per cent in 1953 to over 90 per cent in 1987. South Korea is now a global player in international trade. In 2015 South Korea was the seventh leading trading country in the world.[104]

Challenges

The South Korean economy faces long-term challenges including a rapidly aging population. A study released in 2017 projects that women in South Korea will by 2030 be the first to claim an average lifespan of more than 90 years.[105] Only 551,000 Koreans or 2.9 per cent of the population were aged 65 or above when the Korean War broke out in 1950.[106] 19 percent of South Korea's population, were aged 60 or above in 2015.[107] By 2026 an astounding 10.7 million Koreans - 20.5 per cent of the population - are expected to be aged 65 or above.[108] It is going to take something radical to arrest South Korea's demographic and social decline; immigration is a possible solution.[109] Other challenges are the inflexible labor market, the dominance of large conglomerates (chaebols), and the heavy reliance on exports, which comprise about half of GDP.[110] To address the long-term challenges and sustain economic growth, the current leaders have prioritized structural reforms, deregulation, promotion of entrepreneurship and creative industries, and the competitiveness of small- and medium-sized enterprises.[111]

Lessons from South Korea for African countries

South Korea has been able to prioritize economic development over politics. Unlike the case in many African countries, changes in government did not affect the rolling out of the development plans. During the seven rounds of the five-year economic planning periods, five state leaders held the presidential office in Korea.[112] Except for Kim Young Sam, the first civilian to hold the office in over 30 years, all the rest came from military backgrounds. Their politics were typically viewed as dictatorial, whereas in economic terms they were feted as heroes.[113] Their respective military regimes outperformed all previous efforts at economic management. The actual growth rates mostly exceeded their target growth rates. Among the military dictators, President Park ruled Korea for the longest time (18 years) and his economic performance was more outstanding than at any other period of Korea's history.[114]

Korea's development path has been thinking intensive. Six agents are integral to the functioning of Korea's system of economic planning: the state leader, the planning office, the budget office, the statistical office, the media, and the nation's think tanks.[115] Korea's industrialization commenced in 1962 and reached its pinnacle during the fifth economic planning period (1982-1986). In the aftermath of the financial crisis in the mid-1990s, policy efforts were made to transform the South Korean economy into a knowledge-based one in which innovation could thrive, enhancing overall productivity and thereby sustaining economic growth.

While American think tanks, most of which are private put forward policy ideas and customarily need close political connection, Korea's think tanks have tended to be more involved in research.[116] The South Korean experience shows that if there is focused leadership, frugality in the governing class, openness to guidance from the intelligentsia, and national discipline, it is possible to transition from the ravages of war and the dereliction of poverty within one generation.

THE SINGAPOREAN EXPERIENCE

It is paradoxical that of all the countries discussed in this chapter, Singapore has been the most successful. What was the secret to Singapore's phenomenal success? Unlike all the countries considered so far, Singapore has no natural resources (that is apart from fish and deep water ports). Singapore's population as of July 2016 was estimated to be 5,781,728.[117] A 2013 estimate distributed the population as follows: Chinese 74.2 percent, Malay 13.3 percent, Indian 9.2 percent, other 3.3 percent.[118]

Geography

Singapore is a small island city-state located in southeastern Asia between Malaysia and Indonesia.[119] Its total area is 697 square kilometers of which 687 square kilometers is the land area, and 10 square kilometers is covered by water. It has 193 kilometers of coastline.[120] Only 1 percent of the land is arable, and 3.3 percent is forest-covered.

Background

The modern history of Singapore started in 1819 with the arrival on the island at the southern tip of the Malayan Peninsula of Sir Stamford Raffles from the British East India Company. After being bought by the British in 1824, Singapore grew to be a major port by 1825, with its amount of trade exceeding that of Malaya's Penang and Malacca combined.[121] 1826 saw the merging of Singapore, Penang, and Malacca into the Straits Settlements, an outlying residency of the British East India Company. In 1867 the Strait Settlements were formally made into a British Crown Colony.[122]

The opening of the Suez Canal in 1869 boosted the importance of Singapore as the regional port of South East Asia. Singapore claimed its identity as one of the major ports in the world by the beginning of the twentieth century. This was due to the increased demands of rubber and tin, which are abundant in the region, resulting from the expansion of the automobile and packaging industries in the developed world.[123] In 1921, the British built a naval base and soon supplemented the island with an air base.

During World War II, Singapore was under Japanese occupation from 1942 to 1945 before returning to become a separate British Crown Colony in 1946. It first gained self-governance in 1959 before seceding from the British crown and joining the Federation of Malaya, Sabah, and Sarawak to form Malaysia in 1963. Social strife due to racial tensions filled the following two years spent as part of Malaysia. Street riots and violence became widespread.[124] The Chinese in Singapore outnumbered the Malay three-to-one. However, as Lee Kuan Yew, the first Prime Minister of Singapore and leader of the ruling People's Action Party (PAP) later recalled, "Singapore was a tiny Chinese island in a large Malay sea".[125] The Malay politicians in Kuala Lumpur feared that the growing Chinese population throughout the island and peninsula was threatening their heritage and political ideologies. Therefore, as a way of ensuring a Malay majority within Malaysia-proper and phasing out communist sentiments within the country, the Malaysian Parliament voted to expel Singapore from Malaysia. Singapore separated from Malaysia on August 9, 1965, and has been an independent republic since then.[126]

Earlier, Indonesia had adopted a policy of confrontation against the formation of Malaysia by prohibiting trade of goods involving Indonesia within the region. This policy affected

Singapore substantially since Indonesia had been the island's second-largest trading partner.[127] Political disputes with Indonesia soon ended, and trade resumed from 1966 onwards.

Status at Independence

At the time of the expulsion of Singapore from the Malaysian Federation in 1965, an independent Singapore was not considered viable.[128] Two large, unfriendly states, Malaysia and Indonesia, sandwiched the territory. It lacked natural resources, sanitation, proper infrastructure, and adequate water supply. It depended on the outside world for food, energy, and even water. The primary challenge for Singapore in its early years was to overcome its high unemployment problem.[129] Much of the city-state's three million people were unemployed. More than two-thirds of its population was living in slums and squatter settlements on the city's fringe. The majority of its labor force was in trade and services with no labor tradition. During colonial times, Singapore's economy centered on being an entrepôt trade for the East India Company, and as a result, the manufacturing sector was undeveloped. This economic activity offered little prospect for job expansion in the post-colonial period. The withdrawal of the British bases that were contributing about 20 per cent of the GDP further aggravated the unemployment situation. [130] Industrial strife was common. Prime Minister Lee Kuan Yew sought international assistance, but his pleas went unanswered, leaving Singapore to fend for itself.

The Role of Leadership and Think Tanks

The history of modern Singapore is intertwined with its first prime minister, Lee Kuan Yew and his People's Action Party (PAP). Leadership and governmental institutions played pivotal roles in the development of the island city-state. Lee led Singapore for thirty years while the PAP has ruled the country since it became independent. He left with an intact reputation, a testament to the integrity that characterized his tenure of office.

At his swearing-in ceremony to become the prime minister of the self-governing state of Singapore in 1959, his cabinet all dressed in white:

> One important decision we made before May 1959 general election highlighted our position on corruption…. When we took the oath of office at the ceremony in the city council chamber in June 1959, we all wore white shirts and white slacks to symbolize purity and honesty in our personal behavior and public life. The people expected this from us, and we were determined to live up to their expectations".[131]

The first-generation leaders such as Lee Kuan Yew, S. Rajaratnam, and Goh Keng Swee of the ruling PAP viewed Singapore's strategic predicament as a function of its minuscule size and lack of resources and hinterland, as well as the country's turbulent history and a multi-ethnic population surrounded by larger, and potentially hostile neighbors.[132]

Faced with a fight for their survival on all fronts with very limited options, these leaders concluded that if Singapore was to survive, it had to do extraordinary things.[133] It took a while for the leaders to figure out a strategy for the development of the city-state. After a sabbatical at Harvard, several meetings with American executives in search of investors and several years of trial and error, Lee Kuan Yew reports that they gradually settled on a two-prong strategy that paid off.[134] The first was to leapfrog the hostile region much as Israel, faced with boycotting and hostile neighbors, had done. Singapore set out to connect and trade with the developed world and to convince their multinational corporations to manufacture in Singapore. The second was to create a "First World oasis in a Third Word region".[135] They set out to create an environment that was safe, corruption-free, low in taxation, and unimpeded by unions, to attract investors. Singaporeans were trained and equipped to provide First World standards of service.

Getting the best brains into Government

Singapore's first generation leaders set out to recruit the best brains into their PAP party and into the government.[136] They shunned simply going along with the political activists who joined the party many of who did not have the requisite qualities for the kind of leadership the party was looking for.[137] They were aware of the fact that often the brightest minds shun politics because of the messiness involved. So they went out of their way to scout for able, dynamic, dependable, and hard-driving people to recruit into their political party. They systematically scanned the top echelons of all sectors in Singapore - the professions, commerce, manufacturing, and trade unions- to look for men and women they could persuade to stand as their candidates.[138]

> In the 1968 general election, we fielded several Ph.D.'s, bright minds, teachers at universities, professionals including lawyers, doctors, and even top administrators as candidates. We needed people who were activists with sound judgment and interpersonal skills, To do this, I had to find and get into office a group of men to provide Singapore with effective and creative leadership. Had I left it to chance, depending on activists coming forward to join us, I would never have succeeded. We set out to recruit the best into government.[139]

So high was the premium that Lee and his team put on the quality of leadership that they went to the extent of hiring a psychologist and a psychiatrist to test their candidates to find out if they had what it took to provide leadership for Singapore![140] With the best brains in the country at the helm of leadership, it should not be so surprising what the country was able to achieve.

Development Pathway

The key strategy was to adopt a pro-business, pro-foreign investment, export-oriented economic policy framework, combined with state-directed investments in strategic government-owned corporations.[141] In time Singapore became so attractive that it became a base camp for entrepreneurs, engineers, managers, and other professionals who had business to do in the region.[142] The first foreign minister, S. Rajaratnam, presented the alluring vision of Singapore as a global city that would become a critical node in the international system coordinating global flows of trade, money, materials, goods and people.[143] Singapore's decision to embrace the world economy helped it to become the financial center of Southeast Asia and bolstered its strategic position in the region as well.[144]

Early in its self-governance years, the Singapore government asked the UNDP to send economic advisors who had been working in countries that had similar conditions to Singapore in 1960, especially with regard to its size and economic stage. Dr. Albert Winsemius, a Dutch industrialist who had been a former advisor to Portugal and Greece, led the UNDP team.[145] Based on the Winsemius Report, in 1961 the government drew the State Development Plan, which later became a Five-Year Development Plan. That same year, following the advice given by Winsemius, it set up Singapore's Economic Development Board (EDB) - one of the oldest investment agencies in Southeast Asia. It was established as a statutory board under the Ministry of Trade and Industry. The EDB's responsibility was steering the growth of industry especially in manufacturing and trade by rendering financial assistance, technical advice and other forms of support to local and foreign entrepreneurs in setting up and running manufacturing activities.[146] It was a one-stop agency for investors relating to land, power, water, environmental, and work safety.[147] Its purpose was to ease the transfer of investments into the country by allowing foreign investors to bypass government bureaucracies. The EDB initially had experts from UNDP and ILO but was soon filled with the brightest and best Singaporean scholars who had returned from universities in Britain, Canada, Australia, and New Zealand.[148]

The State Development Plan (1961–1964) represented the first official blueprint for the planned economic development of Singapore following the attainment of self-governance in 1959.[149] The plan was formulated as a means to solve the pressing issues of economic stagnation and high unemployment rates through an expansion in manufacturing. The goal was twofold: first, to increase the national income at a rate that matched the growth in population; second, to create jobs to absorb the additions to the labor force due to a growing population and to alleviate the prevailing levels of high unemployment.[150] Industrial growth was left to the private sector, while the public sector undertook infrastructure and social services development.[151]

The majority of Singapore's working population at the time was in trade and services with no labor tradition. Moreover, there was hardly any capital to finance the growth of the manufacturing sector.[152] Another challenge was that the domestic market was minuscule and due to hostility from their neighbors, regional trade could not be counted on. Nevertheless, the leadership made a strategic decision to embark on a comprehensive program of industrialization, with a focus on labor-intensive industries. Singapore was forced to look for opportunities well beyond its borders to spearhead its industrial development.

The government played a crucial role, initially to jump-start industrialization and increasingly to facilitate economic restructuring.[153] However the government was kept small, efficient and honest - qualities absent in most of Singapore's neighbors.[154] The consumer mentality was held in check as the cost of public administration was kept to a minimum only taking 1.5 percent of the budget. The total amount allocated to development expenditure under the plan was S$871.02 million, of which 58.1 percent would be used for economic development, 40.4 percent for social development and the remaining 1.5 percent for public administration.[155] In 1964, the Economic Planning Unit published an assessment of the progress that had been achieved between 1961 and 1963. According to the review, the plan had more than succeeded in its aim of increasing national income and per capita income inadequate measure to "arrest the threat to the standard of living ... by the growth in population".[156] Other development plans followed this initial planning effort.

Achievements

In the 1970s through the 1990s, Singapore experienced sustained economic growth. Along with Hong Kong, South Korea, and Taiwan, it was called one of the "Four Tigers" of Asian economic prosperity.[157] By the end of the 1970s, the unemployment rate was as low as 3.5 percent while the manufacturing sector continued to grow to about 25 percent of GDP.[158] Singapore's high annual GDP growth rate was beginning to gain international recognition. By 1972, just seven years after independence, twenty-five percent of Singapore's manufacturing firms were either foreign-owned or joint-venture companies, and both the U.S. and Japan were major investors. As a result of Singapore's steady climate, favorable investment conditions and the rapid expansion of the world economy from 1965 to 1972, the country's Gross Domestic Product (GDP) experienced annual double-digit growth.

Without the presence of any natural resource, the Singapore government has always understood that their only available resources are the people of Singapore.[159] As such, the development of human capital throughout the years has been a crucial role that the Singapore government plays in ensuring that the various economic strategies succeed. There has been strong emphasis on developing human resources, and continuously significant investments in human capital as reflected in the strategic thrusts of its Strategic Economic Plan.[160]

Many technical schools were set up and international corporations paid to train local unskilled workers in information technology, petrochemicals, and electronics.[161] Those who could not get industrial jobs were enrolled in labor-intensive untradeable services, such as tourism and transportation. The strategy of letting multinationals educate Singapore's workforce paid high dividends for the country.[162] In the 1970s, Singapore was primarily exporting textiles, garments, and basic electronics. By the 1990s, they were engaging in wafer fabrication, logistics, biotech research, pharmaceuticals, integrated circuit design, and aerospace engineering.[163] Due to considerable economic progress, the IMF recognized Singapore as an advanced economic entity in 1997.[164]

Despite the challenges it faced at independence and the fact that it was a small country, Singapore has become one of the most developed countries in Asia. Today, Singapore has transformed into an ultra-industrialized country achieving high economic growth ratesannually. In fact, Singapore has a Gross Domestic Product (GDP) per capita similar to many OECD (Organization for Economic Cooperation and Development) countries. The Port of Singapore has become the world's busiest transshipment port surpassing Hong Kong and Rotterdam.[165] Regarding total cargo tonnage handled, it has become the world's second busiest, behind only the port of Shanghai. The Singapore Tourism Board reported an all-time high of 16.4 million visitors in 2016.[166] That is more than three times the City State's population. With its small land size and a small labor force of 3 million people, Singapore can produce a GDP that exceeds $300 billion dollars annually, higher than three-quarters of the world.[167]

Notwithstanding its small size, as of 2014, Singapore was the 13th largest export market for the USA, and the 17th largest trading partner.[168] The goods trade relation between Singapore and the USA stands at US$30.2 billion for the exports to Singapore and US$16.4 billion for the imports from Singapore.[169] The country has established strong trade agreements with several countries in South America, Europe, and Asia, as well. In 2016 Singapore was ranked the second most competitive economy in the world.[170] Many multinational corporations are operating in the country in addition to tens of thousands of small and medium enterprises. Corruption is minimal and so is the crime.[171,172]

Today, Singapore has a highly developed and successful free-market economy.[173] It enjoys a remarkably open and corruption-free environment, stable prices, and a per capita GDP higher than that of most developed countries.[174] Unemployment is very low. The economy depends heavily on exports, particularly of consumer electronics, information technology products, medical and optical devices, pharmaceuticals, and on its vibrant transportation, business, and financial services sectors.[175] In 2014 electricity production stood at 49.31 billion KWh while consumption was at 47.18 billion kWh. Singapore's GDP per capita (PPP) has risen to an astonishing U.S. $87,100 (2016 estimate) making it the fifth highest in the world.[176]

Lessons from Singapore for African countries

African countries have much to learn from the integrity and hard work ethic of the government and people of Singapore. What is particularly significant is that the country has made extraordinary progress without the help of natural resources. Singapore has demonstrated that intellectual resources yield much higher returns than natural resources when it comes to nation-building and economic development. Singapore has treasured her people and turned them into assets as the launching pad of its economic development.

Realizing that their primary dependence had to be on their human resource, and that dependence on the resources of foreign investors was secondary, both the leaders and the people worked together to safeguard these to ensure that Singapore's economy remained competitive. With relatively stable governments from 1960 onward, Singapore has been able to attract foreign direct investment for its economic progress.

Singapore's commitment to clean government is something to emulate too. The country has consistently been the least corrupt country in Asia, ahead of Hong Kong, Japan, and Taiwan.[177] The leaders of Singapore shunned the use of large sums of money for elections. Such was the disdain of corruption that senior party officers caught in the practice were imprisoned; one even committed suicide rather than be exposed to shame.[178] The leadership in Singapore established a climate of opinion that looked upon corruption in public office as a threat to society.[179]

African countries and their leaders would do well to learn from this example: there is a price to pay for economic development and progress. Tough choices must be made if progress is to be made. A country cannot have it both ways: tolerate corruption and still expect to enjoy healthy economic growth.

Skeptics have often cited that because of its small size, it was easier for the Singaporean government to implement economic strategies, something that is often tough to do in the larger developing countries. The counter argument to this is that if size alone is a major determinant of economic progress, why haven't the smaller African countries emulated Singapore's example, especially since most of them were more endowed than Singapore was?

Conclusion

The East Asian countries used as case studies in this chapter achieved success on the back of visionary, effective national leadership with political will, and think tanks (both state and non-state) manned by indigenous brains. They were able to borrow ideas from others' experiences, and contextualize them for domestic application. They actively managed their economies to national advantage avoiding unnecessary macroeconomic imbalances. While they learned from others, they did not allow others to plan for them. They envisioned possibilities, drew strategies, and designed contextually relevant programs. They monitored progress and took corrective actions as the need arose. None of them followed laissez-faire liberal economic development paradigms nor entirely neglected the signals of the market and international environment.

Though varied in their endowment with natural resources, Malaysia, South Korea, and Singapore, focused on building self-reliant economies through industrialization. The South Korean leadership invested heavily in the energy sector by developing the Korea Electric Company and fostering industrialization in oil refining, cement, synthetic fibers, iron and steel and other areas. Singapore transformed itself into an attractive center for companies from industrialized countries to build their factories. Malaysia used its predominantly agricultural base to build its industrial sector. These countries all focused on export orientation.

The developmental state theory is not a dogma, neither is it a recipe for successful civilizational advancements of a nation. It is, however, a state philosophy, which as demonstrated by the case studies in this chapter, created an adequate ground for the developmental efforts of the East Asian countries cited. The key point here is that the leaders together with indigenous think tanks in these countries analyzed their predicaments and came up with homegrown solutions to get out of them. They exercised independence in their thinking and found solutions that put development in the forefront agenda. These approaches to development were hatched by visionary leaders and nurtured in national think tanks like the Korean Development Institute (KDI), the Economic Development Board of Singapore, and the Malaysian Industrial Development Authority (MIDA) of Malaysia.

African and East Asian nations became independent in the decades following the end of World War II - the Cold War era. The period was marked by the domination of two superpowers, USA and USSR whose influence did much to distort the development path of the new developing countries. That era gradually gave way to a new epoch called globalization, characterized by a dramatic shrinking of the globe in terms of travel and communication, increased participation in global policymaking by a growing array of state and non-state actors and an exploding set of interlinked problems with ever growing consequences.[180] Many occurrences on the African and Asian continents in the last sixty years happened in the milieu of globalization. The radical changes of the last few decades present current and emerging African leaders with challenges unprecedented in history. Before exploring further the impact that leadership and think tanks can make on Africa's development trajectory, it is important to understand the phenomenon of globalization together with the challenges and opportunities it presents.

Notes & References

1   Moyo, D. (2010). *Dead aid: Why aid is not working and how there is a better way for Africa.* New York: Farrar, Straus and Giroux.

2   Herbst, J. (2005, November). *Africa and the challenge of globalization.* Presented at the Conference on Globalization and Economic Success: Policy Options for Africa, Singapore. Retrieved from http://www.thebrenthurstfoundation. org/Files/Globalisation_and_Economic_Success_Singapore_2005   /Africa_ Globalization.pdf

3   Marquardt, M., & Berger, N. O. (2003). The future: Globalization and new roles for HRD. *Advances in Developing Human Resources, 5*(3), 283-295.

4   Woo-Cumings, M. (1999). *The developmental state.* Ithaca, NY: Cornell University Press.

5   ibid.

6   Drabble, J. (2000). *An Economic History of Malaysia, c.1800-1990: The Transition to Modern Economic Growth.* Palgrave Macmillan. Retrieved from https:// faculty.washington.edu/charles/new percent20PUBS/Reviews percent20and percent20Other percent20Publications/R30.pdf

7   Zainal, A. Y., Bhattasali, D., World Bank, & Commission on Growth and Development. (2008). *Economic growth and development in Malaysia, policy making and leadership.* Washington, D.C: International Bank for Reconstruction and Development.

8   CIA World Factbook. (2016c). Country Profile: Malaysia. Retrieved from https:// www.cia.gov/library/publications/the-world-factbook/geos/my.html

9   ibid.

10 Drabble, J. (2000). An Economic History of Malaysia, c.1800-1990: The Transition to Modern Economic Growth.

11 ibid.

12 ibid.

13 ibid.

14 CIA World Factbook. (2016c). Country Profile: Malaysia.

15 ibid.

16 Zainal, A. Y., Bhattasali, D., World Bank, & Commission on Growth and Development. (2008). *Economic growth and development in Malaysia, policy making and leadership.*

17 ibid.

18 Hoffmann, L., & Tan, S. E. (1980). *Industrial growth, employment, and foreign*

investment in peninsular Malaysia. Kuala Lumpur: Oxford University Press.

19 Kind, H. J., & Mohd, N. I. (2001). Malaysia - the lucky man of Asia. Bergen.

20 Zainal, A. Y., Bhattasali, D., World Bank, & Commission on Growth and Development. (2008). *Economic growth and development in Malaysia, policy making and leadership.*

21 ibid.

22 ibid.

23 ibid.

24 ibid.

25 ibid.

26 Daquila, T. C. (2005). *The economies of Southeast Asia: Indonesia, Malaysia, Philippines, Singapore, and Thailand.* New York: Nova Science Publishers.

27 Kamarudi R. P. (2011). Wikileaks: Malaysia's most prominent think tanks. *Malaysia Today*. Retrieved from http://www.malaysia-today.net/wikileaks-malaysias-most-prominent-think-tanks/

28 ibid.

29 ibid.

30 ibid.

31 ibid.

32 Zainal, A. Y., Bhattasali, D., World Bank, & Commission on Growth and Development. (2008). *Economic growth and development in Malaysia, policy making and leadership.*

33 ibid.

34 ibid.

35 ibid.

36 ibid.

37 ibid.

38 Yeats, A. J. (1991). *Do natural resource-based industrialization strategies convey important (unrecognized) price benefits for commodity-exporting developing countries?* Washington, DC (1818 H St., NW, Washington 20433): International Economics Dept., World Bank.

39 Zainal, A. Y., Bhattasali, D., World Bank, & Commission on Growth and Development. (2008). *Economic growth and development in Malaysia, policy making and leadership.*

40 ibid.

41 ibid.

42 ibid.

43 CIA World Factbook. (2016c). Country Profile: Malaysia.

44 ibid.

45 ibid.

46 ibid.

47 ibid.

48 Zainal, A. Y., Bhattasali, D., World Bank, & Commission on Growth and Development. (2008). *Economic growth and development in Malaysia, policy making and leadership.*

49 Drabble, J. (2000). An Economic History of Malaysia, c.1800-1990: The Transition to Modern Economic Growth.

50 Zainal, A. Y., Bhattasali, D., World Bank, & Commission on Growth and Development. (2008). *Economic growth and development in Malaysia, policy making and leadership.*

51 ibid.

52 CIA World Factbook. (2016e). Country Profile: South Korea.

53 ibid.

54 ibid.

55 Cartwright, M. (2016). *Ancient Korea.* Ancient history encyclopedia. Retrieved from http://www.ancient.eu/Korea/

56 Chung, Y. I. (2007). *South Korea in the fast lane: Economic development and capital formation. Oxford.* New York: Oxford University Press.

57 ibid.

58 ibid.

59 ibid.

60 Kim, I. (2010). Korea's capitalistic planning model: Policy lessons for Mongolia. *The Journal of the Korean Economy, 11*(1), 177-194).

61 Aymes, J. F. L. (2014). Formation and evolution of the knowledge regime and the development process in Korea. *Korean Studies, 38,* 91-123,162.

62 ibid.

63 ibid.

64 ibid.

65 ibid.

66 Choi, B. S. (1991). *The structure of the economic policy-making institution in Korea and the strategic role of the economic planning board.* In Caiden, G. E. & Kim, B. W. (Eds), *A Dragon's progress: Development administration in Korea.* Hartford, CT: Kumarian Press.

67 ibid.

68 Aymes, J. F. L. (2014). Formation and evolution of the knowledge regime and the development process in Korea.

69 ibid.

70 ibid.

71 ibid.

72 ibid.

73 ibid.

74 ibid.

75 ibid.

76 ibid.

77 ibid.

78 ibid.

79 Choi, B. S. (1991). *The structure of the economic policy-making institution in Korea and the strategic role of the economic planning board.*

80 ibid., p.102

81 ibid.

82 O, W. (2009). *The Korea story: President Park Jung-hee's leadership and the Korean industrial revolution.* Seoul, Korea: Wisdom Tree.

83 Brazinsky, G., & Brazinsky, G. (2010). Nation building in South Korea: Koreans, Americans, and the making of a democracy. ACN: Accessible Publishing Systems PTY.

84 Aymes, J. F. L. (2014). Formation and evolution of the knowledge regime and the development process in Korea.

85 Osabuohien, E.S. & Ike, D.N. (2011, September). *Economic transformation and institutional framework in Nigeria - lessons from Botswana and South Korea.* Paper presented at the 52nd Annual Conference of the Nigerian Economic Society, Covenant University, Ota..

86 Chung, Y. I. (2007). *South Korea in the fast lane: Economic development and capital formation.*

87 Federal Research Division (1992). *South Korea A Country Study.* Washington D.C.: Library of Congress.

88 U.S. Library of Congress (2012). The Government Role in Economic Development. Retrieved from http://countrystudies.us/south-korea/47.htm.

89 Chung, Y. I. (2007). *South Korea in the fast lane: Economic development and capital formation.*

90 U.S. Library of Congress (2012). The Government Role in Economic Development.

91 Kim, I. (2010). Korea's capitalistic planning model: Policy lessons for Mongolia.

92 ibid.

93 ibid.

94 Kim, I. (2010). Korea's capitalistic planning model: Policy lessons for Mongolia.

95 CIA World Factbook. (2016e). Country Profile: South Korea.

96 ibid.

97 Chung, Y. I. (2007). *South Korea in the fast lane: Economic development and capital formation.*

98 ibid.

99 ibid.

100 ibid.

101 ibid.

102 Schwab, K., Porter, M. E., Sachs, J. D., Cornelius, P. K., McArthur, J. W., World Economic Forum (2002). (Geneva). *The global competitiveness report 2001-2002.* New York: Oxford University Press.

103 Education in South Korea. (2011). *Education in South Korea: Understanding South Korea's education system.* Retrieved from http://sites.miis.edu/southkoreaeducation/diversity-and-access/).

104 World Trade Organization. (2015). Retrieved from https://www.wto.org/english/res_e/statis_e/its2015_e/its2015_e.pdfv

105 Kontis, V. et al. (2017). Future life expectancy in 35 industrialised countries: Projections with a Bayesian model ensemble. *The Lancet.* Retrieved from http://www.thelancet.com/journals/lancet/article/PIIS0140-6736(16)32381-9/abstract

106 Lee S. O., & Tan T. B. (2016, March). South Korea's demographic dilemma. East Asia Forum. Retrieved from http://www.eastasiaforum.org/2016/03/25/south-koreas-demographic-dilemma.

107 United Nations World Population Prospects. (2015). World Population Prospects 2015. *United Nations.* Retrieved from https://esa.un.org/unpd/wpp/publications/Files/WPP2015_DataBooklet.pdf

108 Lee S. O., & Tan T. B. (2016, March). *South Korea's demographic dilemma.* East Asia Forum. Retrieved from http://www.eastasiaforum.org/2016/03/25/south-koreas-demographic-dilemma.

109 Hundt, D. (2017, February). *Immigration is South Korea's only solution.* East Asia Forum. Retrieved from http://www.eastasiaforum.org/2017/02/21/immigration-is-south-koreas-only-solution/

110 CIA World Factbook. (2016e). Country Profile: South Korea.

111 ibid.

112 Kim, I. (2010). Korea's capitalistic planning model: Policy lessons for Mongolia.

113 ibid.

114 ibid.

115 ibid.

116 ibid.

117 CIA World Factbook. (2016d). Country Profile: Singapore.

118 ibid.

119 ibid.

120 ibid.

121 U.S. Department of State, (2011). Singapore (12/02/11). Retrieved from https://2009-2017.state.gov/outofdate/bgn/singapore/191973.htm

122 ibid.

123 ibid.

124 Lee, K. Y. (2000). *From third world to first: The Singapore story, 1965-2000.* New York, NY: Harper Collins Publishers Inc.

125 ibid., p.25

126 ibid.

127 U.S. Department of State, (2011). Singapore (12/02/11).

128 Lee, K. Y. (2000). *From third world to first: The Singapore story, 1965-2000.*

129 ibid.

130 ibid., p.33

131 ibid., p.157, 158

132 Heng, Y. (2013). A global city in an age of global risks: Singapore's evolving discourse on vulnerability. *Contemporary Southeast Asia, 35*(3), 423-446.

133 Lee, K. Y. (2000). *From third world to first: The Singapore story, 1965-2000.*

134 ibid.

135 ibid., p.58

136 ibid.

137 ibid.

138 ibid.

139 ibid., pp. 664-667

140 ibid., p.667

141 Bock, C.C. (2002). *Heart Work*. Singapore: Singapore Economic Development Board and EDB society.

142 Lee, K. Y. (2000). *From third world to first: The Singapore story, 1965-2000.*

143 Heng, Y. (2013). A global city in an age of global risks: Singapore's evolving discourse on vulnerability.

144 Kefela, G. T. (2011). Driving forces of globalization in emerging market economies developing countries. *Asian Economic and Financial Review, 1*(2), 83.

145 Wong, T. (1999). The transition from physical infrastructure to infostructure: Infrastructure as a modernizing agent in Singapore. *GeoJournal, 49*(3), 279-288.

146 Singapore. (1964). *State of Singapore first development plan, 1961-1964: Review of progress for the three years 1961-1963*. Singapore: Economic Planning Unit, Prime Minister's Office.

147 Lee, K. Y. (2000). *From third world to first: The Singapore story, 1965-2000.*

148 ibid.

149 Singapore. (1964). *State of Singapore first development plan, 1961-1964: Review of progress for the three years 1961-1963.*

150 ibid.

151 Le Blanc. R. (2008). Singapore: *The socio-economic development of a city-state [1960-1980]*. Maarheeze, the Netherlands: Cranendonck Coaching.

152 Bock, C.C. (2002). *Heart Work.*

153 Yue, C. S., & Das, S. B. (2015). The AEC beyond 2015: Implementation and challenges for Singapore. *Journal of Southeast Asian Economies, 32*(2), 239-259.

154 Lee, K. Y. (2000). From third world to first: *The Singapore story, 1965-2000.*

155 Singapore. (1964). *State of Singapore first development plan, 1961-1964: Review of progress for the three years 1961-1963.*

156 ibid., pp. 23–24.

157 Cahyadi, G., Kursten, B., Weiss, M. and Yang G. (2004). *Singapore Metropolitan Economic Strategy Report: Singapore's Economic Transformation*. Czech Republic: Global Urban Development Prague. Retrieved from http://www.globalurbandevelopment.org/GUD percent20Singapore percent20MES percent20Report.pdf

158 ibid.

159 Lee, K. Y. (2000). *From third world to first: The Singapore story, 1965-2000.*

160   Kam, W. P., & Yuen, N. C. (1993). Singapore coping with a maturing economy. *Southeast Asian Affairs,* 313-324.

161   Lee, K. Y. (2000). *From third world to first: The Singapore story, 1965-2000.*

162   ibid.

163   ibid.

164   ibid.

165   World Library Foundation. (2017). List of world's busiest transshipment ports. Retrieved from http://www.worldlibrary.org/articles/list_of_world's_busiest_ transshipment_ports

166   Singapore Tourism Board (2017, February). Singapore Achieves Record Tourism Sector Performance in 2016. Retrieved from https://www.stb.gov.sg/news-and-publications/lists/newsroom/dispform.aspx?ID=696&AspxAutoDetectCo okieSupport=1.

167   Zhou, P. (2017, March). Singapore's Economic Development. *ThoughCo.* Retrieved   from   http://geography.about.com/od/economic-geography/a/ Singapore-Economic-Development.htm.

168   Acunzo. A. (2016, January 25). On the Singapore-USA trade relation and the TPP. *Singapore Business Review.* Retrieved from http://sbr.com.sg/economy/ commentary/singapore-usa-trade-relation-and-tpp.

169   ibid.

170   World Economic Forum (2016). Global Competitiveness Report 2015-2016. *World Economic Forum* Retrieved from http://reports.weforum.org/global-competitiveness-report-2015-2016/

171   Numbeo (2017). Crime in Singapore, Singapore. *Numbeo.* Retrieved from https://www.numbeo.com/crime/in/Singapore

172   Transparency International (2016). Country profile: Singapore. Retrieved from https://www.transparency.org/country/SGP

173   CIA World Factbook. (2016d). Country Profile: Singapore.

174   ibid.

175   ibid.

176   ibid.

177   Lee, K. Y. (2000). *From third world to first: The Singapore story, 1965-2000.*

178   ibid.

179   ibid.

180   Harf, J. E., & Lombardi, M. O. (2007). *Taking sides.* Dubuque, IA: McGraw Hill Contemporary Learning Series.

5

The Globalization Shock Wave

"You can't stop the waves, but you can learn to surf."

Jon Kabat-Zinn

For millennia, trade routes have operated between different parts of the world transporting ideas, as well as goods. The 20th century experienced a marked increase in the scope and scale of this exchange. The momentous changes that swept the world found the newly formed African and Asian countries in a fledgling state. As the years progressed these countries found themselves in a radically different global playfield from the one they entered at independence. The aftermath of the Second World War was a bipolar world - roughly divided into West (capitalist) and East (communist). Two main players, the United States and the Soviet Union, influenced most of the foreign policy of the countries. By the end of the century the world had swung through a unipolar state and was swiftly moving to multiple power centres.

The globalization phenomenon became prominent in the last part of the 20th century. Though there had been progressively closer interactions between societies over millennia, as the last century came to an end, the pace of change accelerated radically. Unprecedented changes in communications, transportation, and computer technology gave the process new impetus and made the world more interdependent than ever.

Globalization: What is it?

Globalization is the process of increasing integration in world civilization, resulting from the interchange of trade, products, ideas, culture among the people, companies, and governments of different nations. It is a process driven by international trade and investment and aided by information technology. The term defines a combination of factors - a single marketplace with growing free trade among nations, the increasing flow and sharing of information, connections, or links of people around the world, and the opportunity for organizations and people to shop around the world unconstrained by national boundaries.[1] It has also been described as the "relentless economic force which integrates national markets, financial services, and labor" and is characterized by "an unrestricted and massive flow of financial information, capital, goods, and services in virtually every part of the world".[2]

Theodore Levitt, a longtime professor of marketing at Harvard Business School is widely credited with coining the term "globalization" in a 1983 article entitled, *The Globalization of Markets*,[3] though others assert that the term had been in use before. His thesis was that new technological facilities (especially in communication) drive consumers' wants and wishes into global commonality. The term was increasingly used in the 80s and 90s to explain the rapid changes in the world as countries became more and more inter-connected.

The main driving forces behind globalization have been attributed to four main factors: technology, travel, trade, and television.[4] Globalization is multi-dimensional, affecting all aspects of life: economic, cultural, environmental, social, and political.[5] Through it ideas, people, goods, services, and capital integrate economies and societies worldwide resulting in an increase in the flow of trade, information, and money, and the mobility of people.[6] It has caused more and more of the world to share common tastes in foods, fashion, and leisure.[7] It has also brought about the integration of production and investment decisions, breakdown of trading and investment barriers, truly global companies with a large capital base, sharing of international trade, and heightened mobility.

Gradually it has brought about the development of a global frame of reference or global level consideration for activities that would usually occur at a local, national or regional level.[8] Globalization has drawn every nation into a single economic system, and through social media, the world is connected in a mediated social system as well. Globalization, therefore, is an intricate network of countries, institutions, and people that have given rise to an interdependent world.[9] It has been facilitated by the ease of exchanging and processing information because of breakthroughs in computer and telecommunications technologies.[10] This has expanded the services that can be traded, moving the world toward a globally integrated economy.

The globalization of the English language is a unique fact in the history of the evolution of languages. Futurists predict that children will no longer speak half of the roughly 6,000 languages spoken today in 2030.[11] Most other languages will have lost users as well, as the languages of developed nations with the most open cultures increasingly take their place.[12] They predict that English, the global language of business today, will benefit the most.[13]

Post World War II Advances

From the end of World War II, international trade among free market economies moved forward through liberalization efforts. In the 1960s the General Agreement on Tariffs and Trade (GATT) was launched with the aim of ensuring a free and global commercial regime for capitalist states.[14] The steps that were taken at the time were measures in accomplishing a form of "integrated capitalism".[15] Then in the 1990s, a second wave of globalization occurred on the back of various technologies (microelectronics, computers, robots, telecommunication, new materials and biotechnology) that have generated a new form of economy, i.e. "knowledge-based economy".[16] Corporations, which perform their activity at a global level, understood the forces of new technology and promoted them as new vectors of progress.[17] The Europe 1992 movement, the Uruguay Round of GATT (1993) and North American Free Trade Agreement, NAFTA (1994) were all part of this wave. The end of the Cold War constituted a major breakthrough for globalization.[18] Growths in the world trade, foreign direct investment, and international financial flow have been the primary manifestations of the increasing globalization of the global economy.[19]

The Pros

Proponents of globalization see it as the key to an inter-connected, independent, and prosperous world. They argue that globalization promotes a trend towards economic equality and poverty reduction.[20, 21, 22] They point to increased global interconnection and economic growth, advancement in education, dynamic interaction of different cultures, higher standards of living, poverty alleviation, and improved healthcare.[23] They propound the view that globalization contributes to the lessening of economic inequalities, pointing to the shift of manufacturing activities to developing countries. However, in this case, the employees who live in the states where manufacturing has moved to benefit while those in the countries it has moved from are the losers.

Paul Goodman advances several other arguments for globalization.[24] He states that it enhances productivity in countries that open up their markets and integrate with external economies. Wealthy countries gain access to emerging economies while developing countries gain access to rich economies where they can sell their goods and services. Developing countries benefit from the increase in investment from foreign countries both financially and through jobs. Innovation occurs at a global level due to the open economies. Global competition and cheap imports help to keep inflation down. Countries can specialize more in what they produce and what they do best. On the cultural front, intermingling encourages countries to learn more about other cultures, strengthening international bonds, and making the peoples of the world more open and tolerant towards each other. Shared financial interests mean that corporations and governments attempt to solve ecological problems together. Finally, with regard to sourcing people and competencies that are needed to support strategy, globalization opens up new strategic possibilities to an increasingly borderless world. It provides as many opportunities to source globally and market locally as it does to source locally and sell globally. While there are merits to various arguments supporting global integration and cooperation, there are others who are vehemently opposed to it.

The Cons

The opponents of globalization, on the other hand, regard it with hostility, even fear, pointing out that the benefits have not accrued equally across countries. They believe that globalization, which is implicit in capitalism, not only destroys heritage and tradition but is also incredibly unstable.[25] They assert that it increases inequality within and between nations, threatens employment and living standards, and thwarts social progress.[26] This perceived injustice explains the resistance to the global movement by countries that prefer to preserve their customs and political beliefs.[27]

Some challenge the notion of globalization being a process of inclusion and equitability pointing out the increasing inequalities and exploitation in the global marketplace reflected in the growing inequalities between and within societies.[28, 29] For example, a recently released 2017 report indicates that eight men now own the same wealth as the 3.6 billion people who make up the poorest half of humanity.[30] Others point to the fact that the competitive business environment resulting from the integration of markets, elimination of restrictions on the transnational flow of goods and services has negatively affected the local employee.[31] For example 100,000 jobs were lost when the mining sector in South Africa was reengineered to adjust to market prices and global competition.[32] Similarly, when the clothing and textile industries downsized in response to world pressure, employment dropped drastically from 300,000 to 185,000 workers.[33] Also, the effect on wages, working conditions, and social security are devastating. Wages and working conditions everywhere worsen as companies gravitate towards countries with the lowest wages and the worst workers' rights. Higher unemployment results in the developed countries, breeding instability in those countries. Social welfare schemes are threatened as countries with no safety net, and poor safety records undercut prices of goods and services.[34]

The environment in the poorer countries, which also have less strict rules and regulations about controlling pollution and deforestation, suffers as production moves there.[35] The interconnectedness of the world economy means that economic problems in one part of the world can spread quickly and create a worldwide recession as happened in the 2008 subprime mortgage crisis in the US.[36, 37] Another argument is that many of the deals made by developed countries with developing countries are unfairly weighted for the former.[38] For example subsidies for agricultural production in the developed countries are maintained making competition in agriculture with the developing countries unfair.[39] Finally globalization undermines national sovereignties and governments, as individual countries are increasingly at the mercy of international markets, and multinational corporations grow more powerful and influential.[40]

The opponents argue that globalization has therefore favored the rich countries and has worsened the plight of the poorer ones. Many developed countries, which were historically net importers of food, are now net exporters. Heavily subsidized farmers in the developed world are seeking outlets for their surplus. International trade agreements apply pressure on African countries to open their borders to food imports. Similarly, by subsidizing their exports of manufactured goods and dumping scrap and second-hand goods at unbeatable prices, rich countries create highly unfavorable conditions for the development of small businesses as well as for the development of the craft industry on the continent.[41] An example is the dumping of used clothes on the African market that has strangulated the textile industry on the continent.

In summary, globalization is creating new ties among peoples and nations and is transforming the world into an interconnected village. However, its global impact has strengthened the superiority of the developed and intensified the dependency of the undeveloped nations.[42] It has brought to the forefront the inequalities both within and between cultures where many people can see the impact, but not everyone gets the benefits.[43]

Impact of Globalization on Africa

To a large extent, Africa has not maximized the benefits of globalization. To the contrary, the downsides have been more evident. The problems come from a deep and widespread development crisis in Africa. Africa's plight with regard to globalization has been attributed to several factors including the legacies of colonialism and neo-colonialism, the politics of the post-colonial state, poverty, foreign domination, instability, institutional and infrastructure decay, and dislocation.[44]

Most of the developed countries enjoyed the luxury of addressing in a gradual way issues such as competitiveness, environmental protection, poverty, governance, democratization, and regional integration one by one over the span of centuries. In the case of Africa, rapid globalization in the recent decades has meant that African countries have been forced to deal with the same issues all at once.[45] African economies based on agricultural and mineral commodity exports were plunged into the world markets and into a level of economic competition for which they were unprepared. This function worked well up until the end of the 1970s.

Africa experienced an economic peak in the late 1970s when all natural resource prices were relatively high.[46] Faced with the mounting needs of a growing population, and the challenge to build modern countries most countries continued to base economic growth on natural assets that could be readily exploited.[47] Paradoxically, weak economic development was mainly the result of exploitation of the region's natural comparative advantage: raw materials or tropical agricultural commodities.[48] The problem has been that there was hardly any value addition to the natural assets. While technological progress in the developed world made it possible to use fewer raw materials and more substitutes in industrial production, the supply of raw materials from the developing countries continued to increase. The entry of Asian producers into the market further compounded the situation.

From 1970 to 1990, the share of primary products in export earnings fell from 53 percent to 20 percent in the developing countries of South and Southeast Asia, from 90 percent to 68 percent in those of Latin America, but only from 93 percent to 89 percent in sub-Saharan Africa.[49] Furthermore, unlike Malaysia, African leaders made few investments to diversify the revenue services of their national economies. While the continent was experiencing the "lost decades" of the 1980s and 1990s, other regions were making dramatic gains.

One prominent manifestation of globalization was the Structural Adjustment Programs discussed in Chapter 2. They were designed by the International Monetary Fund and the World Bank to realign developing economies to the emergent, global neo-liberal hegemony. This package of macroeconomic conditionalities imposed on developing countries in crisis failed to achieve their objectives.[50]

The recession that hit sub-Saharan Africa during the 1980s resulted in a demoralizing loss of confidence in the future. Destabilized and discredited, African governments overladen with debt and advice responded by relegating the driver's seat to foreign advisers.[51] In this situation, aid programs were bound to fail since the countries assisted were unable to clearly (and independently of official doctrine) express their vision. Also, the assistance programs bore increasingly complex conditions. As a result, there was a tendency towards the spread of "Afro-pessimism".[52] Thus the forces of economic globalization deepened the marginalization of Africa.

Africa has had slow economic growth in recent times and has lagged behind other continents. It is the least integrated into the global economy. African nations are progressively getting the short end of the stick. The chances for Africa's integration into the global economy are unfavorable and further marginalization may increase.[53] The only remedy for this is African leaders styling up and cleaning up their act.

Impact of Globalization on Asia

Asia on the whole embraced globalization. With few exceptions like Burma and North Korea, Asian countries chose to mitigate the downsides of globalization and maximize the benefits. Behind this move was the assumption that economics could be separated from politics. So Asian governments sought to liberalize their economies even as they worked to protect existing political systems, institutions, and practices – an effort that proved remarkably successful during their boom years.[54] Improving living standards resulted in populations willing to tolerate governments that were authoritarian as globalization helped to give legitimacy to ruling regimes across Asia. In countries like Indonesia, Malaysia, and even South Korea, growing prosperity and authoritarianism walked hand-in-hand.[55] Greater openness to trade, foreign investors and visitors, and information from the outside world all have contributed to the erosion of sovereignty in Asia. Asian states chose to accept these costs in order to reap the benefits of globalization.[56] Singapore's decision to embrace the world economy helped it to become the financial center of Southeast Asia, and bolstered its strategic position in the region.

During the 1970s, the system of industrial subcontracting by locating manufacturing activities in developing countries with abundant cheap labor provided a development model for a number of countries in Asia.[57] Most of these countries have consequently enjoyed remarkable growth rates and improved living standards. In South Korea, globalization contributed to the nurturing of knowledge capacity and then to the rise of think tanks.[58] It provided non-state actors with more opportunities for agenda-setting and making inputs to policymakers, both in domestic and international affairs. President Kim Young-Sam's Administration declared *segyehwa* (literally meaning globalization) in 1994 and made efforts for Korea to join the Organization for Economic Cooperation and Development (OECD) in 1996.[59] With *segyehwa* and OECD membership, the Kim Administration undertook liberalization of the economic system, in accordance with international standards.[60] To meet the need for enhanced knowledge capacity due to the rapid economic growth, the Kim Administration made efforts to improve the university research environment and raise a new breed of intellectuals. One such effort that produced many young scholars with higher education degrees, both doctoral and master's degrees was *Brain Korea 21,* a major higher education reform project initiated by the South Korean government to prepare Korean human resources for the 21st century.[61] This new breed of intellectuals enriched not only the elite pool in the society but also the overall culture of professionalism.[62]

Riding the Globalization Wave

Often the adverse impact of globalization on African countries is articulated as if African countries do not exist in the same world as the countries that succeeded. So why did Asia ride the wave of globalization while Africa went under? Both Africa and Asia were in similar circumstances and faced the benefits and adverse effects of globalization in the same period; the results were different. As with surfing, the answer lies in the positioning of the surfer (the leadership), connection with the surfboard (institutions like think tanks) and the timing of the wave (the ability to anticipate global events and adjust in a timely way). Of the three, the most important factor is the surfer (the leadership). Leaders have the responsibility of ensuring that their countries maximize the opportunities that globalization brings and mitigate its attendant negative impacts. Asian leaders were able to surf the same wave that took African leaders and their countries under.

The fact is that the global market is ruthless (WTO trade negotiations notwithstanding) and runs on a "survival of the fittest" model. Judging from the trends in the past few decades, the pace of change in the world will continue to accelerate. Globalization is inevitable and irreversible. More and possibly bigger waves are coming. The world will be further diversified. The 21st century promises an age of rapid change and unpredictability. The power and impact of globalization mean that it's essential for every country to understand the current and future impacts of worldwide trends and to develop a globalization strategy to optimize opportunities availed by various markets around the world. No country in this era will thrive without addressing globalization and its effects.

African nations cannot afford to continue functioning as if they are isolated from the rest of the world; they are not. The days of the African village that is totally disconnected and oblivious to the rest of the world are long gone. The world has come to Africa like never before. It is not unusual now to find foreigners in the remotest parts of Africa, or to find Africans in very remote areas connected to the rest of the world through the media. Globalization has increased cross-border sharing of information and perspectives leading to more standard approaches and use of creative ideas irrespective of the origin. It has transferred global pressures to national and local governments. For African nations to prosper in the future, they will need to position themselves to deal with the specter of globalization. The increasing interlinking of the world requires the joining of minds for African countries to ride the tide.

Given the growing level of globalization, all leaders must acquire global leadership acumen. African leaders of the 21ˢᵗ century must be well versed with globalization and its effects. As globalization continues to gain momentum, it is a necessity for leaders in Africa to be equipped both at the national and local levels with the skills, knowledge, and ability to manage a diverse world, and get ready to compete in a globally inclusive market. Over the years, as globalization and competition have pushed traditional boundaries, nations have sought ways of measuring and improving effectiveness which begins by uncovering the dynamics and application of leadership.

In this day and age, ignorant leaders are a huge liability to the people they lead. The answer is building national capacities, and the key to that is developing leadership with certain qualities, together with empowered national and non-state think tanks. It is such leadership that will set organizations, governments, and other collective bodies apart, giving them the much-needed advantage to progress and be proactive in what they do. This was evident in the rise of the East Asian countries. Leadership is where it all begins, but what type of leadership?

Notes & References

1   Marquardt, M., & Berger, N. O. (2003). The future: Globalization and new roles for HRD. *Advances in Developing Human Resources, 5*(3), 283-295.

2   Mir, U. R. (2014). Understanding globalization and its future: An analysis. *Pakistan Journal of Social Sciences, 34* (2), 607-624.

3   The globalization of markets. (1983). *The International Executive (Pre-1986), 25*(3), 17.

4   Marquardt, M., & Berger, N. O. (2003). The future: Globalization and new roles for HRD.

5   Daouas, M. (2001). Africa faces challenges of globalization. *Finance and Development 38* (4): 4- 5.

6   Aninat, E. (2002). Surmounting the challenges of globalization. *Finance and Development 39*(1), 4- 7.

7   Marquardt, M., & Berger, N. O. (2003). The future: Globalization and new roles for HRD.

8   Hicks D. A. (2010). *Globalization*. In Hickman, G. R. (Ed.), *Leading organizations: Perspectives for a new era* (pp.14-20). Thousand Oaks, CA: Sage Publications.

9   Ivancevich, J., Konopaske, R., & Matteson, M. T. (2005). *Organizational behavior and management (7th ed.)*. New York: McGraw-Hill Higher Education.

10 Aninat, E. (2002). Surmounting the challenges of globalization.

11 Wagner, C. G. (2013). Top 10 disappearing futures. *The Futurist, 47*(5), 22-39.

12 ibid.

13 ibid.

14 Radoi, M. A., & Olteanu, A. (2015). Globalization - chances or risks. *Global Economic Observer, 3*(1), 75-79.

15 ibid.

16 ibid.

17 ibid.

18 Yardeni, E. (1997). *The Economic Consequences of Peace*. Deutsche Morgan Grenfell Topical Study #35. May. New York, U.S.A

19 Rugumamu, S. M. (1999). *Globalization, liberalization, and Africa's marginalization*. Harare: African Association of Political Scientists.

20 Dollar, D. & Kraay, A. (2002). Growth is good for the poor. *Journal of Economic Growth, 7*(3), 195-225.

21 Evenett, S. J. (1999). The world trading system: the road ahead. *Finance and Development, 36*(4) 22.

22 Ulubasoglu, M. A. (2004). Globalisation and inequality. *The Australian Economic Review, 37*(1), 116-22.

23 Canton, J. (2007). *The extreme future: The top trends that will reshape the world for the next 20 years*. New York, NY: Plume.

24 Goodman, P. (2016, November). *The Pros and Cons of Globalization*. Soapboxie. Retrieved from https://soapboxie.com/economy/The-Pros-and-Cons-of-Globalization.

25 Flores, V. (2016). Cuba: The last one to the global economic table. *Law and Business Review of the Americas, 22*(1), 59-67.

26 Marquardt, M., & Berger, N. O. (2003). The future: Globalization and new roles for HRD.

27 Flores, V. (2016). Cuba: The last one to the global economic table.

28 Mittelman, J. H. (1994). The globalisation challenge: surviving at the margins. *Third World Quarterly, 15*(3), 427-43.

29 Wade, R. (2004). Is globalization reducing poverty and inequality? *World Development, 32*(4), 567-89.

30 OXFAM (2017, January). Just 8 men own same wealth as half the world. *Oxfam International*. Retrieved from https://www.oxfam.org/en/pressroom/pressreleases/2017-01-16/just-8-men-own-same-wealth-half-world. Published: 16 January 2017

31 Kazi, T. B., & Indermun, V. (2013). The impact of globalization, mergers, acquisitions, reengineering and downsizing, on individuals and organisations in South Africa. *Interdisciplinary Journal of Contemporary Research in Business, 5*(6), 681-698.

32   ibid.

33   ibid.

34   Goodman, P. (2016, November). *The Pros and Cons of Globalization.*

35   ibid.

36   Shah, (2013) Structural Adjustment a Major Cause of Poverty. *Global Issues.* Retrieved from: (http://www.globalissues.org/article/3/structural-adjustment-a-major-cause-of-poverty)

37   Goodman, P. (2016, November). *The Pros and Cons of Globalization.*

38   ibid.

39   ibid.

40   ibid.

41   Cour, J.-M., Snrech, S., Sahel Club., African Development Bank., & Permanent Inter-State Committee for Drought Control in the Sahel. (1998). West Africa Long Term Perspective Study. Paris: OECD. Retrieved from https://www.oecd.org/swac/publications/38512525.pdf

42   Novakovic, l. (2009). Yet even the dogs eat the crumbs that fall from their masters' table: Matthew's gospel and economic globalisation. *Hervormde teologiese studies, 65*(1), 574-580. doi:10.4102/hts.v65i1.321

43   Glanville, E. (2009). Missiological Reflections on Difference: Foundations in the Gospel of Luke. *Mission Studies: Journal Of The International Association For Mission Studies, 26*(1), 64-79. doi:10.1163/157338309X442308

44   Omoweh, D.A. (2000). *Dynamics of globalization: Impact on Nigeria and Africa.* In Akindele R. A., & Ate, B. E. (Eds.), *Selected readings on Nigeria's foreign policy.* Lagos: Vantage

45   Cour, J.-M., Snrech, S., Sahel Club., African Development Bank., & Permanent Inter-State Committee for DroughtControl in the Sahel. (1998). West Africa Long Term Perspective Study.

46   Kefela, G. T. (2011). Driving forces of globalization in emerging market economies developing countries. *Asian Economic and Financial Review, 1*(2), 83.

47   Cour, J.-M., Snrech, S., Sahel Club., African Development Bank., & Permanent Inter-State Committee for Drought Control in the Sahel. (1998). West Africa Long Term Perspective Study.

48   ibid.

49   ibid.

50   Shah, (2013) Structural Adjustment a Major Cause of Poverty.

51   Cour, J.-M., Snrech, S., Sahel Club., African Development Bank., & Permanent Inter-State Committee for Drought Control in the Sahel. (1998). West Africa Long Term Perspective Study.

52   ibid.

53   Gondwe, G. E. (2001). Making globalization work in Africa. *Finance and Development 38* (4): 31-38.

54   Kefela, G. T. (2011). Driving forces of globalization in emerging market economies developing countries.

55   ibid.

56 ibid.

57 Cour, J.-M., Snrech, S., Sahel Club., African Development Bank., & Permanent Inter-State Committee for Drought Control in the Sahel. (1998). West Africa Long Term Perspective Study.

58 Kim, S. C. (2014). Politics, knowledge, and inter-Korean affairs: Korean public think tanks not as policy advocates but as knowledge producers. *Issues and Studies, 50*(1), 123-151.

59 ibid.

60 ibid.

61 Moon, M., & Kim, K. S. (June 01, 2001). A case of Korean higher education reform: The brain korea 21 project. *Asia Pacific Education Review, 2,* 2, 96-105.

62 Kim, S. C. (2014). Politics, knowledge, and inter-Korean affairs: Korean public think tanks not as policy advocates but as knowledge producers.

6

Leadership - The Game Changer

"Everything rises and falls on leadership."

John Maxwell

One of the most pressing leadership issues facing Africa is the scarcity of transformational leaders across the spectrum of society. Though globally there is greater interest in the subject of leadership than at any other time in history, new books on leadership coming off-press every day, and ubiquitous leadership seminars and courses, the lack of transformational leaders has never been more evident on the African Continent and their need has never been more urgent. In reviewing the last sixty odd years of African independence, it is telling that the type of leadership in the different countries was the primary contributing factor to the destinies of the countries. The contrast with the East Asian case studies underscores the point. Renowned Nigerian novelist, poet, professor, and critic, Chinua Achebe reduced all Africa's problems to the failure of leadership.[1] In 2004 the chairman of the African Union Commission, Alpha Oumar Konare, reminded an African Union summit that the continent had suffered from 186 "coup detats" and 26 major wars in the past 50 years.[2]

The journey from the euphoria of liberation from colonial rule in the 1950s and 1960s, through the darkness and violence of dictators and civil wars until the 1990s, when the path to real democracy and good governance began to open up, has been a tortuous one. It has been a tale of failed leadership characterized by wars, massacres, famines, disease, drought and poverty. Nation after nation provides a litany of incompetent governments, insatiable greed, and exploitation on the part of leaders and their cronies. There are tales of unbelievable power lust, repression, megalomanic leaders with delusions of grandeur, of ridiculous levels of corruption, and the suffering of millions of ordinary people.[3]

So what is leadership? What kind of leadership will lift Africa out of the doldrums and place it firmly on the path of growth and development? This chapter discusses leadership and highlights the need for a new African leadership paradigm characterized by serving followers, credibility, a global and multicultural mindset, foresightedness, systems thinking mindsets generation, nurturing consciousness and proactivity in planning succession.

What is leadership?

For more than a century, scholars and practitioners have failed to get universal consensus on the definition of leadership.[4] Various theories of leadership have been postulated. Theoretical frameworks are built on certain cultural assumptions or presuppositions; the more universal these assumptions, the less likely there will be a cultural bias. It is, therefore, important to ascertain whether an underlying assumption reflects the worldview of the national culture from which it is derived to such a degree that it hinders its use in other worldview systems. The concept of leadership that is in vogue comes from the Anglo-Saxon culture.[5] Whereas there are hundreds of definitions of leadership, there are no global leadership theories. Most leadership theories, although failing to state so explicitly, are domestic ones just masquerading as universal ones.[6] Most commonly, they describe the behavior of leaders in one particular country, the United States, and one particular gender, men.[7]

The dominance of Western thought in theories of leadership and management necessitates the exercise of caution in applying cultural analysis instruments created with Western assumptions to other cultures. Leadership research suggests that the United States is particularly unique in several respects among Western cultures.[8] The extreme individualism of Americans combined with a highly participative managerial climate may render U.S. management practices different from the approaches in most areas of the world.[9] For example, in comparison with people from most other cultures, Americans tend to have a more short-term orientation, a more materialistic orientation, and a more quantitative orientation.[10]

A fitting definition of leadership is given by Peter Northouse in his book, *Leadership Theory and Practice;* he defines leadership as a process whereby an individual influences others to achieve a common goal and is composed of leaders, followers, and situations.[11]

Africa's Post-Independence Experience of Leadership

Leadership in Africa is often seen as an inherently individual phenomenon, yet it is great followers who make great leaders.[12] In sub-Saharan Africa the trait concept of leadership is predominant, evidenced by an emphasis on the leader's characteristics, skills, styles, and behaviors.[13] The use of coercive power has been ubiquitous. This is shown by the prevalence of dictatorships on the continent over the last 50 years, resulting in the leadership image of the "strong man." Coercion involves the use of force to effect change as opposed to the use of influence.[14] Coercive leaders are interested in their own goals and not in those of their followers, and so are not good models of ideal leadership.

The exercise of power comes with privilege and benefits. However, as has often been stated, the control of power has a potentially corrupting influence leading to abuse in several ways.[15] Abuse manifests as unwarranted perception and misuse of privilege; favoritism to one's own group; prejudice against the powerless; bias in evaluating information; and refusal to relinquish control.[16, 17, 18, 19, 20] Followers suffer when leaders abuse power. Instead of being sources of strength and opportunity, groups transform to sources of threat and exploitation.[21] All these abuses have been all too evident in the politics of post-independence Africa. As Africa faces the next 50 years, it is clear that a new leadership paradigm is needed if her nations and peoples are to transition to a better future. But what should constitute this paradigm?

Requisite Qualities for African Leaders in the 21ˢᵗ Century

Global Leadership studies have shown that with minor cultural variations, people all over the world desire similar behavior from their leaders. Jim Kouzes and Barry Posner in their study of what leaders did when they were at their personal best, interviewed thousands of leaders all over the world asking them a basic question, "What did you do when you were at your personal best as a leader?" The interviews covered well over one hundred thousand people: men and women, young and old, representing just about every type of organization there is, at all levels, in all functions, from many different places around the world. The result was the best-selling evidence-based book, *The Leadership Challenge* also nicknamed, *The Leadership Bible*. The research continues on the Internet visited by 500,000 to 750,000 people every year. They discovered that irrespective of culture, gender, age, and other variables, when leaders are at their personal best there are five core practices common to all. Kouzes and Posner crystallized their conclusions as, "The Five Practices of Exemplary Leadership":

1. Model the Way
2. Inspire a Shared Vision
3. Challenge the Process
4. Enable Others to Act
5. Encourage the Heart

Their findings are similar to those found by another groundbreaking research project initiated in 1991 by House and his global team of 170 research associates.[22] They studied the perceived characteristics of effective leaders across the globe. The now world famous project was named the *Global Leadership and Organizational Behavior Effectiveness (GLOBE)* research program. The study that covered all continents except Antarctica showed that transformational leadership occurs in one form or another at all levels and in all cultures. It identified many cultural differences but also revealed four universal facilitators and three global hindrances of leadership effectiveness. The facilitators were:

1. Being trustworthy, just, and honest [being credible];
2. Having foresight and planning ahead [being visionary];
3. Being positive, dynamic, encouraging, motivating, and building confidence [empowering followers]; and,
4. Being communicative, informed, a coordinator, and team integrator [being interactive].

The hindrances were identified as:

1. Being a loner and asocial (being self-protective);
2. Being non-cooperative and irritable (being malevolent); and,
3. Being dictatorial (being autocratic).

Transformational Versus Transactional Leadership

The GLOBE research program and the global studies by Jim Kouzes and Barry Posner have established that despite cultural differences, both good leadership characteristics and follower expectations are universal: people all over the world desire similar behavior from their leaders. The country case studies used so far demonstrate that the first precondition for development is quality transformational servant leadership. The African continent needs competent leadership that is committed to serving the African people: credible, with global and multi-cultural competencies, clear-sighted and foresighted, possessing a systems thinking mindset, and proactive in planning. The continent needs transformational servant leaders and not transactional ones. In a transactional leadership approach, the leaders exchange rewards or privileges for desired outcomes. This approach focuses on the exchanges that happen between leaders and followers.[23] The last sixty years of African Independence have been replete with transactional leadership as evidenced by the high level of the following:

1. political patronage (the power to make appointments to government jobs especially for political advantage);

2. patrimonialism (a form of governance in which all power flows directly from the leader);

3. prebendalism (political systems where elected officials, and government workers feel they have a right to a share of government revenues, and use them to benefit their supporters, co-religionists and members of their ethnic group);

4. clientelism (the exchange of goods and services for political support) and,

5. neopatrimonialism (a system of social hierarchy where patrons use resources in order to secure the loyalty of clients in the general population. It can manifest not only in the top levels of the state, but also in the small vilages).

On the other hand, a transformational leadership approach aims at improving the performance of followers and developing them to their fullest potential. It joins leaders and followers in a mutual pursuit to satisfy the higher level needs of self-esteem and self-actualization.[24] Followers are moved to accomplish more than is expected of them. This approach stresses the need for leaders to understand and adapt to the needs and motives of followers. The ensuing relationship of stimulation and elevation so empowers followers that it converts them into leaders.[25] The African continent needs such transformational leaders across the spectrum of its society, with the passion and integrity for delivering economic growth and improving the quality of life of their people.

Leadership That Is Ethical And Credible

Corruption is an issue of major economic and political significance in many countries across the globe, including developed Western states.[26] Though prevalent to some degree in all societies, it is especially daunting for the majority of African countries.[27] A 2017 study concluded that corruption is costing sub-Saharan Africa around $182 billion a year, equivalent to 11.4 percent of its GDP, in revenues from different sources.[28] This revenue loss amounts to over four times the amount of aid allocated to Sub-Saharan Africa by donors. The lost revenues could double combined health and education spending in Sub-Saharan Africa. These statistics imply that if corruption is stopped, donor aid would be unnecessary.

World Bank global estimates of the amount of money misallocated to the personal gain of African leaders including government officials annually are even higher, and additionally, corruption can add anywhere between 25 percent and 100 percent to the cost of a project.[29] In 2002 the African Union estimated that 25 percent of the GDP of African states, was lost to corruption every year.[30] Former UN Secretary General, Koffi Anan described it as an insidious plague that undermines democracy and the rule of law, leads to violations of human rights, distorts markets, erodes the quality of life, and allows organized crime, terrorism and other threats to human security to flourish.[31]

Corruption is a constraint to economic performance.[32] Nowhere else in the world is this more evident than in Africa. It is a paradox that the most resource rich continent on earth is lagging far behind in development. When one considers the difference that embezzled funds could make for education and health, the greatest mass murderers in Africa may well be corrupt public officials. According to the World Bank, the average income in countries with a high level of corruption is about a third of that of countries with a low degree of corruption.[33] Also, the infant mortality rate in such countries is about three times higher and the literacy rate is 25 percent lower.[34]

The leaders that will move Africa forward must be ethical and credible. Empirical data confirms that credibility is the foundation of leadership. Jim Kouzes and Barry Posner's extensive global research found that when leaders are at their best, they inspire trust in their followers.[35] Similarly, the GLOBE Project empirically verified ten culture clusters and concluded that being trustworthy, just, and honest was a Universal Leadership Facilitator.[36] A leader's character is what generates trust among followers. When leaders effectively model their values, the potential for authentic followership increases.[37] Hence, moral leadership is tantamount to the wellbeing of society itself.[38] In reviewing post-independence Africa, historian, journalist, and biographer, Martin Meredith notes that not all of Africa's leaders were corrupt and greedy when they assumed their roles, but almost all were by the time their rule ended.

Leadership That Listens And Serves

The history of post-independence Africa is replete with monocratic narcissistic leadership. Examples abound of leaders like Idi Amin of Uganda, Fidel Bokassa of the Central African Republic, and Charles Taylor of Liberia. Narcissistic leaders overly focus on themselves, and as a result, they frequently hurt followers.[39] Narcissists are considered to be egotistical, manipulative, and exploitive in their interactions with others.[40] Leaders who base decision making on how to maximally benefit as ethical egoists.[41]

The monocratic or autocratic leader has complete authority. The followers obey the instructions of the leader without questioning and without receiving an explanation or rationale for such instructions. Such a leadership style deems followers to be inherently lazy or averse to work. Therefore they must be closely supervised and controlled. Monocratic leaders assume full responsibility and take full credit for the work. They are forced to work at full capacity, leading to stress and other health problems. MacGregor's Theory X bears this approach.[42] The antithesis of Theory X is Theory Y, which assumes that followers enjoy their work and possess the ability for creative problem solving.

Those who prefer the monocratic leadership approach contend that where the leader assumes full responsibility for the decisions and actions, there is ultimately reduced stress for followers and work gets done in a shorter time with less slack. However, if the leader is competent the organization functions smoothly, but if the leader is incompetent or unethical, the organization suffers. Weak autocratic leaders tend to take decisions based on ego rather than sound management principles and punish followers who dare to disagree with such decisions. This style breeds follower dependence, and in the absence of the leader, things often collapse and breakdown.

Another challenge with monocratic leadership is that because followers are not involved in the decision making process, they do not own the decisions made. Their resulting lack of initiative and enthusiasm often results in leaders trying to get the work done by issuing threats and punishments and evoking fear. An atmosphere of distrust builds between the leader and followers, and the unidirectional one-sided communication flow in an autocratic leadership style restricts the creative and leadership skills of followers and prevents their development.

The authoritarian decision making style is useful when the leader possesses all the necessary information and has the required expertise to make the best decision. The leader decides and followers are simply informed. This style is useful when the leader is the expert, and when a quick decision is required. The leader takes sole responsibility for the decisions.

However, when it comes to national vision and development agenda, many minds are necessary as no single individual has the capacity to think in all sectors on their own. When leaders attempt to do so, they ultimately become dysfunctional not because they necessarily become wicked but because their blind spots or things they cannot see overwhelm their achievements.

The wise leader always creates the "political will" and humility to seek the best advice. It is possible for power and humility to reside in the same person.

One could argue that a young country, much like a young child needs a father figure to lead them in a directive way until they mature. Indeed one of the challenges many African countries face in opening up to democracy is the interruption of well-intentioned projects by activists who in some cases are inadequately informed of the issues at play, or are serving the agenda of interest groups. However, the autocratic leadership style, on the whole, remains a short-term or quick fix approach to leadership.

The servant leadership paradigm is the antidote to the abuse of power. Servant leaders focus on meeting the needs of followers; they put followers first, empowering and developing them to their full capacities.[43] An essential characteristic of the servant leader is humility, which among others manifests as the ability to listen to followers.[44] An African example of the failure of leaders to listen and empathize with the suffering of their citizens is the present power struggle between the President of Southern Sudan and his former Vice President that has resulted in the loss of thousands of lives, and is threatening millions with death from famine.[45] Listening is fundamental in building trust.[46] Effective leaders put aside their personal concerns to engage in empathetic listening. Empathetic listening is an excellent way to build a trusting relationship.[47, 48]

Leadership That Nurtures

People are the intellectual or human capital of a nation (representing its hidden wealth). The experience of resource-poor nations like Singapore and South Korea detailed in Chapter 4 shows that countries with more talented citizens will win over time, while those with less talented citizens will lose. With few or no other resources to rely on, South Korea and Singapore gave the maximum attention to the development of their citizens. Their experience has proved that nurtured and developed citizenry, when given opportunity to exercise their talent, will figure out a way to develop the country. Therefore nations that will succeed in the coming years will be those that invest significantly in the development and proper deployment of their people. With the increasing movement of people and talent across borders, the most prosperous countries of tomorrow will also be those that can attract and retain highly skilled employees.

African countries will have to significantly improve in taking care of their professionals if they are to retain them in the increasingly globalized competitive environment. The United Nations Economic Commission for Africa estimates that between 1960 and 1989, some 127,000 highly qualified African professionals left the continent.[49] According to the International Organization for Migration (IOM), Africa has been losing 20,000 professionals each year since 1990.[50] In addition, the cream of professionals raised and trained in Africa with the scant resources available on the continent continue to leave Africa's shores for work abroad in the developed world, leaving the continent further impoverished in intellectual capital. A 2013 United Nations report shows that one in nine Africans with a tertiary education - 2.9 million people - were living in developed countries in Europe, North America and elsewhere.[51] This indicated a 50 percent growth in the years leading up to 2013, more than any other region in the world.[52]

The United Nations has recognized belatedly that emigration of African professionals to the West is one of the greatest obstacles to Africa's development.[53] Some developed countries wary of increasing migration now filter out undesirable Africans (the uneducated and unskilled) and instead entice for migration skilled Africans on whom precious national resources have been spent in nurturing and training. It is high time leadership on the continent recognized the cerebral and workforce hemorrhage that is occurring and made amends to stop it. Progress without the intellectual input from the best brains from within will be an arduous if not impossible task. To compound the problem, globalization has made the job of retaining intellectual capital even more difficult, but leaders must find solutions; that is why leaders exist.

Leadership That Fosters An Innovative Culture

Science, technology and innovation (STI) are engines of growth in any economy. African countries lag behind the world in innovation, and yet the competitive pressures of the rapidly changing, turbulent and competitive environment necessitate nations to focus on creativity, and to be flexible, adaptive and innovative. [54, 55] An innovative culture encourages followers to think independently and creatively in applying personal knowledge to challenges.[56] It creates a climate where all members of the society have the freedom to express their ideas, opinions, and feelings irrespective of their rank. A culture that does not encourage innovation is at a disadvantage whereas a creative and innovative culture plays a crucial part in long-term survival.[57] Societies whose culture embraces emerging innovations will become more self-reliant, more productive and prosperous than at any time in civilization.[58]

An innovative culture is not achieved quickly and requires intentionality and strategic thinking.[59] If transforming an organization into an engine of innovation is a time-consuming process, it must be much more uphill to do so for an entire country. It requires sustained commitment from national leaders seeking to make that transition. However, countries that desire to be successful do not have much choice. The best place to start is in the education system. The approach to education must emphasize enhancement of innate creative abilities of learners rather than just rote learning.

The African elite will need to wake up from decades long slumber. African countries must review their education systems to ensure that they are producing the kind of intellectuals Africa needs. Colonialists were always wary of the colonized attaining intellectual and economic power and so they designed education systems that ensured the maintenance of the status quo. The legacy of colonialism is an elite of consumption rather than one of production. Nigerian Professor Basil Nwanko succinctly put it concerning the Nigerian elite:

> The post-colonial African elite were more skilled at making money than at creating wealth. They had learnt the techniques of circulating money without a talent for creating new wealth. The colonial impact in Africa had generated urbanization without industrialization, fostered Western consumption patterns without Western productive techniques, cultivated among Africans Western tastes without Western skills, initiated secularization without the scientific spirit.[60]

Chika Onyeani concludes in his highly controversial book, *Capitalist Nigger: The Road to Success,* that the African educated elite is a failure, an individual who is not useful to the society, either in Africa or even as migrants.[61] He states, "The African elite have been a total failure; they cannot raise their heads in the community of scholars or the intelligentsia".[62] This predicament must change.

The big indictment on post-colonial African governments is that they did not, and to a large extent have not yet, recognized and corrected this malady in their education systems. East Asians nations did. Till now, sixty years after independence many African countries still hire consultants from the West (often at exorbitant costs) to write their education curriculums. Failure to think and plan indigenously and with a national, regional, and continental perspective has been very costly in the past and will be disastrous in the future if not addressed.

There are characteristics of a culture that supports innovation: encouraging informal meetings and interactions between leaders and followers; recognizing and rewarding successful outcomes; not punishing the failures; encouraging followers to share knowledge freely; appreciating risk taking; giving permission to risk; providing work flexibility and autonomy; sustaining behaviors that question tradition; promoting flexibility in work schedules, and, focusing on long-term performance.[63] The servant leadership paradigm focuses on followers and seeks to bring out the best from them. It entails encouraging them to be creative and innovative.

Leadership With Global Competencies

Given the increasing interconnectedness of the world through globalization, all leaders have to develop global leadership competencies. Even the once remote African villages are now connected with the world through mobile technology and the increased movement of peoples. It has never been more urgent for African countries to improve the quality of their people and especially of their leaders. Without this, opportunists will continue to exploit the ignorance of national and local leaders. An example of this is the acquisition of large swathes of African land by foreign companies, often without proper contracts in the process displacing millions of small farmers. In some cases, these land deals are with gullible traditional leaders or corrupt government officials. The World Bank estimated that in 2009 alone nearly 60 million hectares, an area the size of France was purchased or leased in land grabs.[64] Investors stated that they could usually get what they wanted in exchange for giving a poor tribal chief a bottle of Johnnie Walker [whiskey].[65] African leaders of the 21ˢᵗ century must be well versed with globalization and its effects.

According to Angel Cabrera & Gregory Unruh, in their book, *Being global: how to think, act, and lead in a transformed world*, successful global leaders are those who have honed the skill of, "crafting solutions by bringing people and resources together across national, cultural and organizational boundaries".[66] The competencies they possess are varied depending on the jobs they do, however from a study of 101 global leaders, Morgan McCall and George Hollenbeck in their book, *Developing Global Executives: The Lessons of International Experience*, describe a global competency set that could be used to describe successful global leaders.[67] According to these criteria, characteristics of successful global leaders could be described as open-mindedness and flexibility in thought and tactics; interest in culture and sensitivity to cultural differences; ability to deal with complexity; resilience, resourcefulness, optimism, and high levels of physical and emotional energy; honesty and integrity; stability in personal life; and, possessing value-added technical or business skills. Similarly, the GLOBE research project referred to earlier found the desirable characteristics to be being visionary, inspirational, team builders and possessing integrity, while avoiding self-protectiveness, malevolence, and autocracy.[68] Such global leaders act as citizens of the world, exercising global entrepreneurship with a global mindset.[69]

Leadership With Multicultural Competencies

Culture is the collective programming of the mind that distinguishes members of one group or category of people from others.[70] It is based on the values and practices of society, a group of people who interact together over time.[71] There is no such monolithic entity as "African culture." Africa is made up of over 3000 distinct ethnic groups speaking over 2000 languages.[72] In addition, both colonization and globalization have brought to the continent people from almost every part of the world. Unfortunately, the introduction of multiparty politics in the postcolonial era just fed into the tribal divide with the result that most political parties were based on tribal groups rather than ideology. A case in point is Congo. Martin Meredith in, *State of Africa*, reports that when the Belgian government announced a program of political reform in the Belgian Congo in January 1959, within ten months more than sixty-three (53) political groups were officially registered.[73] By January 1960, the number reached one hundred and twenty (120) political groups; almost every party sprang from tribal origins.[74] Ethnic conflicts on the continent have been responsible for the death of millions. Some of the more notable ones are the Rwanda genocide of the Tutsis by the Hutu (1994), and the Biafra war in Nigeria (1967-1970). The late President of Mozambique Samora Michel once aptly described tribalism as the Commander-in-Chief of anti-African forces.[75]

Given the level of cultural diversity on the continent, Africa needs leaders that value cultural diversity, seek routes to translate such value into actual responses to cultural plurality, and challenge prejudices and stereotyping against cultural, ethnic, racial, gender, and religious identities. It is dangerous for leaders to operate from mono-cultural assumptions and frameworks in multicultural settings.[76, 77] Tribalistic and mono-culturally minded leaders are blind to - or at least do not appreciate - cultural differences.[78] Such leaders are responsible for much of the suffering African people have endured in the past centuries; they have no place in Africa's future.

Research has shown that the ability to effectively lead followers in different cultural contexts is rare.[79] So not every leader is effective in culturally diverse situations.[80] Those who aspire to be multicultural leaders must commit to becoming avid and continuous learners; they must purpose to find ways to make diversity an asset rather than a liability.[81, 82, 83]

The need to understand the influence of cultures on leadership is increasingly important as globalization gains momentum.[84] Today, leaders are increasingly experiencing diverse cultures with different lifestyles as well as different management and leadership practices.[85] Increased travel has meant that one no longer has to travel to another region or country to have intercultural experiences. It is, therefore, imperative that Africa's current and emerging leaders are prepared to work in a culturally diverse world. The thinking of leaders must adapt to develop a global mindset.[86, 87] It also requires developing a host of competencies of which cultural humility is essential, without it, the leader is unable to display the other requisite skills.

Language is a significant predictor of cultural distance.[88] The language barrier increases the communication challenge in a multicultural context. For a leader, becoming fluent in widely spoken languages is very helpful in multicultural settings.[89]

Leadership That Is Generation Conscious

The dominant system of governance in the pre-colonial era was the monarchy where kings or chiefs ruled for life. However, every king raised a successor in the case of death that could be sudden, natural, or as a result of a protracted illness. Africa's post-independence era has shown that political leaders find it difficult to transition out. The longest serving leaders globally today are found on the African continent. Even Sudanese-British mobile communications entrepreneur and billionaire, Mo Ibrahim's offer of five million US dollars for those who leave power willingly with a good record has failed to get enough recipients.[90] The US$5 million prize is believed to be the world's largest, exceeding the $1.3m Nobel Peace Prize.

A new culture is needed on the continent where incumbent leaders groom followers for succession and then step down in time to see their successors flourish or help them when they flounder. True leadership makes itself increasingly unnecessary.[91] Every leader in every sphere of society needs to make an active and deliberate effort towards building his or her legacy right from the start.[92, 93, 94] It is a deliberate effort through Leadership Development. Succession works out more fluently when leaders take the time to groom and prepare potential successors. Mentoring successors is not negotiable for any leader. Leaders risk losing everything they have worked for when unprepared successors take over. Bahamian international leadership consultant, the late Dr. Myles Munroe referred failure to prepare successors, as the highest violation of leadership responsibility.[95]

Planned succession is what makes human progression and development possible. This is not a passive process. It is so crucial that it cannot be left to circumstances, but rather approached deliberately, consciously and strategically. It calls for collaboration between generations. It requires the deliberate mentoring, coaching, teaching, training and empowerment of a successor or a potential pool of successors. A generational consciousness leader lives with the burden of equipping, empowering and preparing the successive generations with a value system, wisdom and critical competences for future life responsibilities. Such leaders also make decisions with their eyes on the next generation and not just the next elections. The practice of raising and empowering successors must become the norm in African leadership otherwise the hard-earned gains from one administration can be lost in a short time when unprepared successors take over.

Leadership That Is Future Oriented

The need for current leaders to develop a long-term thinking mindset in planning for the next generation cannot be overemphasized. Recent history has shown that Africa is a disaster prone continent. A vicious cycle of poverty and ill health are the reality for many African countries. In 2011 it was reported that almost half of the population of sub-Saharan Africa lives on less than one dollar a day.[96] Moreover, the continent shoulders a disproportionate burden of the world's communicable diseases, including AIDS and malaria. Furthermore, the effects of climate change, extreme weather events are on the rise in many parts of the continent.[97] Though disasters can be unpredictable, some are preventable if the leaders exercise foresight. An example from Ethiopia illustrates the point.

In 1984 as President Mengistu Haile Mariam became increasingly captivated by the opulent details of the tenth anniversary of his reign, Ethiopia was heading for its greatest disaster of the twentieth century - the famine of 1984.[98] Though forewarned of the impending catastrophe, he refused to act and even blocked attempts to prepare for the disaster. The lavish celebrations went ahead as he made every attempt to hide the disaster from the world. No one knows how many people died in the Ethiopian famine of 1983-1985; estimates put the number at about one million.[99] This is an example of the lack of foresight and even callousness that has all too often been displayed by political leaders in post-independence Africa.

As the continent addresses the future, it is imperative that its leaders across the spectrum of society but especially at the highest levels cultivate foresight or future orientation. Foresight is the ability to predict what is coming based on what is occurring in the present and what happened in the past.[100] Exercising foresight enables a leader to look out for and take advantage of emerging developments inside and outside their domain of leadership.[101] At the same time, it enables a leader to recognize the warning signs or "prodromes" that indicate that a crisis is brewing and so enable better preparation.[102] As a result of foresight, in Malaysia, as early as the 1960s the national leaders focused on diversifying the economy away from reliance on (declining) commodity prices, shifting resources from low-productivity to high-productivity agriculture, and the beginnings of the push towards industrialization.[103]

The most successful leaders have a keen sense of the future and the ability to see what is next.[104] Strategic foresight is essential for success in today's fast-changing world[105] and must become a fundamental part of leadership in Africa. Foresight allows leaders to take advantage of future challenges and opportunities. Leading with foresight is pivotal in the twenty-first century.

Africa's checkered history has resulted in fatalism, which is one of the greatest challenges to exercising foresight. The failures of the last sixty years have led to a loss of confidence. Fatalism encourages people to believe they have absolutely no controls on their futures and so they just live for the moment.[106] It holds the view that what happens in some sense has to happen.[107] It rationalizes shortsightedness and discourages exploration of future possibilities.[108] In so doing, it reduces both shame about past failures, as well as guilt for continuing to do little to gain success.[109] Scientists have challenged fatalism by refining methods that help to access possible future events like weather forecasts.[110]

Edward Cornish, the founder and former President of the World Futures Society in his book, *Futuring: The Exploration of the Future,* suggests that three half-truths support fatalism.[111] First is the mindset that nothing can be known about the future. It ignores the fact that whatever knowledge we can gain about the future is valuable in helping improve the future. Second is the improvability of the future which states that nothing can be done about the future. It ignores the fact that individuals have the power of choice to determine better futures. The third is the urgency of the future, which states that due to many immediate problems, time should not be wasted thinking about the future. It ignores the fact that time spent thinking about the future is an investment to reduce the problems to be faced in that future.

Foresight, in contrast to fatalism, gives increased power to shape the future, even in the most turbulent of times.[112] People who think ahead live much better lives than those who do not. Thinking ahead prepares them to take advantage of all the new opportunities that rapid social and technological progress is creating.[113]

James Kouzes and Barry Posner affirm that it is the quality of focusing on the future that most differentiates people who are leaders from those who are not.[114] A leader is working proactively using foresight when they move their country "from crisis-prone to crisis ready".[115] Better foresight would enable African leaders to act in preventing predictable crises and to take mitigation steps in dealing with threats to their countries. There is an ethical dimension to foresight because leaders should be held accountable for any failures to anticipate what reasonably could be foreseen and to act on that understanding.[116] Africa desperately needs foresighted leaders that are free from a fatalistic approach to the future, and have developed mechanisms within their countries to scan the internal and external environments continually.

It is important to note though that there will always be unexpected occurrences in the future. These are called "wild cards".[117] Foresight methodologies help in preparing for these future surprises. Wild-card scenarios are, by definition, unlikely to happen.[118] However when they do occur, they have the power to dramatically affect the outlooks on the future and upset almost everything.[119] In the last one hundred years, the optimism that existed at the dawn of the twentieth century was dealt severe blows by two World Wars, the Russian Revolution, the market collapse of 1929, and the Great Depression. These wild card events gave birth to pessimism about the future that still lingers today.

Wild cards can also be positive. Edward Cornish uses the word "benestrophes" to describe an event that is the opposite of a catastrophe.[120] Benestrophes in the last one hundred years include the invention and commercialization of air travel, progress in telecommunication, the emergence of the Internet, and the sudden end of the Cold War.[121] The most useful aspect of thinking about wild cards is, in the case of bad ones, taking the time to explore ways of preventing them from happening, and, in the case of benestrophes, preparing for their success through changes in social systems.[122] In this way, foresight methodologies help to stabilize strategy formation against future shocks.

Leadership With A Systems Mindset

Africa's problems like poverty, disease, ignorance, unemployment, crime, and urban decay are all interlinked. What appear as isolated disasters brought about by drought or conflict in different countries are - in reality - systemic problems.[123] A systems thinking approach realizes from the outset that all stable systems have ways of resisting change. Instead of fighting against the system, the negative feedback loops are identified, together with how they work, and where they are vulnerable. A systems approach is then applied by changing the way the pieces interact.[124] Understanding systems help a leader avoid systems traps: structures that commonly cause problematic behavior.

One such trap is the addiction trap where a system over-relies on interventions to reach the desired state as measured by the system goals. An intervention is a short-term fix that makes everything look like it is working in the short run, however when the intervention is removed the state reverts to where it was or even worse.[125] Examples are industry addictions to government subsidies, and the addiction of many African countries to foreign aid to balance their budgets. Once the aid is removed, everything reverts back to the status quo.

Whether planned or not, the actions leaders take today will influence global economic development, the world's trading system, environmental protection, the spread of epidemics, the fight against terrorism, and, the handling of new biological and genetic technologies.[126] Powerful analytic tools like the International Futures model now exist to help assess risks and improve decision making in business, government, and private life. But almost universally, systematic quantitative analysis rarely extends more than a few decades into the future.[127] Leaders on the continent require an understanding of a systems approach to finding solutions to avoid unintended consequences. The implementation of SAPs and PSRPs with the "one size fits all" approach displayed an astonishing lack of understanding of systems from the Bretton Woods organizations.

Leadership That Understands What It Takes To Lead

The requirements to get into leadership at the national platform in many African countries are shockingly low. For example, information from the Electoral Commission of Zambia indicates that the only educational requirement to become a Member of Parliament or President is that one is literate and conversant with the official language of Zambia.[128] When compared with the rigor that the first Prime Minister of Singapore, Lee Kuan Yew applied to candidates for national elections in Singapore as described in Chapter 4, is it any wonder that African nations are still floundering?

Also, the falsification of qualifications for leadership is not managed robustly. The result is that individuals that are inadequately prepared to grapple with issues at both the local and global levels end up in key leadership positions. This indiscretion has to change if Africa is to claim the 21st Century. Top leaders must purpose to deliberately get people with strength of character and the brightest minds into positions of leadership and policymaking while aiding those with talent but without the necessary education to get the additional training they need. It is only secure leaders, not threatened when others excel, who can do this. Former Singapore Premier Lee Kuan Yew understood this principle and stated:

> Running a government is not unlike conducting an orchestra. No prime minister can achieve much without an able team. While he himself need not be a great player, he has to know enough of the principal instruments from the violin to the cello to the French horn and the flute, or he would not know what he can expect from each of them. My style was to appoint the best man I had to be in charge of the most important ministry at that period, usually finance, except at independence when defense became urgent.... It worked best when the minister was resourceful and could innovate when faced with new, unexpected problems. My involvement in their ministries would be only on questions of policy.[129]

Singapore has unequivocally proved that the quality of national and local leadership is the greatest determiner of societal progress. As long as countries are content with mediocrity from their leaders, and leaders are content with mediocrity from their senior leadership, remarkable societal progress will remain a distant dream.

If Africa is to claim the 21st Century, African leaders and countries must learn to ride the waves that are coming upon the world. While the first precondition for development is quality transformational servant leadership, one of the first acts of all transformational leaders is building think tank capacity and using it for the design, implementation, and monitoring of development. Professor John Paul Kotter of the Harvard Business School refers to it as a guiding coalition.[130] At the national level, such a guiding coalition is a think tank. That is the topic of the next chapter.

Notes & References

1   Achebe, C. (1984). *The trouble with Nigeria*. London, UK: Heinemann Educational Books.

2   Plaut, M. (2006, January). Africa's hunger: A systemic crisis. *BBC News*. Retrieved from: http://newsvote.bbc.co.uk/mpapps/pagetools/print/news.bbc.co.uk/2/hi/africa/4662232.stm

3   Meredith, M. (2006). *The state of Africa: A history of sixty years of independence*. London, UK: Simon & Schuster, Inc.

4   Northouse, P.G. (2013). *Leadership Theory and Practice*. Thousand Oaks, CA, Sage.

5   Igue, J. O. (2010). A new generation of leaders in Africa: what issues do they face? *International Development Policy*. The Graduate Institute Geneva. Retrieved from https://poldev.revues.org/139

6   Adler, N. J. (1996). Global women political leaders: An invisible history, an increasingly important future. *Leadership Quarterly, 7*, 133-161.

7   ibid.

8   Howell, J., Dorfman, P., Hibino, S., Lee, J., & Tate, U. (1994). *Leadership in western and Asian countries: Commonalities and differences in effective leadership processes and substitutes across cultures*. New Mexico State University: Center for Business Research

9   Hofstede, G. (1991). *Cultures and Organizations: Software of the Mind*. London, UK: McGraw-Hill.

10   Hofstede, G. (1980). Motivation, leadership, and organization: Do American theories apply abroad? *Organizational Dynamics, 9*(1), 42-63.

11   Northouse, P.G. (2013). *Leadership Theory and Practice*.

12   Bennis, W. (1999). The end of leadership: Exemplary leadership is impossible without full inclusion, initiatives, and cooperation of followers. *Organizational Dynamics, 28*(1), 71-79.

13   Haruna, P. F. (2009). Revising the leadership paradigm in sub-Saharan Africa: A study of community-based leadership. *Public Administration Review, 69*(5), 941-950.

14   Northouse, P.G. (2013). *Leadership Theory and Practice*.

15   Kipnis, D. (1972). Does power corrupt? *Journal of Personality and Social Psychology, 24*, 33-41.

16   Molm, L. D., Quist, T. M., Wiseley, P. A., (1994). Imbalanced structures, unfair strategies: Power and justice in social exchange. *American Sociological Review, 59*(1), 98-121.

17 Sachdev, I., Bourhis, R. Y. (1991). Power and status differentials in minority and majority group relations. *European Journal of Social Psychology, 21*(1), 1-24. doi: 10.1002/ejsp.2420210102

18 Goodwin, S. A., Gubin, A., Fiske, S. T., Yzerbyt, V. Y. (2000). Power can bias impression processes: Stereotyping subordinates by default and by design. *Group Processes & Intergroup Relations, 3*(3), 227-256. doi: 10.1177/1368430200003003001

19 Bolden, R., Petrov, G., & Gosling, J. (2009). Distributed leadership in higher education: Rhetoric and reality. *Educational Management Administration & Leadership, 37*(2): 257–277.

20 Ebenbach, D. H., & Kelthner, D. (1998). Power, emotion, and judgmental accuracy in social conflict: Motivating the cognitive miser. *Basic and Applied Social Psychology, 20*(1), 7-21. doi: 10.1207/s15324834basp2001_2

21 Maner J. K. & Mead, N. L. (2010). The essential tension between leadership and power: when leaders sacrifice group goals for the sake of self-interest. *Journal of Personality and Social Psychology, 99*(3), 482-492. doi: 10.1037/a0018559

22 Javidan, M., Dorfman, P. W., Sully de Luque, M., & House, R. J. (2006). In the eye of the beholder: Cross cultural lessons in leadership from project GLOBE. *Academy of Management Perspectives, 20*(1), 67–90.

23 Hackman, M. Z., & Johnson, C. E. (2009). *Leadership: A Communication Perspective.* Long Grove, IL. Waveland Press Inc.

24 Northouse, P.G. (2013). *Leadership Theory and Practice.*

25 Burns, J. M. (1978). *Leadership.* New York: Harper & Row.

26 Edward, F. A. (2008). The fight against corruption and its implications for development in developing and transition economies. *Journal of Money Laundering Control, 11*(1), 76-87. doi:http://dx.doi.org/10.1108/13685200810844514

27 Asongu, S. A. (2013). Fighting corruption in Africa: Do existing corruption-control levels matter? *International Journal of Development Issues, 12*(1), 36-52.

28 Curtis, M., & O'Hare, B. A-M. (2017). *Lost revenues in low income countries.* Retrieved from http://curtisresearch.org/wp-content/uploads/Lost-revenues. pdf

29 Cabrera A. & Unruh G. (2012). *Being global: how to think, act, and lead in a transformed world.* Boston, MA: Harvard Business Review Press

30 GNA (2013, March). *More than $148bn is lost to corruption in Africa - AU Report.* GhanaWeb. Retrieved from http://www.ghanaweb.com/GhanaHomePage/NewsArchive/More-than-148bn-is-lost-to-corruption-in-Africa-AU-Report-267336

31 Edward, F. A. (2008). The fight against corruption and its implications for development in developing and transition economies.

32 Svensson, J. (2005). Eight questions about corruption. *Journal of Economic Perspectives, 19*,(3), 19-42.

33 Mirzayev, E. (2015, January 22). *How corruption affects emerging economies.* Retrieved from http://www.investopedia.com/articles/investing/012215/how-corruption-affects-emerging-economies.asp?lgl=rira-baseline-vertical

34 ibid.

35 Kouzes, J. M., & Posner, B. Z. (2012). *The leadership challenge: How to make extraordinary things happen in organizations.* San Francisco, CA: Jossey-Bass.

36 Javidan, M., Dorfman, P. W., Sully de Luque, M., & House, R. J. (2006). In the eye of the beholder: Cross cultural lessons in leadership from project GLOBE.

37 Gardner, W. L., Avolio, B. J., Luthans, F., May, D. R., Walumbwa F. (2005). Can you see the real me? A self-based model of authentic leader and follower development. *Leadership Quarterly, 16*, 343-372.

38 Kretzschmar, L. (2007). The formation of moral leaders in South Africa: A Christian-ethical analysis. *Journal of Theology for Southern Africa, 128*, 18-36.

39 Campbell, J. L., & Pederson, O. K. (2014). *The national origins of policy ideas: Knowledge regimes in the United States, France, Germany, and Denmark.* Princeton, New Jersey: Princeton University Press.

40 Rosenthal, S. A., Pittinsky, T. L. (2006). Narcissistic leadership. *The Leadership Quarterly, 17*, 617-633.

41 Fedler, K. D. (2006). *Exploring Christian Ethics: Biblical foundations for morality.* Louisville, KE: Westminster John Knox Press.

42 Northouse, P.G. (2013). *Leadership Theory and Practice.*

43 ibid.

44 ibid.

45 Dumo, D. (2016, July). *South Sudan leaders order ceasefire as civil war fears grow.* Reuters News AgencyRetrieved from http://www.reuters.com/article/us-south-sudan-security-casualties-idUSKCN0ZQ08J

46 Denning, S. (2007). *The secret language of leadership: How leaders inspire action through narrative.* San Francisco: Jossey-Bass.

47 Covey, S. R. (1989). *The 7 habits of highly effective people.* New York: Free Press.

48 Hackman, M. Z., & Johnson, C. E. (2009). *Leadership: A Communication Perspective.*

49 Tebeje A. (n.d.) *Brain drain and capacity building in Africa.* International Development Research Centre. Retrieved from https://www.idrc.ca/en/article/brain-drain-and-capacity-building-africa

50 ibid.

51 OECD-UNDESA (2013). World Migration in Figures. OECD-UNDESA Retrieved from http://www.oecd.org/els/mig/World-Migration-in-Figures.pdf

52 ibid.

53 ibid.

54 UNCTAD (2016, January 12). *UNCTAD Technology report: Africa lags behind. Afrikonomics.* Retrieved from http://www.afrikonomics.com/unctad-technology-report-africa-lags-behind/

55 Rijal, S. (2016). Leadership style and organizational culture in learning organization: A comparative study. *International Journal of Management & Information Systems* (Online), 20(2), 17-n/a. Retrieved from https://www.cluteinstitute.com/ojs/index.php/IJMIS/article/viewFile/19/17

56 Kalyani, M. (2011). Innovative culture: An intervention strategy for sustainable growth in changing scenario. *International Journal of Business Administration, 2*(4), 84.

57 Rijal, S. (2016). Leadership style and organizational culture in learning organization: A comparative study.

58   Canton, J. (2007). *The extreme future: The top trends that will reshape the world for the next 20 years.* New York, NY: Plume.

59   Alexe, C.G. (2008). What is an innovative culture and how can we build it? *Upb Scientific Bulletin, Series D: Mechanical Engineering, 70*(1), 127-136.

60   Nwankwo, B. C. (1999). Politics of local government budgeting: Financial manipulation in the local government system. *International Journal of Studies in the Humanities, 12*(2), 63-76.

61   Onyeani, C. (2012). *Capitalist Nigger: A Spider Web Doctrine.* Cork: BookBaby

62   ibid.

63   Alexe, C.G. (2008). What is an innovative culture and how can we build it?

64   Fisher, S. (2011). Africa For Sale. *World Rivers Review 26*(3). Berkeley, CA: International Rivers. Retrieved from https://www.internationalrivers.org/resources/africa-for-sale-1657

65   BBC News (2011, June). Hedge funds 'grabbing land' in Africa. *BBC News Services.* Retrieved from http://www.bbc.com/news/world-africa-13688683.

66   Cabrera A. & Unruh G. (2012). *Being global: how to think, act, and lead in a transformed world.*

67   McCall, M. W. (Jr) & Hollenbeck, G. P. (2002). *Developing global executives: The lessons of international experience.* Boston, MA: Harvard Business School Press

68   Javidan, M., Dorfman, P. W., Sully de Luque, M., & House, R. J. (2006). In the eye of the beholder: Cross cultural lessons in leadership from project GLOBE.

69   Cabrera A. & Unruh G. (2012). *Being global: how to think, act, and lead in a transformed world.*

70   Hofstede, G., Hofstede, G. J., & Minkov, M. (2010). *Cultures and organizations: Software of the mind.* New York, NY: McGraw-Hill.

71   Murmu, N. (2014). Cultural diversity in global workforce: Issues and challenges. *Review of HRM, 3,* 67-72.

72   People of Africa (n.d.). *Africa Code.* Retrieved from: http://www.africanholocaust.net/peopleofafrica.htm

73   Meredith, M. (2006). *The state of Africa: A history of sixty years of independence.*

74   ibid.

75   Museveni, Y. K. (2000). *What is Africa's problem?* Minneapolis, MN: University of Minnesota Press

76   Dimmock, C, & Walker A. (2002). Societal culture and school leadership, charting the way ahead. *Asia Pacific Journal of Education, 2*(2), 110-16.

77   Shahin, A. I., & Wright P. L. (2004). Leadership in the context of culture: An Egyptian perspective. *Leadership & Organization Development Journal, 25*(5), 499-511

78   Canen, A. G., & Canen, A. (2008): Multicultural leadership: The costs of its absence in organizational conflict management. *International Journal of Conflict Management, 19*(1), 4-19.

79   Kets de Vries, M. & Florent-Treacy E. (1999). *The New Global Leaders.* San Francisco: Jossey Bass.

80   Robinson, D. A., & Harvey, M. (2008). Global leadership in a culturally diverse world. *Management Decision, 46*(3), 466-480.

81   Canen, A., & Peters, M. A. (2005). Issues and dilemmas of multicultural education: Theories, policies and practices. *Policy Futures in Education, 3*(4).

82   Cseh, M., Davis, E. B., & Khilji, S. E. (2013). Developing a global mindset: Learning of global leaders. *European Journal of Training and Development, 37*(5), 489-499.

83   Hickling, H. A. (2005). White, ethnic and indigenous: Pre-service teachers reflect on discourses of ethnicity in Australian culture. *Policy Futures in Education, 3*(4), 340-58

84   Hsieh, S. (2010). Literature review on global leadership competency. *The Journal of Human Resource and Adult Learning, 6*(2), 99-109.

85   Javidan, M., & House, R. J. (2001). Cultural acumen for the global manager: Lessons from Project GLOBE. *Organizational Dynamics, 29*(4): 289-305.

86   Robinson, D. A., & Harvey, M. (2008). Global leadership in a culturally diverse world.

87   Werhane, P. H. (2007). Women leaders in a globalized world. *Journal of Business Ethics, 74*(4), 425-435.

88   West, J., & Graham, J. L. (1998). *Language's consequences: A test of linguistic-based measures of culture using Hofstede's dimensions.* Paper presented at the Annual Meeting of the Academic of Management, San Diego, CA.

89   Elmuti, D., Minnis, W., & Abebe, M. (2005). Does education have a role in developing leadership skills? *Management Decision, 43*(7), 1018-1031.

90   Salim, A. S. (2006, June). No one's a winner: Why we haven't given Africa's most prestigious award this year? *Quartz Africa.* Retrieved from http://qz.com/714618/why-we-havent-given-africas-most-prestigious-leadership-award-for-two-years/

91   Munroe, M. (2011). *Passing it on: growing your future leaders.* New York: Hachette Book Group

92   ibid.

93   Galford, R. & Maruca, R. (2006). *Your leadership legacy: Why looking towards the future will make you a better leader today.* Boston, MA: Harvard Business Press

94   Brooks, M., Stark, J., Caverhill, S. (2004). *Your leadership legacy: The difference you make in people's lives.* San Francisco, CA: Berrett-Koehler Publishers. Retrieved from http://www.agweb.com/assets/import/files/brookssparksPR.pdf

95   Munroe, M. (2011). *Passing it on: growing your future leaders.*

96   IFRCRCS, (2011). *Disasters in Africa: The case for legal preparedness.* Geneva, Switzerland: International Federation of Red Cross and Red Crescent Societies.

97   ibid.

98   Meredith, M. (2006). *The state of Africa: A history of sixty years of independence.*

99   ibid.

100 Northouse, P.G. (2013). *Leadership Theory and Practice.*

101 Kouzes, J. M., & Posner, B. Z. (2012). *The leadership challenge: How to make extraordinary things happen in organizations.*

102 Hackman, M. Z., & Johnson, C. E. (2009). *Leadership: A Communication Perspective,* p. 404

103 Zainal, A. Y., Bhattasali, D., World Bank, & Commission on Growth and Development. (2008). *Economic growth and development in Malaysia, policy making and leadership.* Washington, D.C: International Bank for Reconstruction and Development.

104 Canton, J. (2007). *The extreme future: The top trends that will reshape the world for the next 20 years.*

105 Hines, A. (2006). Strategic foresight: The state of the art. *The Futurist, 40*(5), 18-21.

106 Cornish, E. (2004). *Futuring: The exploration of the future.* Bethesda, MD: World Future Society.

107 Solomon, R. C. (2003). On fate and fatalism. *Philosophy East and West, 53*(4), 435-454.

108 Cornish, E. (2004). *Futuring: The exploration of the future.*

109 ibid.

110 ibid.

111 Cornish, E. (2004). *Futuring: The exploration of the future.*

112 The art of foresight. (2004). *The Futurist38*(3), A1-A2, A4-A7.

113 ibid.

114 Kouzes, J. M., & Posner, B. Z. (2012). *The leadership challenge: How to make extraordinary things happen in organizations.*

115 Hackman, M. Z., & Johnson, C. E. (2009). *Leadership: A Communication Perspective.*

116 Northouse, P.G. (2013). *Leadership Theory and Practice.*

117 Cornish, E. (2004). *Futuring: The exploration of the future.*

118 Wagner, C. G. (2009). How to play a wild card. *The Futurist, 43*(3), 3

119 Cornish, E. (2004). *Futuring: The exploration of the future.*

120 ibid., p.117

121 Rockfellow, J. D. (1994). Wild cards: preparing for 'the big one'. *The Futurist, 28*(1), 14.

122 Wagner, C. G. (2009). How to play a wild card.

123 Plaut, M. (2006, January). Africa's hunger: A systemic crisis. *BBC News.*

124 Kauffman Jr., D. L. (1980). *Systems one: An introduction to systems thinking.* St. Paul, MN: Future Systems / TLH Associates.

125 Dean, S. (2014, Oct 31). System thinking and UX part 2: System traps and advice on how to avoid them. Retrieved from http://ux.stewdean.com/system-thinking-and-ux-part-2-traps-and-advice-to-avoid-them/

126 Lempert, R. J., Popper, S. W., & Bankes, S. C. (2003). *Shaping the next one hundred years: New methods for quantitative, long-term policy analysis.* Santa Monica, CA: RAND.

127 ibid.

128 Electoral Commission of Zambia. (2017). *Endorsing your choice: Are you a candidate?* Electoral Commission of Zambia. Retrieved from https://www.elections.org.zm/candidate.php

129 Lee, K. Y. (2000). *From third world to first: The Singapore story, 1965-2000.* New York, NY: HarperCollins Publishers Inc. p. 200

130 Kotter, J. P. (2012). *Leading change.* Boston, MA: Harvard Business Review Press.

7

Think Tanks In Positioning Africa For The Future

"You can learn from the brains of others, but you cannot borrow a brain, as there is none on the market"

Professor Stephen Adei

The jelly-like mass of tissue called the brain, located in every human head is the most complex organ in the body. Weighing around 1.4 kilograms, with billions of nerve cells, it is the source of thoughts and actions. [1] While one can do without some parts of the body, without the brain or with a damaged one, meaningful life cannot exist. A national think tank is to a nation what the brain is to the human body. For a country to make sense of its local and global environments and respond in the most appropriate way, there must be a collective thinking center or an interconnected one that receives and processes information and then comes out with actionable recommendations. The first precondition for development is transformational servant leadership. A fundamental responsibility of such leadership is to building national think tank capacity and using it for the design, implementation, and monitoring of development.

Due to the abundance of capacity in all fields in developed countries, the role of think tanks may not be well appreciated there. Even then, there is always an identifiable center such as the

National Economic Council of the USA to advise the leadership. Leaders of developed nations depend a lot on information coming out of think tanks when making decisions. Former President Ronald Reagan of the USA and former Prime Minister Margaret Thatcher of the UK, in particular, relied heavily on both state and non-state think tanks in their economic policies.[2] Even Russian President Mikhail Gorbachev is reported to have been influenced by an American think tank.[3] The role of think tanks is more fundamental in developing nations.

In almost all the emerging economies the first significant action of visionary leadership was the creation of robust, intellectually autonomous national think tank capacity either in an institute such as the Korean Development Institute (KDI) or as a stand-alone unit of the public sector such as the National Economic Bureaus in many East Asian countries. Additionally, such countries encouraged the development of think tank capacity outside government in academia, independent institutes, and organizations to complement and challenge official think tanks.

Development is knowledge and thinking intensive. The case studies of Botswana and the East Asian nations show the need for having think tank capacity developed at the national level. A country may receive all kinds of help in development advice from external sources but just as the brain of a third person cannot be borrowed wholesale but rather only its expressed thoughts, so is national think tank capacity. The lack of adequate indigenous development think tank capacity has been a major constraint on African development.[4] That constraint must now be removed for African countries to experience accelerated development.

Professor Stephen Adei of Accra, Ghana likens a country without think tank capacity to a human being without a brain.[5] Such countries "without brains" are doomed to be "hewers of stone and drawers of water" for those who think ahead. Just like the brain is dedicated to receiving and processing information, nations need institutions dedicated to analyzing trends, current situations, and planning for the future. Economic planning is essential in fast tracking growth and development. In the case studies used in this treatise, governments took the central role in forecasting and planning at national level. It is hard to achieve good planning when this function is left to chance, to a few individuals, or to outsiders. Africa still trails the world in the presence of think tanks (Figure 7.1).

Figure 7.1: Global Distribution of Think Tanks by Region (2015)

Global Distribution of Think Tanks by Region

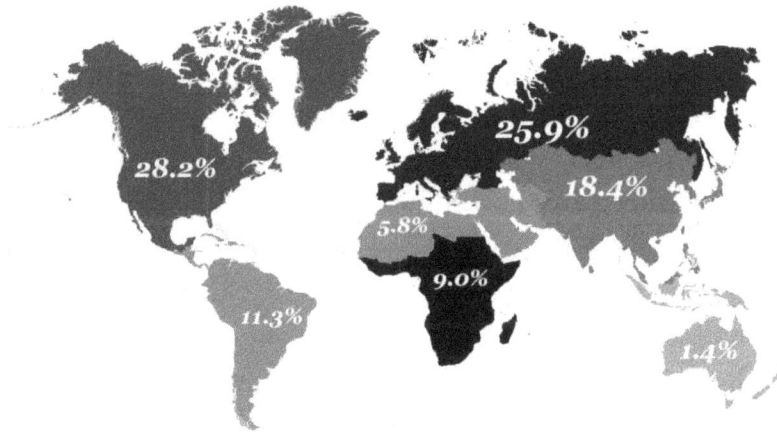

Source: McGann, J. G. (2016). *2016 global go to think tanks report and policy advice:* Philadelphia, PA USA: Think Tanks and Civil Societies Program, International Relations Program, University of Pennsylvania. Retrieved from http:// repository.upenn.edu/cgi/viewcontent.cgi?article=1011&context=think_ tanks

In the past sixty years, African countries have concentrated on trying to catch up with the rest of the world and trying to follow the roads others have walked instead of concentrating on finding their own roads. In the process, ready-made development recipes like SAPS and PRSPs have been followed without regard to prevailing local situations or the aspirations of the people affected. The experience of the developed world and the more recent experiences of East Asian nations show that both state and non-state think tanks have crucial roles in improving the planning frameworks to translate development aspirations and priorities into concrete results. As the case studies have shown, think tanks are critical to the development of effective national policies and programs and their execution.

The Role Think Tanks Played in the Emerging Economies

In his examination of development over the last sixty years, Professor Stephen Adei points out eight factors that combined to generate the fastest growth and improvement in human history:[6]

1. Visionary, transformational leadership within the context of a developmental state.

2. Capable, patriotic and committed national think tanks put in place by the national leaders to elaborate, design and lead in the implementation of credible long-term development vision and agenda backed by "political will."

3. A governance framework that assured peace and national unity for an appreciably long period, enabling the country to implement an agenda of transformation.

4. The building of an efficient, motivated and less corrupt public service especially the core civil service in implementing effective sector policies.

5. Systematic development of the human resources of the country, achieving about a hundred percent enrolment in functional primary schools with a majority of learners progressing through the secondary cycle of education capped by a science and technology biased tertiary education for twenty percent or more of the relevant age groups.

6. Creation of an enabling environment for non-state economic actors to engage in productive activities with active collaboration between the state and non-state actors to create internationally competitive industries and institutions.

7. Systematic sustained and focused improvement in socio-economic infrastructure and institutions resulting in a reduction in the cost of doing business and achievement of international competitiveness.
8. Taking advantage of global trends and niches - developing national capacity to exploit them in a dynamic context.

The catalyst seems always to have been visionary, transformational leadership supported by national think tank capacity. Think tanks have an irreplaceable role in a developmental state. They help in crafting a national vision, elaborating the agenda, assisting in implementation, monitoring, evaluation, and making corrective actions. They are essential in anticipating policy shifts and guiding leadership in taking timely action. No individual leader - let alone busy politician - can do this alone. Politicians do well to create the political will to seek the best advice.

East Asian leaders like Lee Kuan Yew of Singapore and Park Chung-hee of South Korea remained fresh with ideas and guided their countries through quality development policies while many African leaders became dysfunctional over time. One major reason is that the visions of the East Asian leaders soon became owned by capable and trusted think tanks that supported the prosecution of national agenda. In other words, the leaders enlarged their capacity by borrowing the minds of the best thinkers and researchers in the country. The emerging economies of the last sixty years have succeeded on the back of effective national leadership and on the brains of indigenous think tanks able to borrow ideas from others' experiences, which they contextualized for national application.

The development of Africa requires more private think tanks both as sources of new ideas and research, and as alternate sources of thinking about development vision, agenda, policies, and programs.[7] The experience of emerging economies in the last sixty years has shown that development is knowledge and thinking intensive. Lack of capacity in these areas disadvantaged many countries while those that developed strong capabilities in this regard prospered despite the odds. So in what ways can think tanks benefit African countries as they move further into the twenty-first century? Eight areas are examined below.

1. Formulation Of Indigenous African Development Paradigms

The unique role of the brain in the human body has its parallels in building a nation. Every country must develop the capacity to envision, draw strategies, design contextually relevant programs and projects as well as monitor progress and take corrective actions as they become necessary. Development is knowledge and thinking intensive. To date, there is a dearth of indigenous African development paradigms. Leaders have occasionally come up with visions that have not been adequately challenged or developed for lack of think tank capacity. Even the success of Botswana is more of a model for achieving necessary pre-conditions for development since there has not yet been a transformation into modernization.

Every country has unique endowments, constraints, and levers for their development journey. Each society has cultural beliefs, values, and norms some of which constrain the progress of the country, for example, attitude to time, acceptance of corruption by those in authority, and consumption habits. Indigenous think tanks can help African states to unveil the shortcomings of their traditional views on policy matters. Conversely, certain practices are anchors for development such as the community spirit, traditional hospitality, belief in God, and endurance. A foreigner would hardly be adept at identifying these, let alone using them in the policy formulation process; an indigenous think tank can. It is leadership and national think tanks' responsibility to unearth them, utilize and deal with them appropriately. There are no "off the shelf" solutions besides locally thought-through strategies. There are only principles and experiences from which to learn. Contextualizing these is the responsibility of a national development think tank. Perhaps it is in recognition of this fact that since 2013, China's President Xi Jinping has been calling for the establishment of new think tanks with Chinese characteristics.[8]

African countries have tried, often half heartedly, one development recipe after the other. The mantra of industrialization for import substitution soon after independence resulted in weak export orientation. Generations of structural adjustment programs, poverty reduction strategies and debt-forgiveness programs with the underlying development recipe of liberalizing economies followed. More recently the Millennium Development Goals, and now, the Sustainable Development Goals have been on the menu. The intellectual capital behind all these recipes has been externally driven primarily from the Washington-based Bretton-Woods Institutions and their major financiers. Perhaps these approaches would have been more successful if there had been high corresponding national think tank capacities to take them, modify them and ensure that they succeed.

The need for African countries to develop their analytical research and advocacy capacity to advance development paradigms has never been more urgent. Drawing from the success of East Asia there is a need for countries and regional blocks to set up various state-supported think tanks, as was indeed the case in the immediate post-independence era. Unlike at that time, most African countries today have citizens who have trained to the highest levels in some of the best institutions in the world. However often space has not been provided for them to exercise their intellectual capabilities. Sadly, out of frustration many have left the continent to work, where their capabilities are appreciated. Those who remain often end up working for Western companies and NGOs operating on the continent, doing the very things they would have been doing to improve the intellectual capacities of their home countries. Countries that do not need them as desperately as African countries do have continued to reap the benefit.

Think tank capacity as part of government machinery is crucial in enabling countries to develop national vision, policies, and strategies, as well as to support them. It also plays a crucial role in giving the country foresight as the future is continually scanned for emerging trends. In fact, it seems that a robust, intellectually independent and well-resourced officially designated think tank capacity is a necessary pre-requisite to harnessing the contribution of non-state think tanks' research, and advocacy capacity for development. Drawing from the work of non-state and independent think tanks and translating their findings into policy and programs or correcting ongoing ones is the work of official think tanks. Conversely, it is beneficial for state think tanks to have their ideas discussed by independent non-state think tanks. So long as such interchanges are done in an atmosphere of mutual respect, the best decisions and policies ultimately emerge. Aid programs have often failed because the recipient countries were unable to clearly (and independently of official doctrine) express their vision or scrutinize those prescribed by outsiders.

For so long, one of Africa's problems has been that of dependency. The dependency mindset has meant that even intellectually, governments have looked to outsiders (usually the West) for policy solutions that are not rooted in and are not informed by African realities. African governments have been dependent for knowledge production, appropriation, and dissemination - a situation, which undermines the continent's ability to maximize its democratic potentials and development agenda.[9] In fact, the continent is still infested with policymakers who are addressing African realities in borrowed discourses and received paradigms and advocating for outside development models.[10] Without the generation of endogenous knowledge, decision makers and policymakers in Africa will remain dependent on the importation of ideas and expertise.[11] If African countries are to realize their immense potential, the searching out of and collection of indigenous knowledge is indispensable.

African think tanks will need to churn out endogenous, context-sensitive and nationally and continentally relevant policy ideas so as to provide up-to-date independent perspectives and alternative solutions to different policy problems.[12]

2. Development Of Effective Policies And Management Of Policy Shifts

Policies have often failed or had to be backtracked because not enough thinking went into their formulation only for unintended consequences to occur. Think tanks are crucial for the development of effective national policies and programs. The retardation of the growth process in some African countries has been linked to policy failure.[13] Policies should be the result of thoughtful discussion and compromise. Think tanks help to ensure that specific policies are based on facts and research, that they are properly thought through, and that the ensuing programs and projects achieve their intended goals.

Think tanks can improve policymaking and enhance the ability of African legislators to make informed decisions by providing them with information and resources that they would otherwise be lacking.[14] They can also assist governments in applying cost-benefit analysis to public expenditure and proposing policy alternatives to enhance debate.[15] Experts in think tanks need to evaluate and analyze government policies, programs and projects regularly. Through thorough analysis and continuous evaluations, they can formulate plausible hypotheses about possible African futures, develop scenarios and promote the (re) alignment of long-term perspectives to strategic thinking and policymaking in Africa.[16]

Another contribution of think tanks is to anticipate when and how to make policy changes. Governments have to anticipate policies shifts and take timely action. The implications of unanticipated emergencies from drought, to epidemics, to global economic meltdown have to be prudently addressed. That is the work of a think tank, not of an individual leader, nor of the often very busy politicians. Think tanks should be continually scanning the environment to predict changes that would call for policy shifts.

In the absence of think tank capacity, policy changes are determined only by political propaganda and voracious convenience. In the last sixty years of African independence, policy shifts have often occurred without the benefit of scrutiny from many minds. For example, all economic development orthodoxy in the 1950s and 1960s advocated for import substitution to kick-start industrialization. Both East Asian and African countries started by following this approach. The significant difference between the two is that the former had the analytical capacity and political will to make the policy shift from import substitution to export orientation on time while African import substitution factories run aground with losses, lack of raw materials, state interference, managerial inefficiencies, and lack of funding resulting in aborted industrialization ventures. Only now, almost sixty years later are some African countries beginning to realize the need for export orientation and to do something about it. Meanwhile, the global horizon is already shifting to the knowledge economy. It is a case of continually catching the bus late.

For more than 40 years industrial development in Africa has stalled. Today the industries of East Asia are supplying African markets, while all the continent has to offer are the same primary products of sixty years ago. The share of industry in GDP today is the same as it was in the 1970s.[17] Think tanks in the developed world, especially foresight inclined ones, have been very useful in identifying the next important set of issues long before policymakers and journalists realize their significance.[18]

3. Effective Collaboration With Development Partners

Aid programs have often failed because the recipient countries were unable to clearly (and independently of official doctrine) express their vision. The development and maturation of think tank capacity on the continent will be a significant boost towards effective partnerships. There is a need for the analysis and the challenge of recipes of development from sometimes well-meaning development partners. The focus of criticism of development partners' policies has been on the adverse impact of development assistance and of direct foreign investment rather than on the ability of the African countries to enter into the relationship as equal partners and to take advantage of the opportunities aid and foreign investments offer. The main issue is inequity in the partnership stemming primarily from the low level of analytical and research capacity of the recipient nations and lack of political will. In most cases, it is not a question of not having individuals with the requisite training, experience, and orientation as much as the institutional framework to harness such capacity in the form of development think tanks, strong central banks and efficient ministries of planning and finance.

There has been a lack of effective engagement by local counterparts. Why didn't the African countries challenge the recipes and prescriptions being pushed down their throats? What were their counter-offers? What were the African perspectives? Were the nations so desperate that they had to swallow the medicine irrespective of the consequences? It is of utmost importance for African countries not only to develop the capacity to engage development partners but also the ability to formulate and implement their own policies.

Engaging development partners without a homegrown development agenda resulting from deep thinking is a recipe for disaster. At worst it makes countries vulnerable to schemes from outsiders, and at best it leads to the adoption of programs that do not address the most critical needs of the countries. State and non-state think tanks should be the first stop for development partners seeking to engage African leaders. Doing this would safeguard national leaders from being pressurized into signing unscrutinized deals.

4. Improving The African "Ideas Market"

Ideas drive the world. Think tanks and policy research programs believe that ideas matter for politics.[19] Politicians are very sensitive to what the electorate know and think, so they will rarely do things that could jeopardize their political standing. Well-researched reports from think tanks delivered to the public can shift the range of politically acceptable ideas and therefore lead politicians to act differently. Getting new ideas to the public or influencing policymakers, however, requires careful planning in addition to solid research.

The level of democracy and free sharing of ideas across the African continent has improved tremendously over the past two decades. However, the standard of national debates and discussions on the strategic challenges facing the continent and its different countries is deplorable. Currently, in the public space, it is not unusual to hear discussion of development problems, constraints, and solutions in Africa in the media with little thought and analysis. Everybody becomes an expert on how the country should be governed. The views of the expert and the man on the street are sometimes indistinguishable due to lack of adequate research and scenario building. The result is shallow analysis and solutions that often worsen the situation. In many African countries, the political discourses and the media only serve recipes of jaundiced views, insults, and insinuation to the listening public. Occasionally the landscape improves with the launching of a serious publication such as the UNDP's Human Development Report and Transparency International's corruption perception indicators. The fact that when these come out, they are picked by the media shows that the output of local think tanks on relevant national issues can improve the political and media landscape.

Despite the spread of multi-party politics across much of sub-Saharan Africa, few political parties appear to draw on research products to enhance their function as a policy platform.[20]

Research-based information enhances legislative debate. Most cash-strapped opposition parties have little access to research information and are reduced to running bad commentaries on the government to influence the electorate. African political parties have little intellectual support and thus lack the capacity to instigate serious debate and analysis of future scenarios.[21] The alternative to serious debate is rhetoric and sloganeering, which have not done much for the continent in the last sixty years, and as the adage goes, empty tins make the loudest noise. Without a knowledge-based exchange of ideas, the best decisions are not often made, resulting in costly policy failures and the loss of already scarce resources. The answer is good and independent think tanks to improve the 'ideas market" especially for political options and media content to shift the political agenda. Fostering the formation of different types of think tanks can raise the level of debate with consequent improvements in both the public and private sectors. An increase in think tanks and think tank capacity will improve the situation.

In many cases, the target audiences for think tanks are influential policymakers, but they could also be key opinion leaders, other researchers, grassroots organizations, the media, business leaders or the public as a whole. Since the liberalization of the 1990s, power is becoming more diffuse on the continent. Think tanks have the opportunity to positively influence the policymaking process by making their research products available to multiple audiences. These include the executive, legislators, representatives of regional and international organizations, politicians at sub-national level, and even religious leaders who exert a significant influence on African populations.

Another way that think tanks can contribute to the ideas market is in the drafting of credible political party documents – a process that requires considerable intellectual input. Regrettably many political party manifestos are largely an extensive list of wishful thinking devoid of serious debate and analysis of the future.[22] With many democracies across Africa still fledgling, opposition parties, which should be the source of alternative viewpoints to that of government, tend to be weak. Further, civil society research organizations (CSOs) are sometimes reluctant to cooperate too closely with political parties for fear of being seen as partisan and having their research discredited. Therefore, research based CSOs are more likely to work with the executive.[23]

Global experiences from the second half of the last century have shown that leaders who do not have or make use of competent think tanks are prone to becoming dysfunctional. Everyone has blind spots and however intelligent one is, no one can see it all. God gifted humans with a pair of eyes located at the front of the head. Without the use of at least two mirrors, or eyes of others, no one can see the rear. Similarly, in organizational and national planning, wise leaders cover their blind spots by keenly soliciting and listening to the views of others, more especially those that are disagreeable.

Regular use of think tanks is one reason why over the last sixty years East Asian leaders like Lee Kuan Yew of Singapore continued so long and yet seemed to remain fresh with ideas. Such leaders guided their nations through quality development policies while African leaders become dysfunctional over time. The former's vision soon became owned by capable and trusted think tanks (like the Economic Development Board (EDB) for Singapore and Korea Development Institute for South Korea) that supported the prosecution of the national agenda. In entrusting their vision and ideas for further development and analysis by think tanks, these leaders enlarged their capacity by borrowing the minds of the best thinkers and researchers in the country. Lee Kuan Yew's People's Development Party has thus able to win all the elections since Singapore's independence in 1965 not by excessive political intrigue but because of the fruit of their regimes.[24]

5. Riding The Globalization Wave

Globalization is inevitable and irreversible. The 21ˢᵗ century promises an age of rapid change and unpredictability. It has been named the century of the knowledge economy: an economy in which growth is dependent on the quantity, quality, and accessibility of the information available, rather than on the means of production.[25] The focus of economic success has moved to the ability to generate knowledge and to apply that knowledge to create innovations that can provide for the development of communities and human capacities, for greater competitiveness.[26] The power and impact of globalization mean that it is essential for every country to understand the current and future impacts of worldwide trends and to develop a globalization strategy to optimize opportunities availed by various markets around the world. No country in this era will thrive without addressing globalization and its effects.

Globalization has increased cross-border sharing of inform-ation and perspectives leading to more standard approaches and use of creative ideas no matter from where they come. For African nations to succeed, leaders at all levels must understand globalization, and the strategies for nation building in a globalized world formulated. There is a sense of urgency for investing in robust innovation systems, knowledge production infrastructure and on research and development (R&D) systems.[27] Strategies for developing these is the work of think tanks without which countries will not be able to ride the tide. Unfortunately, most African governments currently do not have a capacity to fully comprehend, prepare counter-measures and respond to the challenges that globalization is bringing up.[28]

As globalization increases its reach and grip around the world, it would be prudent for leaders at all levels across Africa to ensure they can draw from the expertise and capacities of think tanks as they grapple with the bewildering decisions in a globalizing world. Globalization means that Africa cannot remain disconnected with the rest of the world. It must stay purposefully connected and proactively engaged. A new generation of Africans must abandon the mindset of servitude. The journey towards this new uncertain future and a knowledge economy is a difficult one, and the experiences elsewhere in the world show that governments on their own can not succeed without assistance from think tanks.[29]

6. Advocacy

Think tanks are not content with producing good quality research; they want people to read the research and use it.[30] The target audiences are varied and so require different approaches. Apart from identifying the specific audience that needs to know about an issue, it is important to choose the most appropriate communication medium to use and how much information to give. To influence policymakers, and decision making in shaping future policies, think tanks need to attractively package their research products such as policy briefs, situation reports and policy papers and share them with the appropriate target audience.

Andrew Selee in his book, *What Should Think Tanks Do? A Strategic Guide to Policy Impact,* gives a useful guide.[31] Books are more suitable for experts and the section of the attentive public that is interested in an issue. They allow for the greatest depth of analysis if well researched, written and marketed. Books tend to be timeless; with a longer shelf life they can shape the field of study they cover over an extended period. Briefs are best for policymakers. They distil a large body of knowledge into a short report that addresses the specific actionable issues that the policymakers are focusing on at the moment. Blogs and short articles are for a general audience and must make a compelling case for action in a popular press fashion to people who may be browsing. Shorter publications and social media tend to be timely, allowing for quick responses to emerging issues.

Other avenues include high-level conferences, seminars, public lectures, research colloquiums, scenario planning policy workshops, brainstorming sessions and other forms of convening, attended by experts and decision makers with the aim of producing policy-relevant outcomes.[32] Through their advocacy role, think tanks can play a role in giving voice and dignity for the downtrodden and thereby providing leadership to civil society. In bringing out the implication of policies, impact analyses and evaluation reports they can become a voice for the silent majority. Think tanks empower the work of advocacy groups, even the work of lone but serious researchers.

Public dialogue is a central feature of most think tanks and is the primary function of some.[33] African think tanks and policy research institutions should increasingly be involved in bringing together university professors, government research units, advocacy organizations, private contractors and the public to intercourse with opinion leaders in policy formulation and decision makers to engage in public debate. These interactions help to remove blind spots and enable the best decisions to be made.

7. Capacity Building And Technical Support

Think tanks are very strategically located on national and regional leadership circuits. They regularly interact with the major leaders and so can play a role in improving the quality of leadership through building capacities of policymakers or by grooming a new caliber of decision makers with the ability to act expeditiously on policy recommendations.[34] Through capacity building and technical support activities, think tanks can, directly and indirectly, influence strategic direction, thus shape possible alternatives.[35]

Capacity building can happen by creating research fellowships opportunities for policymakers, allowing them to spend a short period in the think tank environment as they work with leading experts in particular policy areas. This approach can also be institutionalized through official skills transfer exchange programs between government policy research units and think tanks.[36] Technical support takes various forms including helping them develop certain policy guidelines and doctrines. For example, some think tanks like the South African Institute for Security Studies, are assisting regional organizations like ECOWAS to develop their capacities around conflict analysis and continental early warning systems.[37]

8. Preparing Africa For The Future

The world population is expected to reach 8.6 billion in 2030, 9.8 billion in 2050 and 11.2 billion in 2100, according to a 2017 United Nations report, *World Population Prospects: The 2017 Revision*, published by the UN Department of Economic and Social Affairs.[38] From 2017 to 2050, it is expected that half of the world's population growth will be concentrated in just nine countries, five of which are in Africa: India, Nigeria, the Democratic Republic of the Congo, Pakistan, Ethiopia, the United Republic of Tanzania, the United States of America, Uganda and Indonesia (ordered by their expected contribution to total growth). Between 2017 and 2050, the populations of 26 African countries are projected to expand to at least double their current size. More than half of the anticipated growth in global population between now and 2050 is expected to occur in Africa (Figure 7.2). Of the additional 2.2 billion people who may be added between 2017 and 2050, 1.3 billion will be added in Africa.

Figure 7.2: Population by region: estimates, 1950-2015, and medium-variant projection, 2015-2100

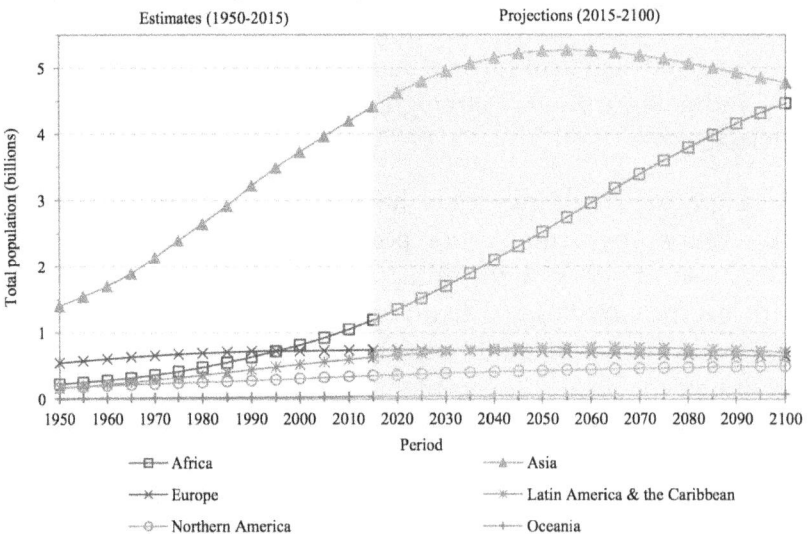

Source: United Nations, Department of Economic and Social Affairs, Population Division (2017). *World Population Prospects: The 2017 Revision.* New York: United Nations.

By 2050, 1.8 billion babies will be born in Africa; the continent's population will double in size; and its under-18 population will increase by two thirds to reach almost 1 billion.[39] Africa is the only region where the population is projected to keep increasing throughout the 21st century.[40] Currently, there are 1.2 billion people on the continent, more than five times the population in 1950.[41] By 2050, Africa's population will double to 2.4 billion, eventually reaching 4.2 billion by the end of the century, just about the entire world population in 1977.[42] Africa is not the first region in the world to undergo such rapid population growth. America in the nineteenth century, China and the Asian sub-continent in the first half of the twentieth also experienced the same.[43] The difference with the African experience is that the growth is happening at a time of the most rapid global socio-economic and political changes ever, and from a rural unskilled population base.[44] A further factor is that progress in medicine and information reduced mortality rates long before the society was ready to reduce its fertility rates.[45] North America's population surge included a proportion of urbanized migrants, businesspeople, and capitalists with skills and savings that helped to build the nation; India and China were able to isolate themselves for a while from the rest of the world while making rudimentary steps towards social and demographic transformation.[46] Africa, on the other hand, is entirely open to outside influences.[47] By around 2020, one out of every two newborn babies could be African.[48] Being home to the world's largest population of youth will require careful foresighted planning to reap this population dividend and avoid it becoming a burden or even worse, a source of instability.

In addition to the rapid population growth is the large-scale migration to urban areas. By 2030 sixty percent of Africans will be living in cities, growing from 36 percent of the population in 2010.[49] Africa's population of potentially productive youth will be the highest in the world. The continent's urbanization rate, the highest in the world, can lead to economic growth and transformation, at par with or even better than the current trajectories of China and other East Asian countries. However, without transformation, it can steer further into increased inequality, urban poverty, the proliferation of slums, and even social chaos such as that of the 'Arab Spring'.[50] Laws, policies, and actions needed to reap real dividends from Africa's urbanization are therefore critical in the continent's transformation. The need for African leaders to develop a long-term thinking mindset in planning for the next generations cannot be overemphasized.

Think tank experts, usually have deep insight on many policy issues. African governments need to harness their expertise for advice on policies, strategies and new approaches.[51] In more recent years, some African countries are returning to more comprehensive development plans that go way beyond the shortsighted PRSPs. These long-term development visions and planning frameworks with far more aggressive growth and social development objectives include Rwanda's Vision 2020, Tanzania's Vision 2025, Kenya's Vision 2030, South Africa's Vision 2025, Namibia's Vision 2030 and Uganda's Vision 2040.

These ambitious plans go beyond the narrow goal of poverty reduction to encompass goals such as accelerated growth, employment creation, structural transformation and sustainable development.[52] Unlike in the preceding years, these plans employ a mix of state and market-based approaches and appreciate the critical role of both the public and the private sector in the development process.[53]

There is ownership from African actors and a more consultative and participatory process involving a broad spectrum of stakeholders, including civil society, the private sector, decentralized constituencies and development partners.[54] These more comprehensive national development plans often take into consideration various global and continental development goals and frameworks such as NEPAD. Think tanks on the continent, especially the future-oriented ones, need to seize the moment because it is their domain. Clear and understandable research outputs that enable policymakers elaborate visions of improved African futures and explore the interventions necessary to move towards those ideals would guarantee the relevance and influence of think tanks in shaping African futures.[55]

Universities are repositories of some of the best and most well developed minds that a nation has. Unfortunately, many universities on the continent are functioning more like glorified high schools and are no longer involved in pioneering research. This has to change. After a long period of neglect, universities of Sub-Saharan Africa seem to be getting renewed attention. This reawakening bodes well for think tanks as many Universities harbor research institutions and policy institutes. State sponsorship of these is good for the general development of think tank capacity in a country.[56]

Think tanks that focus on foresight and future studies are direly needed on the continent if African countries and leaders are to become more proactive and not just reactors to local and global issues. The faster a vehicle moves, the keener the driver must be in scanning the road ahead. The pace of global change requires leaders to be strategic and have a keen eye on the future. Without keen attention to what lies ahead, an accident will occur soon or later. Think tanks like the Institute for Security Studies based in South Africa play a crucial role in finding the next important set of issues long before policymakers and journalists are aware of their significance.

Looking Ahead

The outworking of the full implications of a national vision almost always is beyond the leader's scope, ability, and even time span. Wise leaders therefore efficiently transmit and entrust their ideas to teams of capable leaders not only for analysis and enrichment but also for implementation. When this happens, the vision outlasts the leader. This legacy is exemplified in the continued growth and development of Singapore beyond the initial vision and leadership of the first Prime Minister of Singapore, Lee Kuan Yew. It is also evident in the benefits India is enjoying today in the Information and Communication Technology (ICT) field, which were the initial dreams of India's founding fathers like Jawaharlal Nehru the first Prime Minister. Both of these leaders are deceased, but their ideas live on.

If Africa is to capture the momentum for growth and development in the 21ˢᵗ Century countries need to undertake repositioning exercises to better align themselves with priorities that promote the ultimate objective of promoting economic growth and structural transformation. Effective national planning hinges squarely on the quality and availability of data, which informs the setting of priorities and facilitates the tracking of performance.[57] Countries will need to strengthen institutional structures and processes to address their data challenges. These needs should guide the training of personnel to avoid overdependence on foreigners and foreign institutions.

Success stories are beginning to emerge out of the ashes of the past sixty years. Some countries like Cape Verde, Ghana, Zambia, Botswana, Mauritius, and Kenya have graduated from low-income countries to middle-income countries. Even though the think tank sector in Africa is not as well developed as that of the developed world, it can have a meaningful role to play not only in transforming the policymaking process but also in shaping African futures.[58]

A positive development for the think tank sector in Africa is the holding of an annual Africa Think Tanks Summit organized by African Capacity Building Foundation (ACBF) in partnership with the African Union Commission (AUC), the New Partnership for Africa's Development (NEPAD) and the United Nations Economic Commission for Africa (ECA).[59] These regular meetings will increase the synergies for the growth of the think tank sector on the African continent.

Notes & References

1   Herculano-Houzel, S. (2009). The human brain in numbers: A linearly scaled-up primate brain. *Frontiers in Human Neuroscience, 3*, 31. http://doi.org/10.3389/neuro.09.031.2009

2   Adonis, A. & Hames, T. (1994). *A conservative revolution? The Thatcher-Reagan decade in perspective.* Manchester U.A: Manchester Univ. Press.

3   ibid.

4   Adei, S. (2009, July). *The critical role of the development of think tanks for Africa's development.* Paper presented at the meeting of SALT Institute, Kampala, Uganda.

5   ibid.

6   ibid.

7   ibid.

8   Doyon J. & Godement, F. & Stanzel, A. & Vasselier, A. (2016, August). *A hundred think tanks bloom in China.* London, UK: European Council on Foreign Relations. Retrieved from http://www.ecfr.eu/page/-/hundred_think_tanks.pdf.

9   Arowosegbe, J. O., & Rijksuniversiteit te Leiden. (2008). *Decolonising the social sciences in the global South: Claude Ake and the praxis of knowledge production in Africa.* Leiden: African Studies Centre.

10 ibid.

11 ibid.

12 Mbadlanyana, T., Cilliers, J., & Sibalukhulu, N. (2011). Shaping African futures: Think tanks and the need for endogenous knowledge production in sub-Saharan Africa. *The Journal of Futures Studies, Strategic Thinking and Policy, 13*(3), 64-84.

13 Fosu, A. K. (2011). *Terms of trade and growth of resource economies: A tale of two countries.* Oxford: Centre for the Study of African Economies.

14 Mbadlanyana, T., Cilliers, J., & Sibalukhulu, N. (2011). Shaping African futures: Think tanks and the need for endogenous knowledge production in sub-Saharan Africa.

15 McGann, J. G., & Weaver, R. K. (2009). *Think tanks & civil societies: Catalysts for ideas and action.* New Brunswick, N.J: Transaction Publishers.

16 Mbadlanyana, T., Cilliers, J., & Sibalukhulu, N. (2011). Shaping African futures: Think tanks and the need for endogenous knowledge production in sub-Saharan Africa.

17 Sy, A. N. R., & Africa Growth Initiative at Brookings. (2016). Foresight Africa: Top priorities for the continent in 2016.

18 Selee, A. D. (2013). *What should think tanks do? A strategic guide to policy impact.* Stanford, CA: Stanford Briefs.

19 ibid.

20 Kimenyi, M. S. & Datta, A. (2011). *Think tanks in sub-Saharan Africa: How the political landscape has influenced their origins.* Overseas Development Institute. Retrieved from https://www.odi.org/sites/odi.org.uk/files/odi-assets/publications-opinion-files/7527.pdf

21 Juma, C. & DiSenso, A. (2006, January). Political Parties as Tools of Democracy. *The Daily Nation*. Retrieved from https://www.hks.harvard.edu/news-events/news/news-archive/political-parties-as-tools-for-democracy

22 Kimenyi, M. S. & Datta, A. (2011). *Think tanks in sub-Saharan Africa: How the political landscape has influenced their origins.*

23 ibid.

24 Lee, K. Y. (2000). *From third world to first: The Singapore story, 1965-2000.* New York, NY: HarperCollins Publishers Inc

25 Dang, D., & Umemoto, K. (2009). Modeling the development toward the knowledge economy: A national capability approach. *Journal of Knowledge Management, 13*(5), 359-372.

26 Mbadlanyana, T., Cilliers, J., & Sibalukhulu, N. (2011). Shaping African futures: Think tanks and the need for endogenous knowledge production in sub-Saharan Africa.

27 ibid.

28 ibid.

29 ibid.

30 Selee, A. D. (2013). *What should think tanks do? A strategic guide to policy impact.*

31 ibid.

32 Mbadlanyana, T., Cilliers, J., & Sibalukhulu, N. (2011). Shaping African futures: Think tanks and the need for endogenous knowledge production in sub-Saharan Africa.

33 Selee, A. D. (2013). *What should think tanks do? A strategic guide to policy impact.*

34 Mbadlanyana, T., Cilliers, J., & Sibalukhulu, N. (2011). Shaping African futures: Think tanks and the need for endogenous knowledge production in sub-Saharan Africa.

35 ibid.

36 ibid.

37 ibid.

38 UNDESA, (2017). *World Population Prospects: The 2017 Revision.* Retrieved from https://esa.un.org/unpd/wpp/Publications/Files/WPP2017_KeyFindings.pdf

39 UNCEF. (2014, August). Generation 2030 Africa: Child demographics in Africa. Retrieved from http://data.unicef.org/gen2030/

40 World Population Review. (2013). Africa Population 2015. Retrieved from http://worldpopulationreview.com/continents/africa-population/ 2015-09-13

41 ibid.

42 ibid.

43 Cour, J.-M., Snrech, S., Sahel Club., African Development Bank., & Permanent Inter-State Committee for Drought Control in the Sahel. (1998). West Africa Long Term Perspective Study. Paris: OECD. Retrieved from https://www.oecd.org/swac/publications/38512525.pdf

44 ibid.

45 ibid.

46 ibid.

47 ibid.

48 World Population Review. (2017). Africa Population 2016. Retrieved from http://worldpopulationreview.com/continents/africa-population/

49 Cour, J.-M., Snrech, S., Sahel Club., African Development Bank., & Permanent Inter-State Committee for Drought Control in the Sahel. (1998). West Africa Long Term Perspective Study.

50 Mbadlanyana, T., Cilliers, J., & Sibalukhulu, N. (2011). Shaping African futures: Think tanks and the need for endogenous knowledge production in sub-Saharan Africa. *The Journal of Futures Studies, Strategic Thinking and Policy, 13*(3), 64-84.

51 ibid.

52 Lopes, C. (2013). 50 years of Development Planning in Africa – lessons and challenges. *United Nations Economic Commission for Africa*. Retrieved from: http://www.uneca.org/es-blog/50-years-development-planning-africa---lessons-and-challenges.

53 ibid.

54 ibid.

55 Mbadlanyana, T., Cilliers, J., & Sibalukhulu, N. (2011). Shaping African futures: Think tanks and the need for endogenous knowledge production in sub-Saharan Africa.

56 Lopes, C. (2013). 50 years of Development Planning in Africa – lessons and challenges.

57 ibid.

58 Mbadlanyana, T., Cilliers, J., & Sibalukhulu, N. (2011). Shaping African futures: Think tanks and the need for endogenous knowledge production in sub-Saharan Africa. *The Journal of Futures Studies, Strategic Thinking and Policy, 13*(3), 64-84.

59 Africa Capacity Building Foundation. (2017). *Fourth Africa Think Tank Summit.* [Press Release]. Retrieved from http://www.acbf-pact.org/media/events/4th-africa-think-tank-summit

8

Funding African Think Tanks

"No country can afford to be too poor to fund
its own 'brain center' - the national think tank."

Stephen Adei

One of the major obstacles to the growth of think tanks in Africa is funding - both the lack and nature of it. Fundraising is a source of stress in operating think tanks.[1] Without adequate "no strings attached funding" think tanks cannot function vivaciously. In a country like the USA, private think tanks are well resourced with income coming from foundations, legacies, donations and earned revenue from contract research and policy advice. Policy research organizations constitute a much larger portion of the U.S. knowledge regime than the European ones because these entities and wealthy individuals are able and willing to fund them.[2] The fact that in the U.S. policy research organizations are classified under the federal tax code as educational organizations for which donations are tax deductible[3] also makes them attractive for those seeking to donate.

A source of funding for well-established think tanks in the U.S. is endowments. An endowment fund is created when a donor or the Board of Trustees specify that a gift is to be invested and only the income earned on that gift may be spent for a particular purpose or to further a company's operating process.[4] Traditional think tanks, especially the Washington- and New York- based ones like Brookings Institution and Carnegie Endowment for International Peace have endowments that can support the institution's central infrastructure and fund some key programming priorities.[5] That kind of funding offers the greatest flexibility but is not available in Africa where think tanks are comparably underfunded and not very well resourced.

Fundraising at its core is about building a network of people who share the organization's mission and want to participate, either actively or vicariously, through its work.[6] Sources for African think tanks include government, development partners, the business sector, individuals, and contracts. It is important that think tanks retain their independence. Only then are they believable when seeking to influence policy. This, as can be imagined, may be challenging when donor financing is the largest source of income.

Funding from Government

The state should fully fund government think tanks from its internal revenues. Taking responsibility for the country's future requires this of the state, and shields the institution from external influence. African countries spend a fortune annually on foreign consultants and technical advisers some of whom do not give value commensurate to the expenditure. In 1989 it was reported that there were over 100,000 donor-funded expatriate advisors working in the public sectors of 40 sub-Saharan African countries, at the cost of more than $4 billion, nearly 35 percent of official development assistance to the region.[7] There is no convincing reason why African countries cannot invest sufficiently in thinking for themselves. Professor Stephen Adei adeptly stated that no country can afford to be too poor to fund its "brain center" – the National Think Tank staffed by the best developmental brains in the country.[8] Within the African countries are brilliant minds capable of matching and even outperforming the work done by the foreign experts who in some cases are not as good their local counterparts and do not have the local perspective. African governments ought to increase the funding for think tanks. External support should go to the non-state actors.

Funding from Development Partners

Most African state funding of think tanks is limited to support of universities and national planning authorities where they exist, leaving non-state actors to depend either on support from foreign agencies or contract research. Due to the shortage of funding from domestic sources even for non-state think tanks, dependence on donor funding is inevitable.[9] Funders of economic and policy research in Africa are mostly international agencies and foundations.[10] Bodies such as the African Capacity Building Foundation (ACBF) and Canadian IDRC have provided support to African think tanks in the past. ACBF funded think tanks are often linked to governments and have been until now some of the few with core funding, however, core funding is on its way out.[11] Only a few funders are willing to provide core funding that can be used for long-term programmatic and strategic objectives and even fewer allow for project financing with built-in overhead.[12] Of particular importance is the African Capacity Building Foundation's funding cuts, which have seen many of the largest economic policy think tanks in the continent face significant losses.[13]

Philanthropy

Building a resource base from donors who regularly give to the institutions is common among U.S. organizations with clear ideological agendas like the Heritage Foundation and the Cato Institute.[14] Think tanks whose funding comes from a large number of small donors are more likely to operate with independence than those whose funding comes from a limited number of large donors.[15] Unfortunately, the philanthropic traditions in the continent for support the work of independent public policy research institutions is not yet well developed, though the opportunity exists.

The giving culture is common all across Africa.[16] It is an inherent characteristic of African family life and community but has not yet significantly extended to giving to institutions. According to the World Wealth Report 2014, in 2009 the size of Africa's High-Net-Worth population stood at 107,100, by 2013 this had increased to 140,800, a growth of 31 percent in five years.[17] In 2013, Africa's High-Net-Worth wealth was USD1.3 trillion.[18] The number of Ultra-High Net Worth individuals had risen by 130 per cent between 2003 and 2013; this figure is projected to increase by 53 percent over the next ten-year period – a projected growth rate that is the highest globally.[19] African think tanks are yet to tap from this source.

As indicated earlier, U.S. policy research organizations are classified under the federal tax code as educational organizations for which donations are tax-deductible. This makes them attractive for those seeking to donate. Recognizing the importance of think tanks for the success of the development agenda should lead African governments to enact legislation that encourages businesses and philanthropists to donate to non-state think tanks. Such legislation would go a long way in easing the financial burdens that non-state think tanks carry on the African continent. So long as their activities are well regulated, the ultimate beneficiary would be the government and the citizens.

Other funding sources

African think tanks have to find ways to diversify their funding sources. One major challenge with relying on a single line of income is that donors often have their agenda that can conflict with institutional independence. The world of think tanks has many examples of institutions and policy research programs that either went out of business because their major funder changed priorities or found their mission compromised.[20] Diversifying sources of funding is a hedge against such situations and also ensures that organizations can invest in their internal programs like staff development and adequate infrastructure.[21]

Paid membership can be a source of income, but this may not cover much especially if it requires an invitation to membership. It can, however, provide a good platform from where to develop financially beneficial networks. Another opportunity yet to be tapped is research consultancy with the private sector especially when the research benefits the sector.

It is in the greatest interest of governments and national leaders to ensure that African intellectual resources are put to good use for the benefit of the continent and its peoples. If think tanks fail to survive or cease to function independently, then the quality of the social and political systems that rely on them will also decline. The dream of a prosperous African continent taking its place without shame at the table of nations will remain a mirage - a pipe dream.

Notes & References

1   Selee, A. D. (2013). *What should think tanks do? A strategic guide to policy impact.* Stanford, CA: Stanford Briefs.

2   Campbell, J. L., & Pederson, O. K. (2014). *The national origins of policy ideas: Knowledge regimes in the United States, France, Germany, and Denmark.* Princeton, New Jersey: Princeton University Press.

3   Ibid.

4   Busby, D. (n.d). Effectively Handling endowment gifts. Retrieved from http://www.ecfa.org/Documents/EffectivelyHandlingEndowmentGifts.pdf

5   Selee, A. D. (2013). *What should think tanks do? A strategic guide to policy impact.*

6   ibid.

7   World Bank (1989) *Sub-Saharan Africa: From crisis to sustainable growth.* Washington, DC: IBRD.

8   Adei, S. (2009, July). *The critical role of the development of think tanks for Africa's development.* Paper presented at the meeting of SALT Institute, Kampala, Uganda.

9   McGann, J. G. (2008). *Global Go to Think tanks 2008.* Philadelphia, PA USA: Think Tanks and Civil Societies Program, International Relations Program, University of Pennsylvania.

10 Mendizabal, E. (2015, July). The future of think tanks in Africa: Trends to look out for. *On Think Tanks.* Retrieved from https://onthinktanks.org/articles/the-future-of-think-tanks-in-africa-trends-to-look-out-for/

11 ibid.

12 ibid.

13 ibid.

14 Selee, A. D. (2013). *What should think tanks do? A strategic guide to policy impact.*

15 Campbell, J. L., & Pederson, O. K. (2014). *The national origins of policy ideas: Knowledge regimes in the United States, France, Germany, and Denmark.*

16 Mahomed, H., Julien, L. A. & Samuels, S. (2014). *Africa's wealthy give back: A perspective on philanthropic giving by wealthy Africans in sub-Saharan Africa, with a focus on Kenya, Nigeria, and South Africa.* Trust Africa. Retrieved from https://uhnw-greatwealth.ubs.com/media/7455/ubs-philanthropy-africareport.pdf

17 Capgemini & RBC Management (2014). World Wealth Report 2014. *Capgemini.* Retrieved from https://www.worldwealthreport.com/reports/wealth/africa

18 ibid.

19 ibid.

20 Selee, A. D. (2013). *What should think tanks do? A strategic guide to policy impact.*

21 ibid.

9

Conclusion And Recommendations

"No problem can be solved by the same consciousness that created it. We need to see the world anew."

Albert Einstein

In reviewing the last sixty odd years of African independence, it is evident that political independence did not translate to intellectual freedom. It is also apparent that the type of leaders countries had, determined their destinies. The leaders that maximized the use of the intellectual resources of their countries fared much better than those that did not. Though African nations had the opportunity to design their policies and find their unique paths of development, they largely did not. Instead, they remained dependent on foreign experts, for ideas and strategic advice. Some still do so to this day. The result has been the shackling of the continent by foreign aid, loans and lopsided trade agreements. Donor dependence has provided development partners with significant policy leverage and raises questions as to the extent to which African countries can claim 'ownership' over their economic policy choices. On the global scene, international treaties and development paradigms have influenced the development of domestic policy across sub-Saharan Africa.

Every adult comes to a time when they take responsibility for the decisions they make despite good advice from well-meaning friends. That time is long past for African countries. African leaders must take responsibility for and ultimately prioritize their development agenda; this requires competent national think tank capacity.

Cruel as the legacies of the slave trade, colonialism and more recently the consequences of the SAPs and PRSPs are, Africans must move on and stop the blame game. The season of blaming others for woes suffered has come to an end. It is time for Africa to look within, recognize the mistakes made, make amends and engage the future with a determination not to repeat past mistakes. The age of responsibility has long come. Only when African countries assume ownership of their futures will the continent be able to unshackle the chains - visible and invisible that still restrain it.

In the last sixty years, using one natural resource, Botswana has demonstrated that resources need not be a curse if there is good governance, proper planning, fiscal discipline, and frugality. A new generation of Africans must find ways to leverage the abundant resources on the continent for the future of her peoples. The undertaking is no mean task as many within and without who are benefiting from the status quo will fight to ensure that Africa does not rise to the occasion.

As African countries floundered, their East Asian peers trekked on. Malaysia is an example of how an economy relatively rich in natural resource can transform itself into a more industrialized economy over a period of about 20 years. The Malaysian experience underscores the role of strong national leadership supported by robust institutions, including think tanks, in forecasting, planning and anticipating issues looming on the horizon and making adjustments accordingly.

South Korea displays the pre-eminence of economic development over politics. Despite many changes in government including military dictatorships, the rolling out of development plans continued - unlike the case in many African countries. South Korea also evidences that it is possible to make remarkable progress from the devastation of war.

Singapore has proved that extraordinary progress without the help of natural resources is possible. It has shown that intellectual resources yield much higher returns than natural resources when it comes to nation-building and economic development. Of all the examples given, Singapore, the least endowed country, made the most extraordinary progress.

The examples from East Asia demonstrate that with focused leadership, deep thinking, evidence-based policymaking, and purposeful planning, unbelievable things are possible. Africa can draw comfort from the fact that parts of the world far less naturally endowed have been able to socially and economically transform within one generation. One can only imagine what will happen when the continent finally gets the leadership question sorted and applies its intellectual capabilities to the maximum.

Leadership

The first precondition for development is transformational servant leadership. As Africa journeys into an uncertain future, contemporary and emerging leaders on the continent have the records of sixty years of history to draw from. As in the past, the quality of leadership will continue to be the primary contributing factor to the destinies of countries. How continental leaders handle both negative and positive ideas will be crucial to how the continent turns out. Vital too will be whether the growing intellectual resources will be harnessed or not. The significant difference between the crop of leaders in the last sixty years, and the contemporary and emerging ones is that the latter have the witness of history. Contemporary and emerging leaders have the opportunity to see what has worked and what has not. They also have the witness of other countries that faced similar, and even worse challenges, and spectacularly prevailed. History will judge current leaders harshly should they fail to lead the African people out of the current mire.

Economic development is inseparable from leadership praxis. Leaders across the spectrum of society on the African continent have the responsibility of ensuring that the dominant leadership paradigm becomes one that is congruent with economic development. The transformational leadership paradigm must replace the common transactional one. African people like all peoples around the world are looking, and yearning for leadership that is ethical, credible, listens, and handles followers with an attitude of service. The new leadership paradigm must nurture the continent and its peoples to their highest potential. It must foster the development of an innovative culture in Africa. The continent needs leaders with global competencies to engage the rest of the world at an equal level, and the multicultural competencies to harmoniously lead Africa's diverse peoples. It must be a leadership that governs neither for personal gain nor for political expediency, but rather with its eye on the next generation. It must be a leadership that is not absorbed with consumption, rather one that is frugal and conscious of the need to lay a strong foundation for the 2.4 billion people expected to be living on the continent in 2050. Such leaders must have a keen sense of the future; they must protect and develop Africa's resources for posterity. The new leadership paradigm must have an understanding of what it takes to lead, and a systems understanding of the challenges Africa faces together with the systems approaches needed to solve them. The current generation of leaders owes much to future generations of Africans.

Think Tanks

In almost all the emerging economies the first significant action of the visionary leadership was the creation of robust, intellectually autonomous national think tank capacity. In South Korea, it was the Korean Development Institute (KDI) while in other East Asian countries it was a stand-alone unit of the public sector such as the National Economic Bureau. These institutions were the centers for designing, implementing, and monitoring of development programs. The development catalyst was always visionary, transformational leadership supported by national think tank capacity.

The twenty-first century promises an age of rapid change and unpredictability. The future of the world will be further diversified. The power and impact of globalization mean that it's essential for every country to understand the current and future impacts of worldwide trends and to develop a globalization strategy to optimize opportunities availed by various markets around the world. No country in this era will thrive without addressing globalization and its effects. The complexities of globalization require broad and intense intellectual analysis. No leader, however, brilliant can do that on their own; the brains of others are necessary – the best minds available.

One of the primary constraints to Africa's development has been the shortage of think tank capacity in the last sixty years of African independence. The faster African leaders recognize the critical role both state and non-state think tanks play in national development; the quicker shall be the pace of Africa's transformation. African think tanks have a pivotal role in positioning Africa for the future. By scanning the horizon, plotting development paths and guiding leaders and institutions they can foster a new optimism about African futures. African think tanks should endeavor to produce credible original proposals that are relevant to local contexts. They should also take advantage of emerging technologies to ensure the new tech-savvy generation hears their voice.

Education Systems

African countries must urgently review their education systems to ensure that they are producing the kind of intellectuals and practitioners the continent needs. They should carefully check whether or not the outcome of their educational system is a citizenry that carries the society forward and make the necessary changes. Many African countries are still following educational curricula designed in the colonial era to keep Africans in mental bondage. Why is it that sixty years since independence in most economies in sub-Saharan Africa, there is still a large shortage of entrepreneurs to exploit the abundant natural resources? Why are countries still dependent on "foreign investors and experts" for even core activities like stone quarrying and road construction? What kinds of professionals, technicians, agriculturists and entrepreneurs are our educational institutions producing? There must be a review and overhaul of the education system. African countries must develop new curricula that produce entrepreneurs, and teach critical thinking to create original thinkers. The practice of rote learning for merely passing exams must be discouraged and stopped altogether. The intellectual climate in educational institutions must be tolerant of alternative perspectives.

Universities must move beyond being repositories of research projects developed elsewhere and conduct original research addressing local challenges. Undertaking curriculum reviews must not wait for an international institution to loan a country millions of dollars for hiring a foreign firm, as is often the case. Curriculum writing is a matter of strategic national interest and must be viewed as such. It must be done by indigenous curriculum developers, in consultation with national think tanks, and in light of national development plans.

After a long period of neglect, universities of Sub-Saharan Africa seem to be getting renewed attention. Since universities harbor research institutions and policy institutes, this bodes well for the think tank industry. State sponsorship of these is beneficial for the general development of think tank capacity in a country.

Finally...

Though still faced with significant challenges, Africa has come a long way from the era of slavery and colonialism. The centuries of slave trade, decades of colonial rule, civil wars, ravages of disease, continuous interference from foreign political and economic interests (primarily driven by greed), and the failure of leadership on the continent have left a heavy toll. The continent and its peoples have however displayed remarkable resilience against the challenges they have endured over centuries. Though the nascent years of the post-independence African states were checkered, the future holds great promise.

A new day is dawning over the continent in its leadership and development journey. The continent is poised to become a new center of global growth. Africa and especially sub-Saharan Africa has some of the world's highest growth rates. The IMF forecasts that Africa will be the second-fastest growing region in the world between 2016 and 2020 with an annual growth of 4.3 per cent.[1] If African nations are to sustain the promising gains made in more recent years and diversify their economies into the cadre of industrialized and knowledge-based economies, one thing is definite: a different approach to leadership is needed.

To avoid an abortion of this new promise, the mistakes of the past must be reviewed, understood and avoided. African countries must take firm responsibility for their growth. Intellectual capital must be nurtured, preserved and utilized maximally. Space must be made for civil society input into policymaking and prudent decisions made about the appropriate strategies needed to achieve economic growth and structural transformation. As always, leadership is the greatest game changer. The present generation of leaders across the spectrum of society owes much to future generations of Africans.

Notes & References

1   Burton, D. (2016, May). 3 reasons things are looking up for African economies. *World Economic Forum.* Retrieved from: https://www.weforum.org/agenda/2016/05/what-s-the-future-of-economic-growth-in-africa/

Bibliography

Acemoglu, D., Johnson, S. & Robinson, J. (2003). *Botswana: An African success story.* In Rodrik, D. (Ed.), *In search of prosperity: Analytical narrative on economic growth.* Princeton, NJ: Princeton University Press (pp. 80-122).

Achebe, C. (1984). *The trouble with Nigeria.* London, UK: Heinemann Educational Books.

Acunzo. A. (2016, January 25). On the Singapore-USA trade relation and the TPP. *Singapore Business Review.* Retrieved from http://sbr.com.sg/economy/commentary/singapore-usa-trade-relation-and-tpp.

Adams J. King C., & Hook D. (2010). *Global research report Africa. (2010).* Leeds, UK: Evidence. Retrieved from http://researchanalytics.thomsonreuters.com/m/pdfs/globalresearchreport-africa.pdf

Adei, S. (2009, July). *The critical role of the development of think tanks for Africa's development.* Paper presented at the meeting of SALT Institute, Kampala, Uganda.

Adler, N. J. (1996). Global women political leaders: An invisible history, an increasingly important future. *Leadership Quarterly, 7,* 133-161.

Adonis, A. & Hames, T. (1994). *A conservative revolution? The Thatcher-Reagan decade in perspective.* Manchester U.A: Manchester Univ. Press.

Africa Capacity Building Foundation. (2017). *Fourth Africa Think Tank Summit.* [Press Release]. Retrieved from http://www.acbf-pact.org/media/events/4th-africa-think-tank-summit

Alexe, C.G. (2008). What is an innovative culture and how can we build it? *Upb Scientific Bulletin, Series D: Mechanical Engineering, 70*(1), 127-136.

Anene, J. (1997). Military administrative behavior and democratization: Civilian cabinet appointments in military regimes in sub-Saharan Africa. *Journal of Public Policy, 7*(1), 63-80.

Aninat, E. (2002). Surmounting the challenges of globalization. *Finance and Development 39*(1), 4- 7.

Arowosegbe, J. O., & Rijksuniversiteit te Leiden. (2008). *Decolonising the social sciences in the global South: Claude Ake and the praxis of knowledge production in Africa.* Leiden: African Studies Centre.

Asante, M. K. (2004). *An African Origin of Philosophy: Myth or Reality?* Retrieved from http://www.asante.net/articles/26/afrocentricity/

Asongu, S. A. (2013). Fighting corruption in Africa: Do existing corruption-control levels matter? *International Journal of Development Issues, 12*(1), 36-52.

Ayittey, G. B. N. (1992). *Africa betrayed.* New York: St. Martin's Press.

Aymes, J. F. L. (2014). Formation and evolution of the knowledge regime and the development process in Korea. *Korean Studies, 38,* 91-123,162.

BBC News (2011, June). Hedge funds 'grabbing land' in Africa. *BBC News Services.* Retrieved from http://www.bbc.com/news/world-africa-13688683.

Beaulier, S. A. (2004). *Explaining Botswana's success: The critical role of post-colonial policy.* Retrieved from http://object.cato.org/sites/cato.org/files/serials/files/cato-journal/2003/11/cj23n2-6.pdf

Beaulier, S. A., & Subrick, J. R. (2006). The political foundations of development: The case of Botswana. *Constitutional Political Economy, 17*, 2, 103-115.

Bennis, W. (1999). The end of leadership: Exemplary leadership is impossible without full inclusion, initiatives, and cooperation of followers. *Organizational Dynamics, 28*(1), 71-79.

Biswas, A. K. & Hartley, K. (2015). The Rise of Asia's Think Tanks: Regional think tanks are proliferating. Is the quality keeping pace? *The Diplomat.* Retrieved from http://thediplomat.com/2015/09/the-rise-of-asias-think-tanks/

Bock, C.C. (2002). *Heart Work.* Singapore: Singapore Economic Development Board and EDB society.

Bolden, R., Petrov, G., & Gosling, J. (2009). Distributed leadership in higher education: Rhetoric and reality. *Educational Management Administration & Leadership, 37*(2): 257–277.

Botswana Population. (2015). Increases in Botswana's population. *Expansion.* Retrieved from http://countryeconomy.com/demography/population/botswana

Botswana. (1966). *Transitional plan for social and economic development.* Gaborone: Department of Government Printing.

Braml, J. (2006). U.S. and German Think Tanks in Comparative Perspective. *German Policy Studies, 3*(222-267).

Bratton, M., & van de Walle, N. (1997). *Democratic experiments in Africa: Regime transitions in a comparative perspective.* Cambridge: Cambridge University Press.

Brazinsky, G., & Brazinsky, G. (2010). *Nation building in South Korea: Koreans, Americans, and the making of a democracy.* ACN: Accessible Publishing Systems PTY, [2010] © 2010

Brooks, M., Stark, J., Caverhill, S. (2004). *Your leadership legacy: The difference you make in people's lives.* San Francisco, CA: Berrett-Koehler Publishers. Retrieved from http://www.agweb.com/assets/import/files/brookssparksPR.pdf

Brough, W. T. & Kimenyi, M. S. (1985). On the Inefficient extraction of rents by dictators. *Public Choice 48*(1) 37-48.

Burns, J. M. (1978). *Leadership.* New York: Harper & Row.

Burton, D. (2016, May). 3 reasons things are looking up for African economies. *World Economic Forum.* Retrieved from: https://www.weforum.org/agenda/2016/05/what-s-the-future-of-economic-growth-in-africa/

Busby, D. (n.d). Effectively Handling endowment gifts. Retrieved from http://www.ecfa.org/Documents/EffectivelyHandlingEndowmentGifts.pdf

Cabrera A. & Unruh G. (2012). *Being global: how to think, act, and lead in a transformed world.* Boston, MA: Harvard Business Review Press

Cahyadi, G., Kursten, B., Weiss, M. and Yang G. (2004). *Singapore Metropolitan Economic Strategy Report: Singapore's Economic Transformation.* Czech Republic: Global Urban Development Prague. Retrieved from http://www.globalurbandevelopment.org/GUD percent20Singapore percent20MES percent20Report.pdf

Campbell, J. L., & Pederson, O. K. (2014). *The national origins of policy ideas: Knowledge regimes in the United States, France, Germany, and Denmark.* Princeton, New Jersey: Princeton University Press.

Campbell, W., & Campbell, S. M. (2009). On the self-regulatory dynamics created by the peculiar benefits and costs of narcissism: A contextual reinforcement model and examination of leadership. *Self & Identity, 8*(2/3), 214-232.

Canen, A. G., & Canen, A. (2008): Multicultural leadership: The costs of its absence in organizational conflict management. *International Journal of Conflict Management, 19*(1), 4-19.

Canen, A., & Peters, M. A. (2005). Issues and dilemmas of multicultural education: Theories, policies and practices. *Policy Futures in Education, 3*(4).

Canton, J. (2007). *The extreme future: The top trends that will reshape the world for the next 20 years*. New York, NY: Plume.

Capgemini & RBC Management (2014). World Wealth Report 2014. *Capgemini.* Retrieved from https://www.worldwealthreport.com/reports/wealth/africa

Cartwright, M. (2016). *Ancient Korea*. Ancient history encyclopedia. Retrieved from http://www.ancient.eu/Korea/

Chapman C., & Kagaha, A. (2009). Resolving Disputes using Traditional mechanisms in the Karamoja and Teso Regions of Uganda. *Minority Rights Groups International.* Retrieved from http://www.refworld.org/pdfid/4a97dc232.pdf

Chazan, N., Lewis, P., Mortimer, R. A., Rothchild, D. S., & Stedman, S. J. (1999). *Politics and society in contemporary Africa*. Boulder, CO: Lynne Rienner Publishers.

Choi, B. S. (1991). *The structure of the economic policy-making institution in Korea and the strategic role of the economic planning board.* In Caiden, G. E. & Kim, B. W. (Eds), *A Dragon's progress: Development administration in Korea.* Hartford, CT: Kumarian Press.`

Chung, Y. I. (2007). *South Korea in the fast lane: Economic development and capital formation. Oxford.* New York: Oxford University Press.

CIA World Factbook. (2016a). Country comparison GDPPC (PPP). Retrieved from https://www.cia.gov/library/Publications/the-world-factbook/rankorder/2004rank.html

CIA World Factbook. (2016b). Country profile Botswana. Retrieved from https://www.cia.gov/library/Publications/the-world-factbook/geos/bc.html

CIA World Factbook. (2016c). Country Profile: Malaysia. Retrieved from https://www.cia.gov/library/publications/the-world-factbook/geos/my.html

CIA World Factbook. (2016d). Country Profile: Singapore. Retrieved from https://www.cia.gov/library/publications/the-world-factbook/geos/sn.html

CIA World Factbook. (2016e). Country Profile: South Korea. Retrieved from *https://www.cia.gov/library/publications/the-world-factbook/geos/ks.html*

Colgan, A. L. (2002). Hazards to health: The World Bank and IMF in Africa. *Africa Action.* Retrieved from https://www.africa.upenn.edu/Urgent_Action/apic041802.html

Cornish, E. (2004). *Futuring: The exploration of the future*. Bethesda, MD: World Future Society.

Cour, J.-M., Snrech, S., Sahel Club., African Development Bank., & Permanent Inter-State Committee for Drought Control in the Sahel. (1998). West Africa Long Term Perspective Study. Paris: OECD. Retrieved from https://www.oecd.org/swac/publications/38512525.pdf

Covey, S. R. (1989). *The 7 habits of highly effective people*. New York: Free Press.

Cseh, M., Davis, E. B., & Khilji, S. E. (2013). Developing a global mindset: Learning of global leaders. *European Journal of Training and Development, 37*(5), 489-499.

CSIR (2017). Council for Scientific and Industrial Research. Available at http://www.csir-iir.org/about.html

Curtis, M., & O'Hare, B. A-M. (2017). *Lost revenues in low income countries*. Retrieved from http://curtisresearch.org/wp-content/uploads/Lost-revenues.pdf

Dang, D., & Umemoto, K. (2009). Modeling the development toward the knowledge economy: A national capability approach. *Journal of Knowledge Management, 13*(5), 359-372.

Daouas, M. (2001). Africa faces challenges of globalization. *Finance and Development 38* (4): 4- 5.

Daquila, T. C. (2005). *The economies of Southeast Asia: Indonesia, Malaysia, Philippines, Singapore, and Thailand.* New York: Nova Science Publishers.

Dean, S. (2014, Oct 31). System thinking and UX part 2: System traps and advice on how to avoid them. Retrieved from http://ux.stewdean.com/system-thinking-and-ux-part-2-traps-and-advice-to-avoid-them/

Denning, S. (2007). *The secret language of leadership: How leaders inspire action through narrative.* San Francisco: Jossey-Bass.

Diagne, S. B. (2008). *Toward an intellectual history of West Africa: the meaning of Timbuktu.* In Shamil J. & Diagne S. B. (Eds), *The Meanings of Timbuktu* (pp.19-28). Pretoria, South Africa: The Human Sciences Research Council Press.

Dimmock, C, & Walker A. (2002). Societal culture and school leadership, charting the way ahead. *Asia Pacific Journal of Education, 2*(2), 110-16.

Dollar, D. & Kraay, A. (2002). Growth is good for the poor. *Journal of Economic Growth, 7*(3), 195-225.

Doyon J. & Godement, F. & Stanzel, A. & Vasselier, A. (2016, August). *A hundred think tanks bloom in China.* London, UK: European Council on Foreign Relations. Retrieved from http://www.ecfr.eu/page/-/hundred_think_tanks.pdf.

Drabble, J. (2000). *An Economic History of Malaysia, c.1800-1990: The Transition to Modern Economic Growth.* Palgrave Macmillan. Retrieved from https://faculty.washington.edu/charles/new percent20PUBS/Reviews percent20and percent20Other percent20Publications/R30.pdf

Dumo, D. (2016, July). *South Sudan leaders order ceasefire as civil war fears grow.* Reuters News Agency Retrieved from http://www.reuters.com/article/us-south-sudan-security-casualties-idUSKCN0ZQ08J

Easterly, W. (2002). *The Elusive quest for growth: Economists' adventures and misadventures in the tropics.* Cambridge MA: MIT Press

Ebenbach, D. H., & Kelthner, D. (1998). Power, emotion, and judgmental accuracy in social conflict: Motivating the cognitive miser. *Basic and Applied Social Psychology, 20*(1), 7-21. doi: 10.1207/s15324834basp2001_2

Economic Planning Unit. (1964). *State of Singapore first development plan, 1961–1964: Review of progress for the three years, 1961–1963* (p. 2). Singapore: Economic Planning Unit, Prime Minister's Office. Call no.: RCLOS 338.95957.

Education in South Korea. (2011). *Education in South Korea: Understanding South Korea's education system.* Retrieved from http://sites.miis.edu/southkoreaeducation/diversity-and-access/).

Edward, F. A. (2008). The fight against corruption and its implications for development in developing and transition economies. *Journal of Money Laundering Control, 11*(1), 76-87. doi:http://dx.doi.org/10.1108/13685200810844514

Electoral Commission of Zambia. (2017). *Endorsing your choice: Are you a candidate?* Electoral Commission of Zambia. Retrieved from https://www.elections.org.zm/candidate.php

Elmuti, D., Minnis, W., & Abebe, M. (2005). Does education have a role in developing leadership skills? *Management Decision, 43*(7), 1018-1031.

Eriksen, S. S. (2011). The possibility of state formation: The experience of Botswana in a theoretical perspective. *The European Journal of Development Research, 23*(3), 444-458.

Evenett, S. J. (1999). The world trading system: the road ahead. *Finance and Development, 36*(4) 22.

Bibliography

Federal Research Division (1992). *South Korea: A Country Study.* Washington D.C.: Library of Congress.

Fedler, K. D. (2006). *Exploring Christian Ethics: Biblical foundations for morality.* Louisville, KE: Westminster John Knox Press.

Fisher, S. (2011). Africa For Sale. *World Rivers Review 26*(3). Berkeley, CA: International Rivers. Retrieved from https://www.internationalrivers.org/resources/africa-for-sale-1657

Flores, V. (2016). Cuba: The last one to the global economic table. *Law and Business Review of the Americas, 22*(1), 59-67.

Fosu, A. K. (2011). *Terms of trade and growth of resource economies: A tale of two countries.* Oxford: Centre for the Study of African Economies.

Galford, R. & Maruca, R. (2006). *Your leadership legacy: Why looking towards the future will make you a better leader today.* Boston, MA: Harvard Business Press

Gaolathe, B. (2002). *Budget Speech 2002.* Gaborone: Department of Government Printing. Retrieved from http://www.bankofbotswana.bw/assets/uploaded/ Budget percent20Speech percent202002.pdf

Gardinier, D. E. (1971). *French colonial rule in Africa: A bibliographical essay.* New Haven: Yale University Press.

Gardner, W. L., Avolio, B. J., Luthans, F., May, D. R., Walumbwa F. (2005). Can you see the real me? A self-based model of authentic leader and follower development. *Leadership Quarterly, 16,* 343-372.

Glanville, E. (2009). Missiological reflections on difference: Foundations in the Gospel of Luke. *Mission Studies: Journal Of The International Association For Mission Studies, 26*(1), 64-79. doi:10.1163/157338309X442308

GNA (2013, March). *More than $148bn is lost to corruption in Africa - AU Report.* GhanaWeb. Retrieved from http://www.ghanaweb.com/GhanaHomePage/ NewsArchive/More-than-148bn-is-lost-to-corruption-in-Africa-AU-Report-267336

Gondwe, G. E. (2001). Making globalization work in Africa. *Finance and Development 38* (4): 31-38.

Goodman, P. (2016, November). *The Pros and Cons of Globalization.* Soapboxie. Retrieved from https://soapboxie.com/economy/The-Pros-and-Cons-of-Globalization.

Goodwin, S. A., Gubin, A., Fiske, S. T., Yzerbyt, V. Y. (2000). Power can bias impression processes: Stereotyping subordinates by default and by design. *Group Processes & Intergroup Relations, 3*(3), 227-256. doi: 10.1177/1368430200003003001

Hackman, M. Z., & Johnson, C. E. (2009). *Leadership: A Communication Perspective.* Long Grove, IL. Waveland Press Inc.

Harf, J. E., & Lombardi, M. O. (2007). *Taking sides.* Dubuque, IA: McGraw Hill Contemporary Learning Series.

Hartland-Thunberg, P. (1978). *Botswana: An African Growth Economy.* Boulder, CO: Westview Press.

Haruna, P. F. (2009). Revising the leadership paradigm in sub-Saharan Africa: A study of community-based leadership. *Public Administration Review, 69*(5), 941-950.

Harvey, C. & Lewis Jr. S. R. (1990). *Policy Choice and Development Performance in Botswana.* London: Macmillan in association with the OECD Development Centre.

Hencke, D. (2005, August). Anger as £700,000 of £3m British aid to Malawi spent on US firms. *The Guardian.* Retrieved from https://www.theguardian.com/ politics/2005/aug/29/uk.internationalaidanddevelopment

Heng, Y. (2013). A global city in an age of global risks: Singapore's evolving discourse on vulnerability. *Contemporary Southeast Asia, 35*(3), 423-446.

Herbst, J. (2005, November). *Africa and the challenge of globalization.* Presented at the Conference on Globalization and Economic Success: Policy Options for Africa, Singapore. Retrieved from http://www.thebrenthurstfoundation.org/Files/ Globalisation_and_Economic_Success_Singapore_2005 /Africa_Globalization. pdf

Herculano-Houzel, S. (2009). The human brain in numbers: A linearly scaled-up primate brain. *Frontiers in Human Neuroscience, 3*, 31. http://doi.org/10.3389/ neuro.09.031.2009

Hickling, H. A. (2005). White, ethnic and indigenous: Pre-service teachers reflect on discourses of ethnicity in Australian culture. *Policy Futures in Education, 3*(4), 340-58

Hicks D. A. (2010). *Globalization.* In Hickman, G. R. (Ed.), *Leading organizations: Perspectives for a new era* (pp.14-20). Thousand Oaks, CA: Sage Publications.

Hill, C. (1991). Diamonds or development? A structural assessment of Botswana's forty years of success, *World Development 19*(9), 1,185-96.

Hillbom, E. (2008). Diamonds or development? A structural assessment of Botswana's forty years of success. *The Journal of Modern African Studies, 46*(2), 191-214.

Hines, A. (2006). Strategic foresight: The state of the art. *The Futurist, 40*(5), 18-21.

Hoffmann, L., & Tan, S. E. (1980). *Industrial growth, employment, and foreign investment in peninsular Malaysia.* Kuala Lumpur: Oxford University Press.

Hofstede, G. (1980). Motivation, leadership, and organization: Do American theories apply abroad? *Organizational Dynamics, 9*(1), 42-63.

Hofstede, G. (1991). *Cultures and Organizations: Software of the Mind.* London, UK: McGraw-Hill.

Hofstede, G., Hofstede, G. J., & Minkov, M. (2010). *Cultures and organizations: Software of the mind.* New York, NY: McGraw-Hill.

Holt, K. & Seki, K. (2012). Global leadership: A developmental shift for everyone. *Industrial Organization Psychology, (455)*, 2, 196-215

Hope, K. R., & Somolekae, G. (1998). *Public administration and policy in Botswana.* Kenwyn: Juta

Howell, J., Dorfman, P., Hibino, S., Lee, J., & Tate, U. (1994). *Leadership in western and Asian countries: Commonalities and differences in effective leadership processes and substitutes across cultures.* New Mexico State University: Center for Business Research

Hsieh, S. (2010). Literature review on global leadership competency. *The Journal of Human Resource and Adult Learning, 6*(2), 99-109.

Hundt, D. (2017, February). *Immigration is South Korea's only solution.* East Asia Forum. Retrieved from http://www.eastasiaforum.org/2017/02/21/immigration-is-south-koreas-only-solution/

IFRCRCS, (2011). *Disasters in Africa: The case for legal preparedness.* Geneva, Switzerland: International Federation of Red Cross and Red Crescent Societies.

Igue, J. O. (2010). A new generation of leaders in Africa: what issues do they face? *International Development Policy.* The Graduate Institute Geneva. Retrieved from https://poldev.revues.org/139

Igwe, D. O. (2011). Africa in the age of globalisation. *International Journal of Sociology and Anthropology, 3*(8), 295-303.

Iimi, A., & IMF. (2006). *Did Botswana escape from the resource curse?* Washington, DC: International Monetary Fund, African Dept.

Ivancevich, J., Konopaske, R., & Matteson, M. T. (2005). *Organizational behavior and management (7ᵗʰ ed.).* New York: McGraw-Hill Higher Education.

Javidan, M., & House, R. J. (2001). Cultural acumen for the global manager: Lessons from Project GLOBE. *Organizational Dynamics, 29*(4): 289-305.

Javidan, M., Dorfman, P. W., Sully de Luque, M., & House, R. J. (2006). In the eye of the beholder: Cross cultural lessons in leadership from project GLOBE. *Academy of Management Perspectives, 20*(1), 67–90.

Jefferis, K. (1998). *Botswana and diamond-dependent development*. In Edge, W., & Lekorwe, M. H. (Eds), *Botswana, politics and society*. Pretoria: J.L. van Schaik.

Juma, C. & DiSenso, A. (2006, January). Political Parties as Tools of Democracy. *The Daily Nation*. Retrieved from https://www.hks.harvard.edu/news-events/news/news-archive/political-parties-as-tools-for-democracy

Kalyani, M. (2011). Innovative culture: An intervention strategy for sustainable growth in changing scenario. *International Journal of Business Administration, 2*(4), 84.

Kam, W. P., & Yuen, N. C. (1993). Singapore coping with a maturing economy. *Southeast Asian Affairs*, 313-324.

Kamarudi R. P. (2011). Wikileaks: Malaysia's most prominent think tanks. *Malaysia Today*. Retrieved from http://www.malaysia-today.net/wikileaks-malaysias-most-prominent-think-tanks/

Kariuki, F. (n.d). *Conflict resolution by elders in Africa: Successes, challenges and opportunities*. Retrieved from https://www.ciarb.org/docs/default-source/centenarydocs/speaker-assets/francis-kariuki.pdf?sfvrsn=0

Kauffman Jr., D. L. (1980). *Systems one: An introduction to systems thinking*. St. Paul, MN: Future Systems / TLH Associates.

Kazi, T. B., & Indermun, V. (2013). The impact of globalization, mergers, acquisitions, reengineering and downsizing, on individuals and organisations in South Africa. *Interdisciplinary Journal of Contemporary Research in Business, 5*(6), 681-698.

Kefela, G. T. (2011). Driving forces of globalization in emerging market economies developing countries. *Asian Economic and Financial Review, 1*(2), 83.

Kennedy, J. F. (1961). Special Message to the Congress on Urgent National Needs. [Delivered in person before a joint session of Congress May 25, 1961], *NASA*, Retrieved from https://www.nasa.gov/vision/space/features/jfk_speech_text.html.

Kets de Vries, M. & Florent-Treacy E. (1999). *The New Global Leaders*. San Francisco: Jossey Bass.

Kieh, G.K (2000). Military Rule in Liberia. *Journal of Political and Military Sociology, 28*(2), 327-342.

Kim, I. (2010). Korea's capitalistic planning model: Policy lessons for Mongolia. *The Journal of the Korean Economy, 11*(1), 177-194).

Kimenyi, M. S. & Datta, A. (2011). *Think tanks in sub-Saharan Africa: How the political landscape has influenced their origins*. Overseas Development Institute. Retrieved from https://www.odi.org/sites/odi.org.uk/files/odi-assets/publications-opinion-files/7527.pdf

Kind, H. J., & Mohd, N. I. (2001). Malaysia - the lucky man of Asia. Bergen.

Kipnis, D. (1972). Does power corrupt? *Journal of Personality and Social Psychology, 24*, 33-41. doi: 10.1037/h0033390

Kontis, V. et al. (2017). Future life expectancy in 35 industrialised countries: Projections with a Bayesian model ensemble. *The Lancet*. Retrieved from http://www.thelancet.com/journals/lancet/article/PIIS0140-6736(16)32381-9/abstract

Kotter, J. P. (2012). *Leading change*. Boston, MA: Harvard Business Review Press.

Kouzes, J. M., & Posner, B. Z. (2012). *The leadership challenge: How to make extraordinary things happen in organizations*. San Francisco, CA: Jossey-Bass.

Kposowa, A. J. & Jenkins, J. C. (1993). "The structural sources of military coups in postcolonial Africa, 1957-1984. *The American Journal of Sociology 99*(1), 126-163.

Krause, K. (n.d.). The true size of Africa. Retrieved from http://kai.sub.blue/en/africa.html

Kretzschmar, L. (2007). The formation of moral leaders in South Africa: A Christian-ethical analysis. *Journal of Theology for Southern Africa, 128,* 18-36.

Land, M. A. (2010). *Strengthening of national capacities for national development strategies and their management: An evaluation of UNDP's contribution, Country Study – Botswana.* UNDP. Retrieved from http://web.undp.org/evaluation/documents/thematic/cd/btoswana.pdf

Lawyer, K. (2014, August 6). Biden Calls Continent of Africa a 'Nation'. *CNS News.* Retrieved from http://www.cnsnews.com/mrctv-blog/kelly-lawyer/biden-calls-continent-africa-nation August 6, 2014 | 10:38 AM EDT

Le Blanc. R. (2008). Singapore: *The socio-economic development of a city-state [1960-1980].* Maarheeze, the Netherlands: Cranendonck Coaching.

Lee S. O., & Tan T. B. (2016, March). South Korea's demographic dilemma. East Asia Forum. Retrieved from http://www.eastasiaforum.org/2016/03/25/south-koreas-demographic-dilemma.

Lee, K. Y. (2000). *From third world to first: The Singapore story, 1965-2000.* New York, NY: HarperCollins Publishers Inc

Leith, C. (2005) *Why Botswana prospered.* Montreal, Canada: McGill-Queen's University Press.

Lempert, R. J., Popper, S. W., & Bankes, S. C. (2003). *Shaping the next one hundred years: New methods for quantitative, long-term policy analysis.* Santa Monica, CA: RAND.

Lopes, C. (2013). 50 years of Development Planning in Africa – lessons and challenges. *United Nations Economic Commission for Africa.* Retrieved from: http://www.uneca.org/es-blog/50-years-development-planning-africa---lessons-and-challenges.

Lumpkins, C. (2016). Precolonial African economies. The College of the Liberal Arts., Penn State University. Retrieved from http://elearning.la.psu.edu/afam/100/lesson-2-part1/african-roots-of-african-american-life-under-slavery/pre-colonial-african-economies.

MacLeod, R. M. (2014). The library of Alexandria: Centre of learning in the ancient world. New York, NY: Palgrave Macmillan.

Madsen, S. R., & Gygi, J. (2005). An interview with John H. Zenger on extraordinary leadership. *Journal of Leadership & Organizational Studies, 11*(3), 119-125.

Mafeje, A. (1998). *Kingdoms of the great lakes region.* Kampala, Uganda: CODESRIA.

Mahomed, H., Julien, L. A. & Samuels, S. (2014). *Africa's wealthy give back: A perspective on philanthropic giving by wealthy Africans in sub-Saharan Africa, with a focus on Kenya, Nigeria, and South Africa.* Trust Africa. Retrieved from https://uhnw-greatwealth.ubs.com/media/7455/ubs-philanthropy-africareport.pdf

Maner J. K. & Mead, N. L. (2010). The essential tension between leadership and power: when leaders sacrifice group goals for the sake of self-interest. *Journal of Personality and Social Psychology, 99*(3), 482-492. doi: 10.1037/a0018559

Marquardt, M., & Berger, N. O. (2003). The future: Globalization and new roles for HRD. *Advances in Developing Human Resources, 5*(3), 283-295.

Mbadlanyana, T., Cilliers, J., & Sibalukhulu, N. (2011). Shaping African futures: Think tanks and the need for endogenous knowledge production in sub-Saharan Africa. *The Journal of Futures Studies, Strategic Thinking and Policy, 13*(3), 64-84.

Mboya, T. (1986). *Freedom and after.* Nairobi: Kenya. Heinmann Kenya Ltd.

McCall, M. W. (Jr) & Hollenbeck, G. P. (2002). *Developing global executives: The lessons of international experience.* Boston, MA: Harvard Business School Press

McGann J. G. (2007). *Think tanks and policy advice in the US.* New York: NY: Routledge

McGann J. G. & Sabatini, R. (2011). *Global think tanks: Policy networks and governance.* New York: NY: Routledge

McGann, J. G. (2000). How think tanks are coping with the future. *The Futurist, 34*(6), 16-23.

McGann, J. G. (2008). *Global go to think tanks 2008.* Philadelphia, PA USA: Think Tanks and Civil Societies Program, International Relations Program, University of Pennsylvania.

McGann, J. G. (2012). *2012 global go to think tanks report and policy advice:* Philadelphia, PA USA: Think Tanks and Civil Societies Program, International Relations Program, University of Pennsylvania.

McGann, J. G. (2015). *Global go to think tanks report 2015.* Philadelphia, PA USA: Think Tanks and Civil Societies Program, International Relations Program, University of Pennsylvania.

McGann, J. G. (2016). *2016 Global Go To Think Tank Index Report.* Philadelphia, PA USA: Think Tanks and Civil Societies Program, International Relations Program, University of Pennsylvania. Retrieved from http://repository.upenn.edu/cgi/viewcontent.cgi?article=1011&context=think_tanks

McGann, J. G. (2016). *2016 global go to think tanks report and policy advice.* Philadelphia, PA USA: Think Tanks and Civil Societies Program, International Relations Program, University of Pennsylvania. Retrieved from http://repository.upenn.edu/cgi/viewcontent.cgi?article=1011&context=think_tanks

McGann, J. G., & Weaver, R. K. (2009). *Think tanks & civil societies: Catalysts for ideas and action.* New Brunswick, N.J: Transaction Publishers.

Mehlum, H., Moene, K. & Torvik, R. (2006). Institutions and the resource curse. *Economic Journal, 116,* 1-20.

Mendizabal, E. (2015, July). The future of think tanks in Africa: Trends to look out for. *On Think Tanks.* Retrieved from https://onthinktanks.org/articles/the-future-of-think-tanks-in-africa-trends-to-look-out-for/

Meredith, M. (2006). *The state of Africa: A history of sixty years of independence.* London, UK: Simon & Schuster, Inc.

Miks, J. (2012). India's Think Tank Failure. *The Diplomat.* Retrieved from http://thediplomat.com/2012/01/indias-think-tank-failure/

Mir, U. R. (2014). Understanding globalization and its future: An analysis. *Pakistan Journal of Social Sciences, 34* (2), 607-624.

Mittelman, J. H. (1994). The globalisation challenge: surviving at the margins. *Third World Quarterly, 15*(3), 427-43.

Mkandawire, T. (2000). *Non-organic Intellectuals and 'Learning' in Policy-making Africa.* Stockholm: Learning in Development Co-operation EGDI Publication.

Molm, L. D., Quist, T. M., Wiseley, P. A., (1994). Imbalanced structures, unfair strategies: Power and justice in social exchange. *American Sociological Review, 59*(1), 98-121. doi: 10.2307/2096135

Molutsi, P. (1989). *Whose interests do Botswana's politicians represent?* In Holm, J. & Molutsi, P. (Eds.), *Democracy in Botswana* (pp. 120-131). Athens: Ohio University Press.

Moon, M., & Kim, K.-S. (June 01, 2001). A case of korean higher education reform: The brain korea 21 project. *Asia Pacific Education Review, 2,* 2, 96-105.

Moyo, D. (2010). *Dead aid: Why aid is not working and how there is a better way for Africa.* New York: Farrar, Straus and Giroux.

Mpabanga, D. (1998). *Constraints to industrial development.* In Salkin, J. S. (Ed.), *Aspects of Botswana economy: Selected papers.* Gaborone: Lentswe la lesedi.

Munroe, M. (2011). *Passing it on: growing your future leaders.* New York: Hachette Book Group

Murmu, N. (2014). Cultural diversity in global workforce: Issues and challenges. *Review of HRM, 3,* 67-72.

Museveni, Y. K. (2000). *What is Africa's problem?* Minneapolis, MN: University of Minnesota Press

NASA (2017). July 20, 1969: One Giant Leap For Mankind. Retrieved from https://www.nasa.gov/mission_pages/apollo/apollo11.html

Northouse, P.G. (2013). *Leadership Theory and Practice.* Thousand Oaks, CA, Sage.

Novakovic, I. (2009). Yet even the dogs eat the crumbs that fall from their masters' table: Matthew's gospel and economic globalisation. *Hervormde teologiese studies, 65*(1), 574-580. doi:10.4102/hts.v65i1.321

Numbeo (2017). Crime in Singapore, Singapore. *Numbeo.* Retrieved from https://www.numbeo.com/crime/in/Singapore

Nwankwo, B. C. (1999). Politics of local government budgeting: Financial manipulation in the local government system. *International Journal of Studies in the Humanities, 12*(2), 63-76.

O, W. (2009). *The Korea story: President Park Jung-hee's leadership and the Korean industrial revolution.* Seoul, Korea: Wisdom Tree.

Obadan, M. (2011, September). *Past development plans in Nigeria: Performance, problems and prospects.* Paper presented at the 52ⁿᵈ Annual Conference of the Nigerian Economic Society, Covenant University, Ota.

OECD-UNDESA (2013). World Migration in Figures. OECD-UNDESA Retrieved from http://www.oecd.org/els/mig/World-Migration-in-Figures.pdf

Omoweh, D.A. (2000). *Dynamics of globalization: Impact on Nigeria and Africa.* In Akindele R. A., & Ate, B. E. (Eds.), *Selected readings on Nigeria's foreign policy.* Lagos: Vantage

Onyeani, C. (2012). *Capitalist Nigger: A Spider Web Doctrine.* Cork: BookBaby

Onyewuenyi, I. C. (2010). *The African origin of Greek philosophy: An exercise in afrocentrism.* Nsukka Nigeria: University of Nigeria Press.

Osabuohien, E. & Salami A. (2012). *Planning to fail or failing to plan: Institutional response to Nigeria's development question.* Abidjan: African Development Bank.

Osabuohien, E.S. & Ike, D.N. (2011, September). *Economic transformation and institutional framework in Nigeria - lessons from Botswana and South Korea.* Paper presented at the 52ⁿᵈ Annual Conference of the Nigerian Economic Society, Covenant University, Ota..

Owusu, F. & Samatar, A. I. (1997). Diamonds or development? A structural assessment of Botswana's forty years of success. *Canadian Journal of African Studies 31*(2), 268-99.

OXFAM (2017, January). Just 8 men own same wealth as half the world. *Oxfam International.* Retrieved from https://www.oxfam.org/en/pressroom/pressreleases/2017-01-16/just-8-men-own-own-same-wealth-half-world. Published: 16 January 2017

Pakenham, T., & Abacus. (1994). *The scramble for Africa 1876-1912.* London: Abacus.

Parson, J. (1984) *Botswana: Liberal Democracy and the Labor Reserve in Southern Africa*. Boulder, Co: Westview Press.

People of Africa (n.d.). *Africa Code*. Retrieved from: http://www.africanholocaust.net/peopleofafrica.htm

Perham, M. F. (1960). *Lugard: The years of adventure 1858-1898*. London: Collins.

Pettifor A. (2002). World Bank IMF forces famine on Malawi. *GMWatch*. Retrieved from http://www.gmwatch.org/news/archive/2002/2876-world-bankimf-forces-famine-on-malawi

Picard, L. (1987). *The politics of development in Botswana: A model of success?* Boulder, CO: Lynne Rienner.

Plaut, M. (2006, January). Africa's hunger: A systemic crisis. *BBC News*. Retrieved from: http://newsvote.bbc.co.uk/mpapps/pagetools/print/news.bbc.co.uk/2/hi/africa/4662232.stm

Radoi, M. A., & Olteanu, A. (2015). Globalization - chances or risks. *Global Economic Observer, 3*(1), 75-79.

Rashid, S. (1994). Social sciences and policy-making in Africa: A critical review. *Africa Development, 19*(1), 91-118.

Rijal, S. (2016). Leadership style and organizational culture in learning organization: A comparative study. *International Journal of Management & Information Systems* (Online), 20(2), 17-n/a. Retrieved from https://www.cluteinstitute.com/ojs/index.php/IJMIS/article/viewFile/19/17

Roberts, J. (2009). The global knowledge economy in question. *Critical Perspectives on International Business, 5*(4), 285-303.

Robinson, D. A., & Harvey, M. (2008). Global leadership in a culturally diverse world. *Management Decision, 46*(3), 466-480.

Rockfellow, J. D. (1994). Wild cards: preparing for 'the big one'. *The Futurist, 28*(1), 14.

Rosenthal, S. A., Pittinsky, T. L. (2006). Narcissistic leadership. *The Leadership Quarterly, 17,* 617-633.

Rugumamu, S. M. (1999). *Globalization, liberalization, and Africa's marginalization*. Harare: African Association of Political Scientists.

Sachdev, I., Bourhis, R. Y. (1991). Power and status differentials in minority and majority group relations. *European Journal of Social Psychology, 21*(1), 1-24.

Salim, A. S. (2006, June). No one's a winner: Why we haven't given Africa's most prestigious award this year? *Quartz Africa*. Retrieved from http://qz.com/714618/why-we-havent-given-africas-most-prestigious-leadership-award-for-two-years/

Samatar, A.I. (1999). *An African miracle: State and class leadership and colonial legacy in Botswana*. Portsmouth, UK: Heinemann.

Sayre, A. P. (1999). *Africa*. Twenty-First Century Books.

Schapera, I. (1947). *Migrant labour and tribal life: A study of conditions in the Bechuanaland protectorate*. London: Oxford University Press.

Schwab, K., Porter, M. E., Sachs, J. D., Cornelius, P. K., McArthur, J. W., World Economic Forum (2002). (Geneva). *The global competitiveness report 2001-2002*. New York: Oxford University Press.

Sebudubudu, D. (2005). The institutional framework of the developmental state in Botswana. In Mbabazi, P. & Taylor, I. (Eds.), *The potentiality of developmental states in Africa: Botswana and Uganda compared* (pp. 79-89). Dakar, Senegal: Codesria.

Selee, A. D. (2013). *What should think tanks do? A strategic guide to policy impact*. Stanford, CA: Stanford Briefs.

Shah, (2013) Structural Adjustment a Major Cause of Poverty. *Global Issues.* Retrieved from: http://www.globalissues.org/article/3/structural-adjustment-a-major-cause-of-poverty

Shahin, A. I., & Wright P. L. (2004). Leadership in the context of culture: An Egyptian perspective. *Leadership & Organization Development Journal, 25*(5), 499-511

Shore, D. (2014). *Launching and Leading Change Initiatives in Health Care Organizations.* San Francisco, CA: Jossey-Bass.

Silitshena, R. M. K. & McLeod, G. (1998). *Botswana: a physical, social and economic geography.* Gaborone: Longman Botswana, 2nd edition.

Singapore Tourism Board (2017, February). Singapore Achieves Record Tourism Sector Performance in 2016. Retrieved from https://www.stb.gov.sg/news-and-publications/lists/newsroom/dispform.aspx?ID=696&AspxAutoDetectCookieSupport=1.

Singapore. (1964). *State of Singapore first development plan, 1961-1964: Review of progress for the three years 1961-1963.* Singapore: Economic Planning Unit, Prime Minister's Office.

Siwawa-Ndai, P. (1998). *Industrialisation in Botswana: evolution, performance and prospects.* In Salkin, J. S. (Ed.), *Aspects of Botswana economy: Selected papers.* Gaborone: Lentswe la lesedi.

Soest, C. (2009). *Stagnation of a "miracle": Botswana's governance record revisited.* Hamburg: German Institute of Global and Area Studies.

Soll J. (2017). How think tanks became engines of royal propaganda. *Tablet Magazine.* Retrieved from http://www.tabletmag.com/jewish-news-and-politics/222421/think-tanks-jacob-soll-propaganda.

Solomon, R. C. (2003). On fate and fatalism. *Philosophy East and West, 53*(4), 435-454.

Stiglitz, J. (2002). *Globalization and its Discontents.* New York: W. W. Norton Press.

Stone, D. (2004). *Introduction: think tanks, policy advice and governance.* In Stone, D., & Denham, A, (Eds), *Think Tank Traditions.* Manchester, UK: Manchester University Press.

Stone, D. (2010).Think tank transnationalisation and non-profit analysis, advice and advocacy, *Global Society 14* (2), 154-55.

Svensson, J. (2005). Eight questions about corruption. *Journal of Economic Perspectives, 19,*(3), 19-42.

Sy, A. N. R., & Africa Growth Initiative at Brookings. (2016). *Foresight Africa: Top priorities for the continent in 2016.* Retrieved from https://www.brookings.edu/research/foresight-africa-top-priorities-for-the-continent-in-2016-2/

Tarikh 11. (1970). *Indirect rule in British Africa.* Longman for the Historical Society of Nigeria.

Taylor, I. (2005). Botswana's Developmental State and the Politics of Legitimacy. Retrieved from http://www.rrojasdatabank.info/devstate/Botswana.pdf

Tebeje A. (n.d.) *Brain drain and capacity building in Africa.* International Development Research Centre. Retrieved from https://www.idrc.ca/en/article/brain-drain-and-capacity-building-africa

The art of foresight. (2004). *The Futurist, 38*(3), A1-A2, A4-A7.

The Bretton Wood Project, (2001, June). *PRSPs just PR say civil society groups.* Bretton Woods Project. Retrieved from http://www.brettonwoodsproject.org/2001/06/art-15999/

The Economist. (2017). *Farm subsidies milking tax payers.* The Economist. Retrieved from http://www.economist.com/news/united-states/21643191-crop-prices-fall-farmers-grow-subsidies-instead-milking-taxpayers

Bibliography

The globalization of markets. (1983). *The International Executive (Pre-1986), 25*(3), 17.

Transparency International (2016). Country profile: Singapore. Retrieved from https://www.transparency.org/country/SGP

Tsie, B. (1998). *The state and development policy in Botswana.* In Hope, K.R. & Somolekae, G. (Ed.), *Public Administration and Policy in Botswana.* Johannesburg: Juta Press.

U.S. Department of State, (2011). Singapore (12/02/11). Retrieved from https://2009-2017.state.gov/outofdate/bgn/singapore/191973.htm

U.S. Library of Congress (2012). The Government Role in Economic Development. Retrieved from http://countrystudies.us/south-korea/47.htm.

Ulubasoglu, M. A. (2004). Globalisation and inequality. *The Australian Economic Review, 37*(1), 116-22.

UNCEF. (2014, August). Generation 2030 Africa: Child demographics in Africa. Retrieved from http://data.unicef.org/gen2030/

UNCTAD (2016, January 12). *UNCTAD Technology report: Africa lags behind. Afrikonomics.* Retrieved from http://www.afrikonomics.com/unctad-technology-report-africa-lags-behind/

UNDESA, (2017). *World Population Prospects: The 2017 Revision.* Retrieved from https://esa.un.org/unpd/wpp/Publications/Files/WPP2017_KeyFindings.pdf

UNDP. (2005). Botswana Human Development Report 2005. Retrieved from http://hdr.undp.org/sites/default/files/botswana_2005_en.pdf

UNICEF. (2000, September). Balance sheet of human progress in Africa. Retrieved from http://www.unicef.org/miscellaneous/balance.htm

United Nations World Population Prospects. (2015). World Population Prospects 2015. *United Nations.* Retrieved from https://esa.un.org/unpd/wpp/publications/Files/WPP2015_DataBooklet.pdf

Van de Walle, N. (1999). Economic Reform in a Democratizing Africa. *Comparative Politics 32*(1), 21-41.

Van Wyk, J. (2010). Double diamonds, real diamonds: Botswana's national competitiveness. *Academy of Marketing Studies Journal, 14*(2), 55-76.

Wade, R. (2004). Is globalization reducing poverty and inequality? *World Development, 32*(4), 567-89.

Wagner, C. G. (2009). How to play a wild card. *The Futurist, 43*(3), 3

Wagner, C. G. (2013). Top 10 disappearing futures. *The Futurist, 47*(5), 22-39.

Warner, A. M., Sachs, J. D., & National Bureau of Economic Research. (1995). *Natural Resource Abundance and Economic Growth.* Cambridge, Mass: National Bureau of Economic Research.

Weidenbaum, M. L. (2009). *The competition of ideas: the world of the Washington think tanks.* New Brunswick: NJ: Transaction Publishers

Werhane, P. H. (2007). Women leaders in a globalized world. *Journal of Business Ethics, 74*(4), 425-435.

West, J., & Graham, J. L. (1998). *Language's consequences: A test of linguistic-based measures of culture using Hofstede's dimensions.* Paper presented at the Annual Meeting of the Academic of Management, San Diego, CA.

Wong, T. (1999). The transition from physical infrastructure to infostructure: Infrastructure as a modernizing agent in Singapore. *GeoJournal, 49*(3), 279-288.

Woo-Cumings, M. (1999). *The developmental state.* Ithaca, NY: Cornell University Press.

World Bank (1989) *Sub-Saharan Africa: From crisis to sustainable growth.* Washington, DC: IBRD.

World Bank (2002). *World Development Indicators Online Database*. Washington: World Bank.

World Bank (2016a). Literacy Rate, Adult Total for Botswana [SEADTLITRZSBWA]. Retrieved from https://fred.stlouisfed.org/series/SEADTLITRZSBWA

World Bank. (1994). *Adjustment in Africa: Reforms, results, and the road ahead*. New York, N.Y: Oxford University Press.

World Bank(2016b). Country overview: Botswana. Retrieved from https://www.worldbank.org/en/country/botswana/overview

World Economic Forum (2016). Global Competitiveness Report 2015-2016. *World Economic Forum* Retrieved from http://reports.weforum.org/global-competitiveness-report-2015-2016/

World Library Foundation. (2017). List of world's busiest transshipment ports. Retrieved from http://www.worldlibrary.org/articles/list_of_world's_busiest_transshipment_ports

World Population Review. (2013). Africa Population 2015. Retrieved from http://worldpopulationreview.com/continents/africa-population/ 2015-09-13

World Population Review. (2017). Africa Population 2016. Retrieved from http://worldpopulationreview.com/continents/africa-population/

World Trade Organization. (2015). Retrieved from https://www.wto.org/english/res_e/statis_e/its2015_e/its2015_e.pdfv

Xiangwei, W. (2017, February). China's think tanks overflow, but most still think what they're told to think. *South China Morning Post*. Retrieved from http://www.scmp.com/week-asia/opinion/article/2069944/chinas-think-tanks-overflow-most-still-think-what-theyre-told

Yang, K. S. (1992). *Chinese social orientation: From the social interaction perspective*. In Yang K. S. & Yu, A. B. (Eds.), *Chinese psychology and behavior* (87-142). Taipei, Taiwan: Laurel.

Yardeni, E. (1997). *The Economic Consequences of Peace*. Deutsche Morgan Grenfell Topical Study #35. May. New York, U.S.A

Yeats, A. J. (1991). *Do natural resource-based industrialization strategies convey important (unrecognized) price benefits for commodity-exporting developing countries?* Washington, DC (1818 H St., NW, Washington 20433): International Economics Dept., World Bank.

Yue, C. S., & Das, S. B. (2015). The AEC beyond 2015: Implementation and challenges for Singapore. *Journal of Southeast Asian Economies, 32*(2), 239-259.

Zainal, A. Y., Bhattasali, D., World Bank, & Commission on Growth and Development. (2008). *Economic growth and development in Malaysia, policy making and leadership*. Washington, D.C: International Bank for Reconstruction and Development.

Zhou, P. (2017, March). Singapore's Economic Development. *ThoughCo*. Retrieved from http://geography.about.com/od/economic-geography/a/Singapore-Economic-Development.htm

Index

M

MacGregor's
156
Macroeconomic
56, 107, 108, 123, 140
Madagascar
39
Madrasa
27
Mafikeng
71
Malaria
166
Malawi
37, 39, 59, 67, 92, 94, 223, 229
Malawian
59
Mali
39, 46, 51
Management
1, 23, 47, 49, 63, 79-81, 84, 88, 107,
112, 145, 150, 151, 157, 164,
173-176, 187, 202, 210, 220-222,
224-226, 229, 231
Manufacture
116
Manufacturing
74, 81, 84, 96, 99-102, 109, 110, 115,
117-120, 136, 142
Marginalization
141, 145, 229
Market
37, 71, 76, 80, 88, 94, 97, 104, 109,
112, 119, 121, 123, 130, 135,
137-140, 143, 144, 146, 169, 179,
190, 191, 225
Market-based
74, 198
Marketplace
9, 33, 58, 134, 137
Marxist
51
Mauritania
39
Mauritius
39, 84, 200
Maximally
156, 217
Medical
62, 122
Medicine
189, 197
Mediocrity
171

Medium-sized
110, 112
Medium-term
79
Methodologies
169
Metropolitan
130, 220
Microelectronics
110, 135
Middle-income
74, 95, 100, 200
Migrant
58, 86, 229
Migrants
96, 161, 197
Migration
159, 174, 197, 228
Militants
71
Militaries
54
Military
28, 46, 54-56, 61, 62, 66, 71, 104, 107,
112, 213, 219, 225, 226
Millennia
133
Millennium
60, 185
Minority
64, 173, 221, 229
Misallocated
155
Mismanagement
74, 79
Modernization
81, 85, 105, 106, 184
Modernizing
108, 130, 231
Monarchs
28, 46, 51, 62
Monetary
56, 66, 85, 140, 224
Money
52, 71, 104, 118, 122, 134, 155, 161,
173, 222
Monitoring
31, 76, 172, 179, 183, 215
Monocratic
52, 156, 157
Mono-cultural
164
Mono-culturally
164

Index

Single-party
52, 54, 62
Skilled
20, 72, 73, 76, 81, 109, 159, 161
Skills
14, 79, 117, 144, 151, 157, 161, 163,
164, 176, 195, 197, 222
Slave
38, 55, 56, 212, 216
Slavery
216
Slums
115, 198
Socialist
52, 57
Socialists
52
Societies
20, 28, 31, 35, 36, 39-42, 46, 47, 51,
133, 134, 137, 155, 160, 176, 181,
201, 209, 224, 227
Society
27, 29, 30, 34, 38, 41, 53, 54, 62, 64,
65, 67, 72, 83, 88, 95, 97, 122, 128,
130, 142, 149, 154, 156, 160, 161,
163, 165, 167, 168, 177, 184, 192,
195, 197, 198, 214, 216, 217, 220,
221, 225, 228, 230
Socio-economic
94, 109, 130, 183, 197, 226
Sociological
172, 227
Sociology
66, 224-226
Socrates
27
Somalia
39
Songhay
46
Sovereign
43
Sovereignties
138
Sovereignty
141
Soviet
13, 35, 57, 133
State-sponsored
55
State-supported
19, 53, 185
Statistics
52, 76, 107, 155

Strategic
2, 14-16, 41, 48, 98, 99, 101, 116-120,
127, 128, 137, 141, 160, 167, 177,
187, 190, 194, 195, 199, 201-203,
207, 209-211, 216, 221, 224, 227, 229
Strategically
15, 166, 195
Strategies
2, 15, 25, 30, 78, 88, 98, 120, 123,
126, 172, 184-186, 193, 198, 217,
226, 227, 232
Strategy
13, 15, 16, 57, 60, 74, 97-100, 104,
116, 117, 120, 130, 137, 143, 169,
174, 193, 215, 220, 225
Sub-saharan
23, 35, 37, 38, 40-42, 56, 58-60, 62-
67, 69, 80, 83, 92, 140, 151, 155, 166,
172, 190, 199, 201-203, 206,
209-211, 216, 217, 219, 223,
225-227, 231
Subsidies
59, 67, 138, 170, 230
Subsidized
138
Subsidizing
59, 139
Subsistence
71
Succession
150, 165
Successor
165, 166
Successors
165, 166
Sudanese-British
165
Suez
114
Sustainability
57, 83
Swaziland
39, 46
Switzerland
36, 176, 224

T

Taiwan
81, 120, 122, 232
Tanzania
2, 21, 38, 39, 61, 196
Tanzania's
52, 198
Tariff
100

Index

U

Uganda
2, 6, 9, 21, 38, 39, 41, 46, 54, 57, 61,
64, 66, 87, 91, 94, 156, 196, 201, 209,
219, 221, 226, 229
Uganda's
55, 198
Un-colonized
47
Under-developed
110
Under-employment
82
Underfunded
206
UNICEF
67, 202, 231
Unskilled
120, 159, 197
Upper-middle
80
Urban
101, 130, 169, 197, 198, 220
Urban-based
72
Urbanization
101, 161, 197, 198
Urbanized
197
Uruguay
136
USA
1, 9, 31, 35, 36, 38-40, 43, 45, 66, 121,
124, 180, 181, 205, 209, 227
USAID
105
USSR
124

V

Vaccines
77
Value-added
100, 163
Village
46, 105, 139, 143
Vision
2, 13, 14, 17, 19, 21, 25, 31, 97, 98,
106, 118, 141, 152, 157, 182, 183,
186, 188, 192, 198-200, 225
Visionary
105, 123, 124, 153, 163, 180, 182,
183, 214, 215
Visions
14, 16, 183, 184, 198, 199

Voice
30, 32, 38, 194, 195, 215
Voices
30, 35
Volatility
99
Vulnerabilities
100
Vulnerability
58, 130, 223
Vulnerable
56, 169, 189

W

Wars
45, 149, 150, 169, 216
Washington
19, 59, 62, 66, 67, 85, 89, 125, 126,
128, 176, 206, 209, 222-224, 231, 232
Water
14, 75, 77, 82, 95, 103, 113, 115, 118,
180
Waterways
14
Waves
133, 143, 171
West
34, 40, 49, 50, 58, 64, 65, 69-71, 91,
103, 133, 146, 147, 159, 161, 176,
177, 186, 202, 203, 221, 222, 230,
231
Western
33, 34, 45, 51, 59, 69, 75, 150, 151,
155, 161, 172, 185, 224
Westminster
73, 174, 223
Wild-card
169
Windfalls
78
Worldwide
134, 138, 143, 193, 215

Y

Young-Sam's
142

Z

Zambia
39, 69, 94, 170, 177, 200, 222
Zimbabwe
38, 39, 69
102
Zulus
70

www.ingramcontent.com/pod-product-compliance
Lightning Source LLC
Chambersburg PA
CBHW071634200326

41519CB00012BA/2296